W9-CSX-220

1974 Supplement

Sex Roles in

Law and Society

Cases and Materials

Leo Kanowitz
Professor of Law
University of California
Hastings College of the Law

University of New Mexico Press

Albuquerque

3962
K16
S

© 1974 by Leo Kanowitz. All rights reserved.
Manufactured in the United States of America.
Library of Congress Catalog Card No. 72-94656.
International Standard Book No. 0-8263-0328-5.

Preface

Only a year and a half have passed since the main volume of *Sex Roles in Law and Society* first appeared. But important new developments have occurred so rapidly—especially in the areas of constitutional doctrine and equal employment opportunity—that this 1974 Supplement has become necessary for students of the field.

For various forms of assistance in the preparation of this Supplement, I would like to express my sincere appreciation to Joseph Towey and Erika Smith of the Hastings College of the Law. Above all, the encouragement and aid of Dean Marvin J. Anderson of the Hastings College of the Law and Dean Frederick M. Hart of the University of New Mexico School of Law, which made this volume possible, are gratefully acknowledged.

Table of Contents

Numbers at the left indicate where the new material may be fitted into the Casebook; those at the right indicate where it appears in this Supplement. Cases set out substantially in full are in boldface type.

CHAPTER 2
The Law's Traditional View of Sex Roles: An Overview

CHAPTER 3
Sex Roles without Regard to Marital Status

CHAPTER 4
Sex Roles and Marriage

COPY 3

CHAPTER 5

Sex Roles and Employment

CHAPTER 10
Sex Roles and the Media

CHAPTER 11
Sex Roles, Sex Preferences, and Appearance

Table of Cases

The principal cases are in italic type. Cases cited or discussed are in roman type. References are to pages in the Supplement.

1974 Supplement

Sex Roles in Law and Society

Chapter 2

The Law's Traditional View of Sex Roles:
An Overview

Page 74. Following Gruenwald, add:

NOTE

42 U.S.C. § 415(b)(3) has been sex-neutralized since the decision in *Gruenwald.* Pub. L. 92-603, § 104(b) struck out the provisions setting a separate age computation point for women, and reduced from age 65 to age 62 the age computation point for men.

Page 78. Following note 3, add:

4. In Healy v. Edwards, 363 F. Supp. 1110 (E.D. La. 1973), a three-judge federal district court held that the Louisiana jury law of the type upheld in *Hoyt v. Florida,* excusing women from jury service unless they affirmatively volunteer in writing, denies equal protection to women litigants and due process to all litigants. Though *Hoyt* has not been overruled by the United States Supreme Court, the federal district court in *Healy* holds that recent Supreme Court decisions, notably *Reed v. Reed* and *Frontiero v. Richardson* (see 93 below), have so eroded *Hoyt* that it would be improper for it to follow that older case. In the light of *Kahn v. Shevin,* p. 104 *infra* of the Supplement, how should the U.S. Supreme Court rule in *Healy v. Edwards?* Is the conferral of the right not to serve on juries unless they affirmatively volunteer to do so a benefit for women or a burden? A result contrary to the one in *Healy* was reached by the Louisiana Supreme Court in State v. Leichman, La., 286 So.2d 649 (1973).

Chapter 3

Sex Roles without Regard to Marital Status

Page 97. Following note 4, add:

5. Equal-protection and right-of-privacy arguments against prostitution statutes are discussed in Rosenbleet & Pariente, The Prostitution of the Criminal Law, 11 Am. Crim. L. Rev. 373 (1973).

1

Page 159. Delete note 2.

Page 162. After note 11, add:

Roe v. Wade
United States Supreme Court, 1973
410 U.S. 113, 93 S.Ct. 705, 35 L.Ed.2d 147

MR. JUSTICE BLACKMUN delivered the opinion of the Court.

This Texas federal appeal and its Georgia companion, *Doe* v. *Bolton, post,* present constitutional challenges to state criminal abortion legislation. The Texas statutes under attack here are typical of those that have been in effect in many States for approximately a century. The Georgia statutes, in contrast, have a modern cast and are a legislative product that, to an extent at least, obviously reflects the influences of recent attitudinal change, of advancing medical knowledge and techniques, and of new thinking about an old issue.

We forthwith acknowledge our awareness of the sensitive and emotional nature of the abortion controversy, of the vigorous opposing views, even among physicians, and of the deep and seemingly absolute convictions that the subject inspires. One's philosophy, one's experiences, one's exposure to the raw edges of human existence, one's religious training, one's attitudes toward life and family and their values, and the moral standards one establishes and seeks to observe, are all likely to influence and to color one's thinking and conclusions about abortion.

In addition, population growth, pollution, poverty, and racial overtones tend to complicate and not to simplify the problem.

Our task, of course, is to resolve the issue by constitutional measurement, free of emotion and of predilection. We seek earnestly to do this, and, because we do, we have inquired into, and in this opinion place some emphasis upon, medical and medical-legal history and what that history reveals about man's attitudes toward the abortion procedure over the centuries. We bear in mind, too, Mr. Justice Holmes' admonition in his now-vindicated dissent in *Lochner* v. *New York,* 198 U.S. 45, 76 (1905):

> "[The Constitution] is made for people of fundamentally differing views, and the accident of our finding certain opinions natural and familiar or novel and even shocking ought not to conclude our judgment upon the question whether statutes embodying them conflict with the Constitution of the United States."

I

The Texas statutes that concern us here are Arts. 1191-1194 and 1196 of the State's Penal Code. These make it a crime to "procure an abortion," as therein defined, or to attempt one, except with respect to "an abortion procured or attempted by medical advice for the purpose of saving the life of the mother." Similar statutes are in existence in a majority of the States.

[Before examining the merits, Justice Blackmun first considered the "issues of justiciability, standing and abstention," and held that the only challenger entitled to maintain the action was Jane Roe, a pregnant single woman, despite the termination of her 1970 pregnancy. "Pregnancy," stated Justice Blackmun, "provides a classic justification for a conclusion of non-mootness. It truly could be 'capable of repetition, yet evading review.' " By contrast, the other parties challenging the Texas abortion laws were barred from maintaining the action. These were John and Mary Doe, a childless couple, the wife not being pregnant, and Dr. Hallford, a licensed physician, against whom two criminal charges were pending in the state court. The claims of the Does were held to be "too speculative" to come within the "case or controversy" requirement of Article III of the U.S. Constitution. As for Dr. Hallford, the pendency of the state criminal prosectuions precluded direct access to the federal courts under the principles established in Samuels v. Mackell, 401 U.S. 66, 91 S.Ct. 764, 27 L.Ed.2d 688.]

V

The principal thrust of appellant's attack on the Texas statutes is that they improperly invade a right, said to be possessed by the pregnant woman, to choose to terminate her pregnancy. Appellant would discover this right in the concept of personal "liberty" embodied in the Fourteenth Amendment's Due Process Clause; or in personal, marital, familial, and sexual privacy said to be protected by the Bill of Rights or its penumbras, see *Griswold* v. *Connecticut,* 381 U.S. 479 (1965); *Eisenstadt* v. *Baird,* 405 U.S. 438 (1972); *id.,* at 460 (WHITE, J., concurring in result); or among those rights reserved to the people by the Ninth Amendment, *Griswold* v. *Connecticut,* 381 U.S., at 486 (Goldberg, J., concurring). Before addressing this claim, we feel it desirable briefly to survey, in several aspects, the history of abortion, for such insight as that history may afford us, and then to examine the state purposes and interests behind the criminal abortion laws.

VI

It perhaps is not generally appreciated that the restrictive criminal abortion laws in effect in a majority of States today are of relatively recent vintage. Those laws, generally proscribing abortion or its attempt at any time during pregnancy except when necessary to preserve the pregnant woman's life, are not of ancient or even of common-law origin. Instead, they derive from statutory changes effected, for the most part, in the latter half of the 19th century. . . .

VII

Three reasons have been advanced to explain historically the enactment of criminal abortion laws in the 19th century and to justify their continued existence. It has been argued occasionally that these laws were the product of a Victorian social concern to discourage illicit sexual conduct. Texas, however, does not advance this justification in the present case, and it appears that no court or commentator has taken the argument seriously. . . .

A second reason is concerned with abortion as a medical procedure. When most criminal abortion laws were first enacted, the procedure was a hazardous one for the woman. . . .

Modern medical techniques have altered this situation. Appellants and various *amici* refer to medical data indicating that abortion in early pregnancy, that is, prior to the end of the first trimester, although not without its risk, is now relatively safe. Mortality rates for women undergoing early abortions, where the procedure is legal, appear to be as low as or lower than the rates for normal childbirth. Consequently, any interest of the State in protecting the woman from an inherently hazardous procedure, except when it would be equally dangerous for her to forgo it, has largely disappeared. Of course, important state interests in the area of health and medical standards do remain. The State has a legitimate interest in seeing to it that abortion, like any other medical procedure, is performed under circumstances that insure maximum safety for the patient. This interest obviously extends at least to the performing physician and his staff, to the facilities involved, to the availability of after-care, and to adequate provision for any complication or emergency that might arise. The prevalence of high mortality rates at illegal "abortion mills" strengthens, rather than weakens, the State's interest in regulating the conditions under which abortions are performed. Moreover, the risk to the woman increases as her pregnancy continues. Thus, the State retains a definite interest in protecting the woman's own health and safety when an abortion is proposed at a late stage of pregnancy.

The third reason is the State's interest—some phrase it in terms of duty—in protecting prenatal life. Some of the argument for this justification rests on the theory that a new human life is present from the moment of conception. The State's interest and general obligation to protect life then extends, it is argued, to prenatal life. Only when the life of the pregnant mother herself is at stake, balanced against the life she carries within her, should the interest of the embryo or fetus not prevail. Logically, of course, a legitimate state interest in this area need not stand or fall on acceptance of the belief that life begins at conception or at some other point prior to live birth. In assessing the State's interest, recognition may be given to the less rigid claim that as long as at least *potential* life is involved, the State may assert interests beyond the protection of the pregnant woman alone.

Parties challenging state abortion laws have sharply disputed in some courts the contention that a purpose of these laws, when enacted, was to protect prenatal life. Pointing to the absence of legislative history to support the contention, they claim that most state laws were designed solely to protect the woman. Because medical advances have lessened this concern, at least with respect to abortion in early pregnancy, they argue that with respect to such abortions the laws can no longer be justified by any state interest. There is some scholarly support for this view of original purpose. The few state courts called upon to interpret their laws in the late 19th and early 20th centuries did focus on the State's interest in protecting the woman's health rather than in preserving the embryo and fetus. Proponents of this view point out that in many States, including Texas, by statute or judicial interpretation, the pregnant woman herself could not be prosecuted for self-abortion or for cooperating in an abortion performed upon her by another. They claim that adoption of the "quickening" distinction through received common law and state statutes tacitly recognizes the greater health hazards inherent in late abortion and impliedly repudiates the theory that life begins at conception.

It is with these interests, and the weight to be attached to them, that this case is concerned.

VIII

The Constitution does not explicitly mention any right of privacy. In a line of decisions, however, going back perhaps as far as *Union Pacific R. Co.* v. *Botsford,* 141 U.S. 250, 251 (1891), the Court has recognized that a right of personal privacy, or a guarantee of certain areas or zones of privacy, does exist under the Constitution. In varying contexts, the Court or individual Justices have, indeed, found at least the roots of that right in the First Amendment, *Stanley* v. *Georgia,* 394 U.S. 557, 564 (1969); in the Fourth and Fifth Amendments, *Terry* v. *Ohio,* 392 U.S. 1, 8-9 (1968), *Katz* v. *United States,* 389 U.S. 347, 350 (1967), *Boyd* v. *United States,* 116 U.S. 616 (1886), see *Olmstead* v. *United States,* 277 U.S. 438, 478 (1928) (Brandeis, J., dissenting); in the penumbras of the Bill of Rights, *Griswold* v. *Connecticut,* 381 U.S., at 484-485; in the Ninth Amendment, *id.,* at 486 (Goldberg, J., concurring); or in the concept of liberty guaranteed by the first section of the Fourteenth Amendment, see *Meyer* v. *Nebraska,* 262 U.S 390, 399 (1923). These decisions make it clear that only personal rights that can be deemed "fundamental" or "implicit in the concept of ordered liberty," *Palko* v. *Connecticut,* 302 U.S. 319, 325 (1937), are included in this guarantee of personal privacy. They also make it clear that the right has some extension to activities relating to marriage, *Loving* v. *Virginia,* 388 U.S. 1, 12 (1967); procreation, *Skinner* v. *Oklahoma,* 316 U.S. 535, 541-542 (1942); contraception, *Eisenstadt* v. *Baird,* 405 U.S., at 453-454; *id.,* at 460, 463-465 (WHITE, J., concurring in result); family relationships, *Prince* v. *Massachusetts,* 321 U.S. 158, 166 (1944); and child rearing and education, *Pierce* v. *Society of Sisters,* 268 U.S. 510, 535 (1925), *Meyer* v. *Nebraska, supra.*

This right of privacy, whether it be founded in the Fourteenth Amendment's concept of personal liberty and restrictions upon state action, as we feel it is, or, as the District Court determined, in the Ninth Amendment's reservation of rights to the people, is broad enough to encompass a woman's decision whether or not to terminate her pregnancy. The detriment that the State would impose upon the pregnant woman by denying this choice altogether is apparent. Specific and direct harm medically diagnosable even in early pregnancy may be involved. Maternity, or additional offspring, may force upon the woman a distressful life and future. Psychological harm may be imminent. Mental and physical health may be taxed by child care. There is also the distress, for all concerned, associated with the unwanted child, and there is the problem of bringing a child into a family already unable, psychologically and otherwise, to care for it. In other cases, as in this one, the additional difficulties and continuing stigma of unwed motherhood may be involved. All these are factors the woman and her responsible physician necessarily will consider in consultation.

On the basis of elements such as these, appellant and some *amici* argue that the woman's right is absolute and that she is entitled to terminate her pregnancy at whatever time, in whatever way, and for whatever reason she alone chooses. With this we do not agree. Appellant's arguments that Texas either has no valid interest at all in regulating the abortion decision, or no interest strong enough to support any limitation upon the woman's sole determination, is unpersuasive. The Court's decisions recognizing a right of privacy also acknowledge that some state regulation in areas protected by that right is appropriate. As noted above, a State may properly assert important interests in safeguarding health, in maintaining medical standards, and in protecting potential life. At some point in pregnancy, these respective interests become sufficiently compelling to sustain regulation of the factors that govern the abortion decision. The privacy right involved, therefore, cannot be said to be absolute. In fact, it is not clear to us that the claim asserted by some *amici* that one has an unlimited right to do with one's body as one pleases bears a close relationship to the right of privacy previously articulated in the Court's decisions. The Court has refused to recognize an unlimited right of this kind in the past. *Jacobson* v. *Massachusetts,* 197 U.S. 11 (1905) (vaccination); *Buck* v. *Bell,* 274 U.S. 200 (1927) (sterilization).

We, therefore, conclude that the right of personal privacy includes the abortion decision, but that this right is not unqualified and must be considered against important state interests in regulation.

We note that those federal and state courts that have recently considered abortion law challenges have reached the same conclusion. A majority, in addition to the District Court in the present case, have held state laws unconstitutional, at least in part, because of vagueness or because of overbreadth and abridgment of rights. . . .

Others have sustained state statutes. . . .

Although the results are divided, most of these courts have agreed that the right of privacy, however based, is broad enough to cover the abortion decision; that the right, nonetheless, is not absolute and is subject to some limitations; and that at some point the state interests as to protection of health, medical standards, and prenatal life, become dominant. We agree with this approach.

Where certain "fundamental rights" are involved, the Court has held that regulation limiting these rights may be justified only by a "compelling state interest," . . . and that legislative enactments must be narrowly drawn to express only the legitimate state interests at stake. . . .

In the recent abortion cases, cited above, courts have recognized these principles. Those striking down state laws have generally scrutinized the State's interest in protecting health and potential life, and have concluded that neither interest justified broad limitations on the reasons for which a physician and his pregnant patient might decide that she should have an abortion in the early stages of pregnancy. Courts sustaining state laws have held that the State's determinations to protect health or prenatal life are dominant and constitutionally justifiable.

IX

The District Court held that the appellee failed to meet his burden of demonstrating that the Texas statute's infringement upon Roe's rights was necessary to support a compelling state interest, and that, although the appellee presented "several compelling justifications for state presence in the area of abortions," the statutes outstripped these justifications and swept "far beyond any areas of compelling state interest." 314 F. Supp., at 1222-1223. Appellant and appellee both contest that holding. Appellant, as has been indicated, claims an absolute right that bars any state imposition of criminal penalties in the area. Appellee argues that the State's determination to recognize and protect prenatal life from and after conception constitutes a compelling state interest. As noted above, we do not agree fully with either formulation.

A. The appellee and certain *amici* argue that the fetus is a "person" within the language and meaning of the Fourteenth Amendment. In support of this, they outline at length and in detail the well-known facts of fetal development. If this suggestion of personhood is established, the appellant's case, of course, collapses, for the fetus' right to life is then guaranteed specifically by the Amendment. The appellant conceded as much on reargument. On the other hand, the appellee conceded on reargument that no case could be cited that holds that a fetus is a person within the meaning of the Fourteenth Amendment.

The Constitution does not define "person" in so many words. Section 1 of the Fourteenth Amendment contains three references to "person." The first, in defining "citizens," speaks of "persons born or naturalized in the United States." The word also appears both in the Due Process Clause and in the Equal Protection Clause. "Person" is used in other places in the Constitution: in the listing of qualifications for Representatives and Senators, Art. I, § 2, cl. 2, and § 3, cl. 3; in the Apportionment Clause, Art. I, § 2, cl. 3; in the Migration and Importation provision, Art. I, § 9, cl. 1; in the Emolument Clause, Art. I, § 9, cl. 8; in the Electors provisions, Art. II, § 1, cl. 2, and the superseded cl. 3; in the provision outlining qualifications for the office of President, Art. II, § 1, cl. 5; in the Extradition provisions, Art. IV, § 2, cl. 2, and the superseded Fugitive Slave Clause 3; and in the Fifth, Twelfth, and Twenty-second Amendments, as well as in § § 2 and 3 of the Fourteenth Amendment. But in nearly all these instances, the use of the word is such that it has application only postnatally. None indicates, with any assurance, that it has any possible pre-natal application.[54]

---

54. When Texas urges that a fetus is entitled to Fourteenth Amendment protection as a person, it faces a dilemma. Neither in Texas nor in any other State are all abortions prohibited. Despite broad proscription, an exception always exists. The exception contained in Art. 1196, for an abortion procured or attempted by medical advice for the purpose of saving the life of the mother, is typical. But if the fetus is a person who is not to be deprived of life without due process of law, and if the mother's condition is the sole determinant, does not the Texas exception appear to be out of line with the Amendment's command?

There are other inconsistencies between Fourteenth Amendment status and the typical abortion statute. It has already been pointed out, n. 49, *supra,* that in Texas the woman is not a principal or an accomplice with respect to an abortion upon her. If the fetus is a person, why is the woman not a principal or an accomplice? Further, the penalty for criminal abortion specified by Art. 1195 is significantly less than the maximum penalty for murder prescribed by Art. 1257 of the Texas Penal Code. If the fetus is a person, may the penalties be different?

All this, together with our observation, *supra*, that throughout the major portion of the 19th century prevailing legal abortion practices were far freer than they are today, persuades us that the word "person," as used in the Fourteenth Amendment, does not include the unborn.[55] This is in accord with the results reached in those few cases where the issue has been squarely presented. . . . Indeed, our decision in *United States* v. *Vuitch,* 402 U.S. 62 (1971), inferentially is to the same effect, for we there would not have indulged in statutory interpretation favorable to abortion in specified circumstances if the necessary consequence was the termination of life entitled to Fourteenth Amendment protection.

This conclusion, however, does not of itself fully answer the contentions raised by Texas, and we pass on to other considerations.

B. The pregnant woman cannot be isolated in her privacy. She carries an embryo and, later, a fetus, if one accepts the medical definitions of the developing young in the human uterus. See Dorland's Illustrated Medical Dictionary 478-479, 547 (24th ed. 1965). The situation therefore is inherently different from marital intimacy, or bedroom possession of obscene material, or marriage, or procreation, or education, with which *Eisenstadt, Griswold, Stanley, Loving, Skinner, Pierce,* and *Meyer* were respectively concerned. As we have intimated above, it is reasonable and appropriate for a State to decide that at some point in time another interest, that of health of the mother or that of potential human life, becomes significantly involved. The woman's privacy is no longer sole and any right of privacy she possesses must be measured accordingly.

Texas urges that, apart from the Fourteenth Amendment, life begins at conception and is present throughout pregnancy, and that, therefore, the State has a compelling interest in protecting that life from and after conception. We need not resolve the difficult question of when life begins. When those trained in the respective disciplines of medicine, philosophy, and theology are unable to arrive at any consensus, the judiciary, at this point in the development of man's knowledge, is not in a position to speculate as to the answer. . . .

In areas other than criminal abortion, the law has been reluctant to endorse any theory that life, as we recognize it, begins before live birth or to accord legal rights to the unborn except in narrowly defined situations and except when the rights are contingent upon live birth. For example, the traditional rule of tort law denied recovery for prenatal injuries even though the child was born alive. That rule has been changed in almost every jurisdiction. In most States, recovery is said to be permitted only if the fetus was viable, or at least quick, when the injuries were sustained, though few courts have squarely so held. In a recent development, generally opposed by the commentators, some States permit the parents of a stillborn child to maintain an action for wrongful death because of prenatal injuries. Such an action, however, would appear to be one to vindicate the parents' interest and is thus consistent with the view that the fetus, at most, represents only the poten-

55. Cf. the Wisconsin abortion statute, defining "unborn child" to mean "a human being from the time of conception until it is born alive," Wis. Stat. § 940.04(6) (1969), and the new Connecticut statute, Pub. Act No. 1 (May 1972 special session), declaring it to be the public policy of the State and the legislative intent "to protect and preserve human life from the moment of conception."

tiality of life. Similarly, unborn children have been recognized as acquiring rights or interests by way of inheritance or other devolution of property, and have been represented by guardians *ad litem*. Perfection of the interests involved, again, has generally been contingent upon live birth. In short, the unborn have never been recognized in the law as persons in the whole sense.

X

In view of all this, we do not agree that, by adopting one theory of life, Texas may override the rights of the pregnant woman that are at stake. We repeat, however, that the State does have an important and legitimate interest in preserving and protecting the health of the pregnant woman, whether she be a resident of the State or a nonresident who seeks medical consultation and treatment there, and that it has still *another* important and legitimate interest in protecting the potentiality of human life. These interests are separate and distinct. Each grows in substantiality as the woman approaches term and, at a point during pregnancy, each becomes "compelling."

With respect to the State's important and legitimate interest in the health of the mother, the "compelling" point, in the light of present medical knowledge, is at approximately the end of the first trimester. This is so because of the now-established medical fact, referred to above at 149, that until the end of the first trimester mortality in abortion may be less than mortality in normal childbirth. It follows that, from and after this point, a State may regulate the abortion procedure to the extent that the regulation reasonably relates to the preservation and protection of maternal health. Examples of permissible state regulation in this area are requirements as to the qualifications of the person who is to perform the abortion; as to the licensure of that person; as to the facility in which the procedure is to be performed, that is, whether it must be a hospital or may be a clinic or some other place of less-than-hospital status; as to the licensing of the facility; and the like.

This means, on the other hand, that, for the period of pregnancy prior to this "compelling" point, the attending physician, in consultation with his patient, is free to determine, without regulation by the State, that, in his medical judgment, the patient's pregnancy should be terminated. If that decision is reached, the judgment may be effectuated by an abortion free of interference by the State.

With respect to the State's important and legitimate interest in potential life, the "compelling" point is at viability. This is so because the fetus then presumably has the capability of meaningful life outside the mother's womb. State regulation protective of fetal life after viability thus has both logical and biological justifications. If the State is interested in protecting fetal life after viability, it may go so far as to proscribe abortion during that period, except when it is necessary to preserve the life or health of the mother.

Measured against these standards, Art. 1196 of the Texas Penal Code, in restricting legal abortions to those "procured or attempted by medical advice for the purpose of saving the life of the mother," sweeps too broadly. The statute makes no distinction between abortions performed early in pregnancy and those performed later, and it limits to a single reason, "saving" the mother's life, the legal justification for the procedure. The statute, therefore, cannot survive the constitutional attack made upon it here.

This conclusion makes it unnecessary for us to consider the additional challenge to the Texas statute asserted on grounds of vagueness. See *United States* v. *Vuitch*, 402 U.S., at 67-72.

XI

To summarize and to repeat:

1. A state criminal abortion statute of the current Texas type, that excepts from criminality only a *lifesaving* procedure on behalf of the mother, without regard to pregnancy stage and without recognition of the other interests involved, is violative of the Due Process Clause of the Fourteenth Amendment.

(a) For the stage prior to approximately the end of the first trimester, the abortion decision and its effectuation must be left to the medical judgment of the pregnant woman's attending physician.

(b) For the stage subsequent to approximately the end of the first trimester, the State, in promoting its interest in the health of the mother, may, if it chooses, regulate the abortion procedure in ways that are reasonably related to maternal health.

(c) For the stage subsequent to viability, the State in promoting its interest in the potentiality of human life may, if it chooses, regulate, and even proscribe, abortion except where it is necessary, in appropriate medical judgment, for the preservation of the life or health of the mother.

2. The State may define the term "physician," as it has been employed in the preceding numbered paragraphs of this Part XI of this opinion, to mean only a physician currently licensed by the State, and may proscribe any abortion by a person who is not a physician as so defined.

In *Doe* v. *Bolton, post,* . . . procedural requirements contained in one of the modern abortion statutes are considered. That opinion and this one, of course, are to be read together.[67]

This holding, we feel, is consistent with the relative weights of the respective interests involved, with the lessons and examples of medical and legal history, with the lenity of the common law, and with the demands of the profound problems of the present day. The decision leaves the State free to place increasing restrictions on abortion as the period of pregnancy lengthens, so long as those restrictions are tailored to the recognized state interests. The decision vindicates the right of the physician to administer medical treatment according to his professional judgment

---

67. Neither in this opinion nor in *Doe* v. *Bolton, post,* p. — do we discuss the father's rights, if any exist in the constitutional context, in the abortion decision. No paternal right has been asserted in either of the cases, and the Texas and the Georgia statutes on their face take no cognizance of the father. We are aware that some statutes recognize the father under certain circumstances. North Carolina, for example, N.C. Gen. Stat. § 14-45.1 (Supp. 1971), requires written permission for the abortion from the husband when the woman is a married minor, that is, when she is less than 18 years of age, 41 N.C. A.G. 489 (1971); if the woman is an unmarried minor, written permission from the parents is required. We need not now decide whether provisions of this kind are constitutional.

up to the points where important state interests provide compelling justifications for intervention. Up to those points, the abortion decision in all its aspects is inherently, and primarily, a medical decision, and basic responsibility for it must rest with the physician. If an individual practitioner abuses the privilege of exercising proper medical judgment, the usual remedies, judicial and intra-professional, are available.

XII

Our conclusion that Art. 1196 is unconstitutional means, of course, that the Texas abortion statutes, as a unit, must fall. The exception of Art. 1196 cannot be stricken separately, for then the State would be left with a statute proscribing all abortion procedures no matter how medically urgent the case.

Although the District Court granted plaintiff Roe declaratory relief, it stopped short of issuing an injunction against enforcement of the Texas statutes. The Court has recognized that different considerations enter into a federal court's decision as to declaratory relief, on the one hand, and injunctive relief, on the other. *Zwickler* v. *Koota,* 389 U.S. 241, 252-255 (1967); *Dombrowski* v. *Pfister,* 380 U.S. 479 (1965). We are not dealing with a statute that, on its face, appears to abridge free expression, an area of particular concern under *Dombrowski* and refined in *Younger* v. *Harris,* 401 U.S., at 50.

We find it unnecessary to decide whether the District Court erred in withholding injunctive relief, for we assume the Texas prosecutorial authorities will give full credence to this decision that the present criminal abortion statutes of that State are unconstitutional.

The judgment of the District Court as to intervenor Hallford is reversed, and Dr. Hallford's complaint in intervention is dismissed. In all other respects, the judgment of the District Court is affirmed. Costs are allowed to the appellee.

It is so ordered.

MR. JUSTICE STEWART, concurring.

In 1963, this Court in *Ferguson* v. *Skrupa,* 372 U.S. 726, purported to sound the death knell for the doctrine of substantive due process, a doctrine under which many state laws had in the past been held to violate the Fourteenth Amendment. As Mr. Justice Black's opinion for the Court in *Skrupa* put it: "We have returned to the original constitutional proposition that courts do not substitute their social and economic beliefs for the judgment of legislative bodies, who are elected to pass laws." *Id.,* at 730.

Barely two years later, in *Griswold* v. *Connecticut,* 381 U.S. 479, the Court held a Connecticut birth control law unconstitutional. In view of what had been so recently said in *Skrupa,* the Court's opinion in *Griswold* understandably did its best to avoid reliance on the Due Process Clause of the Fourteenth Amendment as the ground for decision. Yet, the Connecticut law did not violate any provision of the Bill of Rights, nor any other specific provision of the Constitution. So it was clear to me then, and it is equally clear to me now, that the *Griswold* decision can be rationally understood only as a holding that the Connecticut statute substantively invaded the "liberty" that is protected by the Due Process Clause of the Fourteenth Amendment. As so understood, *Griswold* stands as one in a long line of pre-*Skrupa* cases decided under the doctrine of substantive due process, and I now accept it as such.

"In a Constitution for a free people, there can be no doubt that the meaning of 'liberty' must be broad indeed." *Board of Regents* v. *Roth,* 408 U.S. 564, 572. The Constitution nowhere mentions a specific right of personal choice in matters of marriage and family life, but the "liberty" protected by the Due Process Clause of the Fourteenth Amendment covers more than those freedoms explicitly named in the Bill of Rights. . . .

As Mr. Justice Harlan once wrote: "[T] he full scope of the liberty guaranteed by the Due Process Clause cannot be found in or limited by the precise terms of the specific guarantees elsewhere provided in the Constitution. This 'liberty' is not a series of isolated points pricked out in terms of the taking of property; the freedom of speech, press, and religion; the right to keep and bear arms; the freedom from unreasonable searches and seizures; and so on. It is a rational continuum which, broadly speaking, includes a freedom from all substantial arbitrary impositions and purposeless restraints . . . and which also recognizes, what a reasonable and sensitive judgment must, that certain interests require particularly careful scrutiny of the state needs asserted to justify their abridgment." *Poe* v. *Ullman,* 367 U.S. 497, 543 (opinion dissenting from dismissal of appeal) (citations omitted). In the words of Mr. Justice Frankfurter, "Great concepts like . . . 'liberty' . . . were purposely left to gather meaning from experience. For they relate to the whole domain of social and economic fact, and the statesmen who founded this Nation knew too well that only a stagnant society remains unchanged." *National Mutual Ins. Co.* v. *Tidewater Transfer Co.,* 337 U.S. 582, 646 (dissenting opinion).

Several decisions of this Court make clear that freedom of personal choice in matters of marriage and family life is one of the liberties protected by the Due Process Clause of the Fourteenth Amendment. . . .

Clearly, therefore, the Court today is correct in holding that the right asserted by Jane Roe is embraced within the personal liberty protected by the Due Process Clause of the Fourteenth Amendment.

It is evident that the Texas abortion statute infringes that right directly. Indeed, it is difficult to imagine a more complete abridgment of a constitutional freedom than that worked by the inflexible criminal statute now in force in Texas. The question then becomes whether the state interests advanced to justify this abridgment can survive the "particularly careful scrutiny" that the Fourteenth Amendment here requires.

The asserted state interests are protection of the health and safety of the pregnant woman, and protection of the potential future human life within her. These are legitimate objectives, amply sufficient to permit a State to regulate abortions as it does other surgical procedures, and perhaps sufficient to permit a State to regulate abortions more stringently or even to prohibit them in the late stages of pregnancy. But such legislation is not before us, and I think the Court today has thoroughly demonstrated that these state interests cannot constitutionally support the broad abridgment of personal liberty worked by the existing Texas law. Accordingly, I join the Court's opinion holding that that law is invalid under the Due Process Clause of the Fourteenth Amendment.

MR. JUSTICE REHNQUIST, dissenting.

The Court's opinion brings to the decision of this troubling question both extensive historical fact and a wealth of legal scholarship. While the opinion thus commands my respect, I find myself nonetheless in fundamental disagreement with those parts of it that invalidate the Texas statute in question, and therefore dissent. . . .

II

. . . I have difficulty in concluding, as the Court does, that the right of "privacy" is involved in this case. Texas, by the statute here challenged, bars the performance of a medical abortion by a licensed physician on a plaintiff such as Roe. A transaction resulting in an operation such as this is not "private" in the ordinary usage of that word. Nor is the "privacy" that the Court finds here even a distant relative of the freedom from searches and seizures protected by the Fourth Amendment to the Constitution, which the Court has referred to as embodying a right to privacy. *Katz* v. *United States,* 389 U.S. 347 (1967).

If the Court means by the term "privacy" no more than that the claim of a person to be free from unwanted state regulation of consensual transactions may be a form of "liberty" protected by the Fourteenth Amendment, there is no doubt that similar claims have been upheld in our earlier decisions on the basis of that liberty. I agree with the statement of MR. JUSTICE STEWART in his concurring opinion that the "liberty," against deprivation of which without due process the Fourteenth Amendment protects, embraces more than the rights found in the Bill of Rights. But that liberty is not guaranteed absolutely against deprivation, only against deprivation without due process of law. The test traditionally applied in the area of social and economic legislation is whether or not a law such as that challenged has a rational relation to a valid state objective. *Williamson* v. *Lee Optical Co.,* 348 U.S. 483, 491 (1955). The Due Process Clause of the Fourteenth Amendment undoubtedly does place a limit, albeit a broad one, on legislative power to enact laws such as this. If the Texas statute were to prohibit an abortion even where the mother's life is in jeopardy, I have little doubt that such a statute would lack a rational relation to a valid state objective under the test stated in *Williamson, supra.* But the Court's sweeping invalidation of any restrictions on abortion during the first trimester is impossible to justify under that standard, and the conscious weighing of competing factors that the Court's opinion apparently substitutes for the established test is far more appropriate to a legislative judgment than to a judicial one.

The Court eschews the history of the Fourteenth Amendment in its reliance on the "compelling state interest" test. See *Weber* v. *Aetna Casualty & Surety Co.,* 406 U.S. 164, 179 (1972) (dissenting opinion). But the Court adds a new wrinkle to this test by transposing it from the legal considerations associated with the Equal Protection Clause of the Fourteenth Amendment to this case arising under the Due Process Clause of the Fourteenth Amendment. Unless I misapprehend the consequences of this transplanting of the "compelling state interest," the Court's opinion will accomplish the seemingly impossible feat of leaving this area of the law more confused than it found it. . . .

The fact that a majority of the States reflecting, after all, the majority sentiment in those States, have had restrictions on abortions for at least a century is a strong indication, it seems to me, that the asserted right to an abortion is not "so rooted in the traditions and conscience of our people as to be ranked as fundamental," *Snyder* v. *Massachusetts,* 291 U.S. 97, 105 (1934). Even today, when society's views on abortion are changing, the very existence of the debate is evidence that the "right" to an abortion is not so universally accepted as the appellants would have us believe.

There apparently was no question concerning the validity of this provision or of any of the other state statutes when the Fourteenth Amendment was adopted. The only conclusion possible from this history is that the drafters did not intend to have the Fourteenth Amendment withdraw from the States the power to legislate with respect to this matter.

III

Even if one were to agree that the case that the Court decides were here, and that the enunciation of the substantive constitutional law in the Court's opinion were proper, the actual disposition of the case by the Court is still difficult to justify. The Texas statute is struck down *in toto,* even though the Court apparently concedes that at later periods of pregnancy Texas might impose these selfsame statutory limitations on abortion. My understanding of past practice is that a statute found to be invalid as applied to a particular plaintiff, but not unconstitutional as a whole, is not simply "struck down" but is, instead, declared unconstitutional as applied to the fact situation before the Court. *Yick Wo* v. *Hopkins,* 118 U.S. 356 (1886); *Street* v. *New York,* 394 U.S. 576 (1969).

For all of the foregoing reasons, I respectfully dissent.

Doe v. Bolton
United States Supreme Court, 1973
410 U.S. 179, 93 S.Ct. 739, 35 L.Ed.2d 201

MR. JUSTICE BLACKMUN delivered the opinion of the Court.

In this appeal, the criminal abortion statutes recently enacted in Georgia are challenged on constitutional grounds. The statutes are §§ 26-1201 through 26-1203 of the State's Criminal Code, formulated by Georgia Laws, 1968 Session, pp. 1249, 1277-1280. In *Roe* v. *Wade, ante,* we today have struck down, as constitutionally defective, the Texas criminal abortion statutes that are representative of provisions long in effect in a majority of our States. The Georgia legislation, however, is different and merits separate consideration.

I

The statutes in question are reproduced as Appendix A. . . . As the appellants acknowledge, the 1968 statutes are patterned upon the American Law Institute's Model Penal Code, § 230.3 (Proposed Official Draft, 1962), reproduced as Appendix B, . . . The ALI proposal has served as the model for recent legislation in approximately one-fourth of our States. The new Georgia provisions replaced statutory law that had been in effect for more than 90 years. Georgia Laws 1876, No. 130, § 2, at 113. The predecessor statute paralleled the Texas legislation considered in *Roe* v. *Wade, supra,* and made all abortions criminal except those necessary "to preserve the life" of the pregnant woman. The new statutes have not been tested on constitutional grounds in the Georgia state courts.

Section 26-1201, with a referenced exception, makes abortion a crime, and § 26-1203 provides that a person convicted of that crime shall be punished by imprisonment for not less than one nor more than 10 years. Section 26-1202(a) states the exception and removes from § 1201's definition of criminal abortion, and thus makes noncriminal, an abortion "performed by a physician duly licensed" in Georgia when, "based upon his best clinical judgment . . . an abortion is necessary because:

"(1) A continuation of the pregnancy would endanger the life of the pregnant woman or would seriously and permanently injure her health; or

"(2) The fetus would very likely be born with a grave, permanent, and irremediable mental or physical defect; or

"(3) The pregnancy resulted from forcible or statutory rape."

Section 26-1202 also requires, by numbered subdivisions of its subsection (b), that, for an abortion to be authorized or performed as a noncriminal procedure, additional conditions must be fulfilled. These are (1) and (2) residence of the woman in Georgia; (3) reduction to writing of the performing physician's medical judgment that an abortion is justified for one or more of the reasons specified by § 26-1202(a), with written concurrence in that judgment by at least two other Georgia-licensed physicians, based upon their separate personal medical examinations of the woman; (4) performance of the abortion in a hospital licensed by the State Board of Health and also accredited by the Joint Commission on Accreditation of Hospitals; (5) advance approval by an abortion committee of not less than three members of the hospital's staff; (6) certifications in a rape situation; and (7), (8), and (9) maintenance and confidentiality of records. There is a provision (subsection (c)) for judicial determination of the legality of a proposed abortion on petition of the judicial circuit law officer or of a close relative, as therein defined, of the unborn child, and for expeditious hearing of that petition. There is also a provision (subsection (e)) giving a hospital the right not to admit an abortion patient and giving any physician and any hospital employee or staff member the right, on moral or religious grounds, not to participate in the procedure.

II

On April 16, 1970, Mary Doe, 23 other individuals (nine described as Georgia-licensed physicians, seven as nurses registered in the State, five as clergymen, and two as social workers), and two nonprofit Georgia corporations that advocate abortion reform instituted this federal action in the Northern District of Georgia against the State's attorney general, the district attorney of Fulton County, and the chief of police of the city of Atlanta. The plaintiffs sought a declaratory judgment that the Georgia abortion statutes were unconstitutional in their entirety. They also sought injunctive relief restraining the defendants and their successors from enforcing the statutes.

Mary Doe alleged:

(1) She was a 22-year-old Georgia citizen, married, and nine weeks pregnant. She had three living children. The two older ones had been placed in a foster home because of Doe's poverty and inability to care for them. The youngest, born July 19, 1969, had been placed for adoption. Her husband had recently abandoned her and she was forced to live with her indigent parents and their eight children. She and her husband, however, had become reconciled. He was a construction worker employed only sporadically. She had been a mental patient at the State Hospital. She had been advised that an abortion could be performed on her with less danger to her health than if she gave birth to the child she was carrying. She would be unable to care for or support the new child.

(2) On March 25, 1970, she applied to the Abortion Committee of Grady Memorial Hospital, Atlanta, for a therapeutic abortion under § 26-1202. Her application was denied 16 days later, on April 10, when she was eight weeks pregnant, on the ground that her situation was not one described in § 26-1202(a).

(3) Because her application was denied, she was forced either to relinquish "her right to decide when and how many children she will bear" or to seek an abortion that was illegal under the Georgia statutes. This invaded her rights of privacy and liberty in matters related to family, marriage, and sex, and deprived her of the right to choose whether to bear children. This was a violation of rights guaranteed her by the First, Fourth, Fifth, Ninth, and Fourteenth Amendments. The statutes also denied her equal protection and procedural due process and, because they were unconstitutionally vague, deterred hospitals and doctors from performing abortions. She sued "on her own behalf and on behalf of all others similarly situated."

The other plaintiffs alleged that the Georgia statutes "chilled and deterred" them from practicing their respective professions and deprived them of rights guaranteed by the First, Fourth, and Fourteenth Amendments. These plaintiffs also purported to sue on their own behalf and on behalf of others similarly situated.

A three-judge district court was convened. An offer of proof as to Doe's identity was made, but the court deemed it unnecessary to receive that proof. The case was then tried on the pleadings and interrogatories.

The District Court, *per curiam,* 319 F. Supp. 1048 (ND Ga. 1970), held that all the plaintiffs had standing but that only Doe presented a justiciable controversy. On the merits, the court concluded that the limitation in the Georgia statute of the "number of reasons for which an abortion may be sought," *id.,* at 1056, improperly restricted Doe's rights of privacy articulated in *Griswold* v. *Connecticut,* 381 U.S. 479 (1965), and of "personal liberty," both of which it thought "broad enough to include the decision to abort a pregnancy," 319 F. Supp., at 1055. As a consequence, the court held invalid those portions of §§ 26-1202(a) and (b)(3) limiting legal abortions to the three situations specified; § 26-1202(b)(6) relating to certifications in a rape situation; and § 26-1202(c) authorizing a court test. Declaratory relief was granted accordingly. The court, however, held that Georgia's interest in protection of health, and the existence of a *"potential* of independent human existence" (emphasis in original), *id.,* at 1055, justified state regulation of "the manner of performance as well as the quality of the final decision to abort," *id.,* at 1056, and it refused to strike down the other provisions of the statutes. It denied the request for an injunction, *id.,* at 1057.

Claiming that they were entitled to an injunction and to broader relief, the plaintiffs took a direct appeal pursuant to 28 U.S.C. § 1253. We postponed decision on jurisdiction to the hearing on the merits. 402 U.S. 941 (1971). The defendants also purported to appeal, pursuant to § 1253, but their appeal was dismissed for want of jurisdiction. 402 U.S. 936 (1971). We are advised by the appellees, Brief 42, that an alternative appeal on their part is pending in the United States Court of Appeals for the Fifth Circuit. The extent, therefore, to which the District Court decision was adverse to the defendants, that is, the extent to which portions of the Georgia statutes were held to be unconstitutional, technically is not now before us. *Swarb* v. *Lennox,* 405 U.S. 191, 201 (1972).

III

Our decision in *Roe* v. *Wade, ante,* ... established (1) that, despite her pseudonym, we may accept as true, for this case, Mary Doe's existence and her pregnant state on April 16, 1970; (2) that the constitutional issue is substantial; (3) that the interim termination of Doe's and all other Georgia pregnancies in existence in 1970 has not rendered the case moot; and (4) that Doe presents a justiciable controversy and has standing to maintain the action. . . .

IV

The appellants attack on several grounds those portions of the Georgia abortion statutes that remain after the District Court decision: undue restriction of a right to personal and marital privacy; vagueness; deprivation of substantive and procedural due process; improper restriction to Georgia residents; and denial of equal protection.

A. *Roe* v. *Wade, supra,* sets forth our conclusion that a pregnant woman does not have an absolute constitutional right to an abortion on her demand. What is said there is applicable here and need not be repeated. . . .

C. Appellants argue that § 26-1202(a) of the Georgia statutes, as it has been left by the District Court's decision, is unconstitutionally vague. This argument centers on the proposition that, with the District Court's having stricken the statutorily specified reasons, it still remains a crime for a physician to perform an abortion except when, as § 26-1202(a) reads, it is "based upon his best clinical judgment that an abortion is necessary." The appellants contend that the word "necessary" does not warn the physician of what conduct is proscribed; that the statute is wholly without objective standards and is subject to diverse interpretation; and that doctors will choose to err on the side of caution and will be arbitrary.

The net result of the District Court's decision is that the abortion determination, so far as the physician is concerned, is made in the exercise of his professional, that is, his "best clinical," judgment in the light of *all* the attendant circumstances. He is not now restricted to the three situations originally specified. Instead, he may range farther afield wherever his medical judgment, properly and professionally exercised, so dictates and directs him.

The vagueness argument is set at rest by the decision in *United States* v. *Vuitch,* 402 U.S. 62, 71-72 (1971), where the issue was raised with respect to a District of Columbia statute making abortions criminal "unless the same were done as necessary for the preservation of the mother's life or health and under the direction of a competent licensed practitioner of medicine." That statute has been construed to bear upon psychological as well as physical well-being. This being so, the Court concluded that the term "health" presented no problem of vagueness. "Indeed, whether a particular operation is necessary for a patient's physical or mental health is a judgment that physicians are obviously called upon to make routinely whenever surgery is considered." *Id.,* at 72. This conclusion is equally applicable here. Whether, in the words of the Georgia statute, "an abortion is necessary" is a professional judgment that the Georgia physician will be called upon to make routinely.

We agree with the District Court, 319 F. Supp., at 1058, that the medical judgment may be exercised in the light of all factors—physical, emotional, psychological, familial, and the woman's age—relevant to the well-being of the patient. All these factors may relate to health. This allows the attending physician the room he needs to make his best medical judgment. And it is room that operates for the benefit, not the disadvantage, of the pregnant woman.

D. The appellants next argue that the District Court should have declared unconstitutional three procedural demands of the Georgia statute: (1) that the abortion be performed in a hospital accredited by the Joint Commission on Accreditation of Hospitals: (2) that the procedure be approved by the hospital staff abortion committee; and (3) that the performing physician's judgment be confirmed by the independent examinations of the patient by two other licensed physicians. The appellants attack these provisions not only on the ground that they unduly restrict the woman's right of privacy, but also on procedural due process and equal protection grounds. The physician-appellants also argue that, by subjecting a doctor's individual medical judgment to committee approval and to confirming consultations, the statute impermissibly restricts the physician's right to practice his profession and deprives him of due process.

1. *JCAH accreditation.* The Joint Commission on Accreditation of Hospitals is an organization without governmental sponsorship or overtones. No question whatever is raised concerning the integrity of the organization or the high purpose of the accreditation process. That process, however, has to do with hospital standards generally and has no present particularized concern with abortion as a medical or surgical procedure. In Georgia, there is no restriction on the performance of non-abortion surgery in a hospital not yet accredited by the JCAH so long as other requirements imposed by the State, such as licensing of the hospital and of the operating surgeon, are met. See Georgia Code § § 88-1901(a) and 88-1905 (1971) and 84-907 (Supp. 1971). Furthermore, accreditation by the Commission is not granted until a hospital has been in operation at least one year. The Model Penal Code, § 230.3, Appendix B hereto, contains no requirement for JCAH accreditation. And the Uniform Abortion Act (Final Draft, Aug. 1971), approved by the American Bar Association in February 1972, contains no JCAH-accredited hospital specification. Some courts have held that a JCAH-accreditation requirement is an overbroad infringement of fundamental rights because it does not relate to the particular medical problems and dangers of the abortion operation. *Poe* v. *Menghini,* 339 F. Supp., at 993-994; *People* v. *Barksdale,* 96 Cal. Rptr. 265, 273-274 (Cal. App. 1971).

We hold that the JCAH-accreditation requirement does not withstand constitutional scrutiny in the present context. It is a requirement that simply is not "based on differences that are reasonably related to the purposes of the Act in which it is found." *Morey* v. *Doud,* 354 U.S. 457, 465 (1957).

This is not to say that Georgia may not or should not, from and after the end of the first trimester, adopt standards for licensing all facilities where abortions may be performed so long as those standards are legitimately related to the objective the State seeks to accomplish. The appellants contend that such a relationship would be lacking even in a lesser requirement that an abortion be performed in a licensed hospital, as opposed to a facility, such as a clinic, that may be required by the State to possess all the staffing and services necessary to perform an abortion safely (including those adequate to handle serious complications or other emergency, or arrangements with a nearby hospital to provide such services). Appellants and various *amici* have presented us with a mass of data purporting to demonstrate that some facilities other than hospitals are entirely adequate to perform abortions if they possess these qualifications. The State, on the other hand, has not presented persuasive data to show that only hospitals meet its acknowledged interest in insuring the quality of the operation and the full protection of the patient. We feel compelled to agree with appellants that the State must show more than it has in order to prove that only the full resources of a licensed hospital, rather than those of some other appropriately licensed institution, satisfy these health interests. We hold that the hospital requirement of the Georgia law, because it fails to exclude the first trimester of pregnancy, see *Roe* v. *Wade, ante,* at 163, is also invalid. In so holding we naturally express no opinion on the medical judgment involved in any particular case, that is, whether the patient's situation is such that an abortion should be performed in a hospital, rather than in some other facility.

2. *Committee approval.* The second aspect of the appellants' procedural attack relates to the hospital abortion committee and to the pregnant woman's asserted lack of access to that committee. Relying primarily on *Goldberg* v. *Kelly,* 397 U.S. 254 (1970), concerning the termination of welfare benefits, and *Wisconsin* v. *Constantineau,* 400 U.S. 433 (1971), concerning the posting of an alcoholic's name, Doe first argues that she was denied due process because she could not make a presentation to the committee. It is not clear from the record, however, whether Doe's own consulting physician was or was not a member of the committee or did or did not present her case, or, indeed, whether she herself was or was not there. We see nothing in the Georgia statute that explicitly denies access to the committee by or on behalf of the woman. If the access point alone were involved, we would not be persuaded to strike down the committee provision on the unsupported assumption that access is not provided.

Appellants attack the discretion the statute leaves to the committee. The most concrete argument they advance is their suggestion that it is still a badge of infamy "in many minds" to bear an illegitimate child, and that the Georgia system enables the committee members' personal views as to extramarital sex relations, and punishment therefor, to govern their decisions. This approach obviously is one founded on suspicion and one that discloses a lack of confidence in the integrity of physicians. To say that physicians will be guided in their hospital committee decision by their predilections on extramarital sex unduly narrows the issue to pregnancy outside marriage. (Doe's own situation did not involve extramarital sex and its product.) The appellants' suggestion is necessarily somewhat degrading to the conscientious physician, particularly the obstetrician, whose professional activity is concerned with the physical and mental welfare, the woes, the emotions, and the concern of his female patients. He, perhaps more than anyone else, is knowledgeable in this area of patient care, and he is aware of human frailty, so-called "error," and needs. The good physician—despite the presence of rascals in the medical profession, as in all others, we trust that most physicians are "good"—will have a sympathy and an understanding for the pregnant patient that probably is not exceeded by those who participate in other areas of professional counseling.

It is perhaps worth noting that the abortion committee has a function of its own. It is a committee of the hospital and it is composed of members of the institution's medical staff. The membership usually is a changing one. In this way, its work burden is shared and is more readily accepted. The committee's function is protective. It enables the hospital appropriately to be advised that its posture and activities are in accord with legal requirements. It is to be remembered that the hospital is an entity and that it, too, has legal rights and legal obligations.

Saying all this, however, does not settle the issue of the constitutional propriety of the committee requirement. Viewing the Georgia statute as a whole, we see no constitutionally justifiable pertinence in the structure for the advance approval by the abortion committee. With regard to the protection of potential life, the medical judgment is already completed prior to the committee stage, and review by a committee once removed from diagnosis is basically redundant. We are not cited to any other surgical procedure made subject to committee approval as a matter of state criminal law. The woman's right to receive medical care in accordance with her licensed physician's best judgment and the physician's right to administer it are substantially limited by this statutorily imposed overview. And the hospital itself is otherwise fully protected. Under § 26-1202(e), the hospital is free not to admit a patient for an abortion. It is even free not to have an abortion committee. Further, a physician or any other employee has the right to refrain, for moral or religious reasons, from participating in the abortion procedure. These provisions obviously are in the statute in order to afford appropriate protection to the individual and to the denominational hospital. Section 26-1202(e) affords adequate protection to the hospital, and little more is provided by the committee prescribed by § 26-1202(b)(5).

We conclude that the interposition of the hospital abortion committee is unduly restrictive of the patient's rights and needs that, at this point, have already been medically delineated and substantiated by her personal physician. To ask more serves neither the hospital nor the State.

3. *Two-doctor concurrence.* The third aspect of the appellants' attack centers on the "time and availability of adequate medical facilities and personnel." It is said that the system imposes substantial and irrational roadblocks and "is patently unsuited" to prompt determination of the abortion decision. Time, of course, is critical in abortion. Risks during the first trimester of pregnancy are admittedly lower than during later months.

The appellants purport to show by a local study of Grady Memorial Hospital (serving indigent residents in Fulton and DeKalb Counties) that the "mechanics of the system itself forced ... discontinuance of the abortion process" because the median time for the workup was 15 days. The same study shows, however, that 27% of the candidates for abortion were already 13 or more weeks pregnant at the time of application, that is, they were at the end of or beyond the first trimester when they made their applications. It is too much to say, as appellants do, that these particular persons "were victims of a system over which they [had] no control." If higher risk was incurred because of abortions in the second rather than the first trimester, much of that risk was due to delay in application, and not to the alleged cumbersomeness of the system. We note, in passing, that appellant Doe had no delay problem herself; the decision in her case was made well within the first trimester.

It should be manifest that our rejection of the accredited-hospital requirement and, more important, of the abortion committee's advance approval eliminates the major grounds of the attack based on the sytem's delay and the lack of facilities. There remains, however, the required confirmation by two Georgia-licensed physicians in addition to the recommendation of the pregnant woman's own consultant (making under the statute, a total of six physicians involved, including the three on the hospital's abortion committee). We conclude that this provision, too, must fall.

The statute's emphasis, as has been repetitively noted, is on the attending physician's "best clinical judgment that an abortion is necessary." That should be sufficient. The reasons for the presence of the confirmation step in the statute are perhaps apparent, but they are insufficient to withstand constitutional challenge.

Again, no other voluntary medical or surgical procedure for which Georgia requires confirmation by two other physicians has been cited to us. If a physician is licensed by the State, he is recognized by the State as capable of exercising acceptable clinical judgment. If he fails in this, professional censure and deprivation of his license are available remedies. Required acquiescence by co-practitioners has no rational connection with a patient's needs and unduly infringes on the physician's right to practice. The attending physician will know when a consultation is advisable—the doubtful situation, the need for assurance when the medical decision is a delicate one, and the like. Physicians have followed this routine historically and know its usefulness and benefit for all concerned. It is still true today that "[r]eliance must be placed upon the assurance given by his license, issued by an authority competent to judge in that respect, that he [the physician] possesses the requisite qualifications." *Dent* v. *West Virginia*, 129 U.S. 114, 122-123 (1889). See *United States* v. *Vuitch*, 402 U.S., at 71.

E. The appellants attack the residency requirement of the Georgia law, §§ 26-1202(b)(1) and (b)(2), as violative of the right to travel stressed in *Shapiro* v. *Thompson*, 394 U.S. 618, 629-631 (1969), and other cases. A requirement of this kind, of course, could be deemed to have some relationship to the availability of post-procedure medical care for the aborted patient.

Nevertheless, we do not uphold the constitutionality of the residence requirement. It is not based on any policy of preserving state-supported facilities for Georgia residents, for the bar also applies to private hospitals and to privately retained physicians. There is no intimation, either, that Georgia facilities are utilized to capacity in caring for Georgia residents. Just as the Privileges and Immunities Clause, Const. Art. IV, § 2, protects persons who enter other States to ply their trade, *Ward* v. *Maryland,* 12 Wall. 418, 430 (1871); *Blake* v. *McClung,* 172 U.S. 239, 248-256 (1898), so must it protect persons who enter Georgia seeking the medical services that are available there. See *Toomer* v. *Witsell,* 334 U.S. 385, 396-397 (1948). A contrary holding would mean that a State could limit to its own residents the general medical care available within its borders. This we could not approve.

F. The last argument on this phase of the case is one that often is made, namely, that the Georgia system is violative of equal protection because it discriminates against the poor. The appellants do not urge that abortions should be performed by persons other than licensed physicians, so we have no argument that because the wealthy can better afford physicians, the poor should have nonphysicians made available to them. The appellants acknowledged that the procedures are "nondiscriminatory in ... express terms" but they suggest that they have produced invidious discriminations. The District Court rejected this approach out of hand. 319 F. Supp., at 1056. It rests primarily on the accreditation and approval and confirmation requirements, discussed above, and on the assertion that most of Georgia's counties have no accredited hospital. We have set aside the accreditation, approval, and confirmation requirements, however, and with that, the discrimination argument collapses in all significant aspects.

V

The appellants complain, finally, of the District Court's denial of injunctive relief. A like claim was made in *Roe* v. *Wade, ante,* p. 113. We declined decision there insofar as injunctive relief was concerned, and we decline it here. We assume that Georgia's prosecutorial authorities will give full recognition to the judgment of the Court.

In summary, we hold that the JCAH-accredited hospital provision and the requirements as to approval by the hospital abortion committee, as to confirmation by two independent physicians, and as to residence in Georgia are all violative of the Fourteenth Amendment. Specifically, the following portions of § 26-1202(b), remaining after the District Court's judgment, are invalid:

(1) Subsections (1) and (2).

(2) That portion of Subsection (3) following the words "[s]uch physician's judgment is reduced to writing."

(3) Subsections (4) and (5).

The judgment of the District Court is modified accordingly and, as so modified, is affirmed. Costs are allowed to the appellants.

[The concurring opinion of Mr. Justice Douglas is omitted.]

MR. JUSTICE WHITE, with whom MR. JUSTICE REHNQUIST joins, dissenting.

At the heart of the controversy in these cases are those recurring pregnancies that pose no danger whatsoever to the life or health of the mother but are, nevertheless, unwanted for any one or more of a variety of reasons—convenience, family planning, economics, dislike of children, the embarrassment of illegitimacy, etc. The common claim before us is that for any one of such reasons, or for no reason at all, and without asserting or claiming any threat to life or health, any woman is entitled to an abortion at her request if she is able to find a medical advisor willing to undertake the procedure.

The Court for the most part sustains this position: During the period prior to the time the fetus becomes viable, the Constitution of the United States values the convenience, whim, or caprice of the putative mother more than the life or potential life of the fetus; the Constitution, therefore, guarantees the right to an abortion as against any state law or policy seeking to protect the fetus from an abortion not prompted by more compelling reasons of the mother.

With all due respect, I dissent. I find nothing in the language or history of the Constitution to support the Court's judgment. The Court simply fashions and announces a new constitutional right for pregnant mothers and, with scarcely any reason or authority for its action, invests that right with sufficient substance to override most existing state abortion statutes. The upshot is that the people and the legislatures of the 50 States are constitutionally disentitled to weigh the relative importance of the continued existence and development of the fetus, on the one hand, against a spectrum of possible impacts on the mother, on the other hand. As an exercise of raw judicial power, the Court perhaps has authority to do what it does today; but in my view its judgment is an improvident and extravagant exercise of the power of judicial review that the Constitution extends to this Court.

The Court apparently values the convenience of the pregnant mother more than the continued existence and development of the life or potential life that she carries. Whether or not I might agree with that marshaling of values, I can in no event join the Court's judgment because I find no constitutional warrant for imposing such an order of priorities on the people and legislatures of the States. In a sensitive area such as this, involving as it does issues over which reasonable men may easily and heatedly differ, I cannot accept the Court's exercise of its clear power of choice by interposing a constitutional barrier to state efforts to protect human life and by investing mothers and doctors with the constitutionally protected right to exterminate it. This issue, for the most part, should be left with the people and to the political processes the people have devised to govern their affairs.

It is my view, therefore, that the Texas statute is not constitutionally infirm because it denies abortions to those who seek to serve only their convenience rather than to protect their life or health. Nor is this plaintiff, who claims no threat to her mental or physical health, entitled to assert the possible rights of those women whose pregnancy assertedly implicates their health. This, together, with *United States* v. *Vuitch,* 402 U.S. 62 (1971), dictates reversal of the judgment of the District Court.

Likewise, because Georgia may constitutionally forbid abortions to putative mothers who, like the plaintiff in this case, do not fall within the reach of § 26-1202(a) of its criminal code, I have no occasion, and the District Court had none, to consider the constitutionality of the procedural requirements of the Georgia statute as applied to those pregnancies posing substantial hazards to either life or health. I would reverse the judgment of the District Court in the Georgia case.

NOTES

1. Notwithstanding the decisions of the Supreme Court in *Roe v. Wade* and *Doe v. Bolton,* various problems persist. For one thing, the philosophical debate over when life begins (see *Rosen,* p. 132 of main volume) has not quieted. Advocates of the view that life begins at conception have been seeking adoption of a federal constitutional amendment that would embody this principle in the nation's fundamental law. See, e.g., S.J. Res. 119 (1973). A state statute attempting to do the same thing was held unconstitutional in the light of *Roe* and *Doe* in Doe v. Israel, 358 F. Supp. 1193 (1973). Should such a federal constitutional amendment ever be adopted, it would undoubtedly have the effect of overruling *Roe* and *Doe.* But the likelihood that this will occur in the foreseeable future is remote. Not only is the process formidable—only 26 of approximately 1500 attempts to amend the Constitution have succeeded—but American public opinion appears to be strongly in favor of the liberal abortion policies reflected in *Roe* and *Doe.*

2. Another problem concerns the validity of statutes requiring spousal and/or parental consent to abortions. A Florida statute of this type was held invalid by a

three-judge federal court in Coe v. Gerstein,   F. Supp.   (1973), although the court refused to issue an injunction. In a per curiam opinion, the United States Supreme Court has upheld the refusal to issue the injunction, while dismissing for want of jurisdiction the direct of the State of Florida from the declaratory judgment invalidating the statute. Gerstein v. Coe,   U.S.   , 42 L.W. 3666 (June 4, 1974). Compare Jones v. Smith, 278 So. 2d 339 (Fla. App. 1973). The Supreme Court itself has expressly refrained from discussing the question of paternal rights in the abortion decision, since they were not raised in either *Doe* or *Roe*. See footnote 67 in *Roe*, p. 10 of Supplement, *supra*. What reasons are there for and against permitting a state to require parental (in the case of minors) or spousal consent to the abortion decision? For a decision holding that an indigent minor could validly consent to an abortion without parental consent—under a statute which dispensed with any parental consent requirement for "medical and surgical care related to [the] pregnancy" of an unmarried, pregnant minor, Cal. Civ. C. § 34.5 (1954)—see Ballard v. Anderson, 4 Cal. 3rd 873, 484 P.2d 1345, 95 Cal. Rptr. 1 (1971). The Massachussetts Supreme Court has also ruled that a husband cannot prevent his wife from having an abortion if that is her wish. San Francisco Chronicle, March 15, 1974, p. 2.

3. May a hospital validly adopt a policy refusing to perform abortions? No, held a federal court in the case of a public hospital in Nyberg v. Virginia Municipal Hospital, 361 F. Supp. 932 (1973). Should the result be the same for private hospitals? When does a private hospital become invested with a public character? Compare *McCabe*, p. 163 of main volume. What other facts might be relevant in determining the validity *vel non* of a "private" hospital's no-abortion policy? Should an individual physician be permitted to refuse to perform an abortion as a matter of conscience? Should a hospital be permitted to assert an "institutional conscience" as justification for refusing to perform abortions?

4. The directive of the New York State Commissioner of Social Services, discussed in note 9, p. 162 of the main volume, distinguishing "elective" from "medically indicated" abortions for Medicaid coverage, was invalidated as a violation of the equal-protection guarantee in Klein v. Nassau County Medical Center, 347 F. Supp. 496 (1972). Following *Roe* and *Doe*, however, the Supreme Court vacated the judgment and remanded the case for further consideration in the light of those decisions. 412 U.S. 925, 93 S. Ct. 2748, 37 L.Ed.2d 152 (1972).

5. Regardless of what one might think of the results in *Roe* and *Doe*, what problems are presented by the process of judicial reasoning in those cases? See Ely, The Wages of Crying Wolf: A Comment on Roe v. Wade, 82 Yale L.J. 920 (1973); Tribe, The Supreme Court, 1972 Term, Foreword: Toward a Model of Roles in the Due Process of Life and Law, 87 Harv. L. Rev. 1 (1973).

Page 176. Following note 3, add:

3a. Relying upon the passage cited in note 3, *supra,* the Idaho Supreme Court, in Harrigfeld v. District Court, 95 Id. 540, 511 P.2d 822, held that a statute making

18 the age of majority for females and 21 for males violated the equal-protection guarantee of the federal constitution. The issue in *Harrigfeld* was whether the wife and child of a 20-year-old male decedent could sue for his wrongful death in the light of a statute that conferred such rights upon a decedent's heirs only if he were not a minor. In that context, the Idaho Supreme Court held that the disparity, based upon sex, in the age of majority in force at the time the cause of action arose was invalid. In the light of an intervening legislative amendment making 18 the uniform age of majority for both sexes, however, the court held that the earlier statute need not be nullified. Instead, it cured the unconstitutional inequality by making 18 the age of majority for men too.

The Utah Supreme Court reached a contrary result, however, in Stanton v. Stanton, 30 Utah 2d 315, 517 P.2d 1010 (1974), refusing to find an equal-protection violation in a statute making 21 the age of majority for males and 18 for females. In *Stanton,* plaintiff mother, at the time of her divorce from defendant father, had been awarded $100 a month support payments for each of their children—Sherri, born in 1953, and Rick, born in 1955. When Sherri reached majority at age 18, the husband's obligation had terminated, whereas his obligation to pay support for Rick would continue until he reached majority at age 21. Applying a "reasonable basis" test, the court made the following observations:

> It may be that our ancestors for generations before us have been misguided in their belief that there are some fundamental differences between the sexes. But it is remarkable how some of those old notions do continue to prevail as to numerous interesting differences. Included among them is the belief held by many that generally it is the man's primary responsibility to provide a home and its essentials for the family; and that however many exceptions and whatever necessary and proper variations therefrom may exist in differing circumstances, it is a salutary thing for him to get a good education and/or training before he undertakes those responsibilities.

> Perhaps more important than this, there is another widely accepted idea: that girls tend generally to mature physically, emotionally and mentally before boys, and that they generally tend to marry earlier. We realize that as a court made up of men, there is a possibility of masculine bias, which we should endeavor to guard against in considering matters of this character. But we do not regard it as our judicial function to pass upon the soundness or the unsoundness of the ideas just mentioned above. What we do note is our knowledge of their existence; and that they have played an essential role in the history of the development of the law as declared in the statute under attack.

> Should it be deemed the prerogative of the court to initiate a change in the age at which the parental duty of support terminates, it would be appropriate to reflect upon another aspect of the problem: that is, how would the shoe fit on the other foot? Assume that we would take judicial cognizance of the trend in the differing role of women, perhaps we should similarly notice the trend toward the earlier emancipation and fuller freedom of conduct of minors; and that this applies to both boys and girls. One indication of this is

the recent reduction of the age for voting to 18. From this it could be argued with equal logic that instead of extending the defendant's duty of supporting Sherri to 21, he should be relieved of the duty of supporting the son Rick (age 16) when he reaches 18. Thus in a contest between the plaintiff and the defendant as to the support of these children, there would be a net loss to the plaintiff.

Had an equal protection violation been found, how should the inequality have been cured?

Page 182. Following note 3, add:

4. In Friedrich v. Katz, 73 Misc. 2d 663, 341 N.Y.S. 2d 932 (1973), § 15(2) of the New York Domestic Relations Law, setting an 18-year-old minimum for females and 21 for males to be married without parental consent, was upheld by a trial court as against an equal-protection attack. In the court's view, the "natural order ... designates the male as the provider in the usual marriage relation. That duty ... is sufficient reason to require males to be older and generally more suited to their duty before they may independently decide to marry."

Without disputing that basic premise, a contrary result was reached more recently by another New York trial court in Berger v. Adornato, 350 N.Y.S. 2d 520 (1973). Placing its decision on the ground of equal protection (although conceding that due process might have been a more satisfactory basis for its analysis), the court in *Berger* stated:

There is no guarantee of "alike treatment" to all those in the classification. The burden of fulfilling the state need is assigned to the parents. There are no safeguards, guidelines, limitations or assurances that the parents will perform their responsibility within the framework of the allegedly valid state objectives. There is no provision for judicial review, since the authority of the parents is unrestricted, and, therefore, final.

Thus the parents may use their authority to act on behalf of the state interest. Or, they may do whatever they please. What can result is exactly what has occurred in this case. A mature, emancipated man is denied a fundamental right on what appear to be arbitrary grounds wholly unrelated to the alleged state purpose [to assure that below-21-year-old males who marry are financially responsible and emotionally mature] (350 N.Y.S. 2d 523).

Chapter 4

Sex Roles and Marriage

Page 192. Following note 7, add:

8. In Stuart v. Board of Supervisors of Elections, 266 Md. 440, 295 A.2d 223 (1972), the Maryland Court of Appeals reviewed English common law precedents and the common law of Maryland, and concluded that both permitted a married woman to retain her premarital name so long as her use of that name following marriage was consistent and nonfraudulent. Like the factual situation in *State ex rel Krupa v. Green, supra* note 1, the one in Stuart also involved an oral prenuptial agreement that the wife would continue to use her own, and not her husband's, surname after marriage. The California attorney general has issued an opinion stating that a wife need not go to court or file a petition to use her "maiden" name. San Francisco Chronicle, March 15, 1974, p. 2.

9. Further documentation of the position that the common law permitted, but did not require, married women to assume their husbands' surnames appears in MacDougall, Married Women's Common Law Right to Their Own Surnames, 1 Women's Rights L. Rep. #3, 2 (1972/73).

Page 207. Following note 5, add:

6. See also Littlefield, Sex-Based Discrimination and Credit Granting Practices, 5 Conn. L. Rev. 575 (1973).

Page 211. Before New Mexico Stats. 1953, add:

New Mexico voters, in the 1972 general elections, added an Equal Rights Amendment to the state constitution, which became effective on July 1, 1973. That amendment provides: "Equality of rights under law shall not be denied on account of the sex of any person." To implement the State ERA, the New Mexico legislature enacted, among other statutes, the "Community Property Act of 1973," thereby changing many of the community-property principles under state law. A major innovation is found in N.M. Rev. Stats. § 57-4A-7.1 and § 57-4A-8, which provide:

> **57-4-A-7.1 Presumption of management and control of commercial community personal property.**—A. It is presumed that the husband shall have the sole power to manage, control, dispose of or encumber any commercial community personal property, personal property which is part of a community business enterprise or community personal property used in a business, the proceeds of which support the family in whole or in part, unless the wife has

assumed her rights of management of such property, as provided in section 57-4A-8 NMSA 1953, by filing a written statement with the county clerk of the county in which she resides.

B. Any person dealing in good faith with a wife in reliance upon such written statement, shall incur no liability to the husband for so dealing, and shall be under no obligation to recognize the sole authority of the husband to manage, control, dispose of or encumber the property covered by the statement, until such statment has been revoked.

C. As to any third person, such statement may be revoked only by an instrument in writing signed by the wife or by an order of any court having jurisdiction to enter such an order. The revocation shall not be effective as to any third person until such person has been furnished with a copy of the written instrument or order of revocation.

57-4A-8. Management and control of other community personal property. —A. Except as provided in section 57-4A-7.1 NMSA 1953 and except as provided in subsections B and C of this section, either spouse alone has full power to manage, control, dispose of and encumber the entire community personal property.

B. Where only one [1] spouse is:

(1) named in a document of title to community personal property; or

(2) named or designated in a written agreement between that spouse and a third party as having sole authority to manage, control, dispose of or encumber the community personal property which is described in the agreement, whether the agreement was executed prior to or after July 1, 1973; only the spouse so named may manage, control, dispose of or encumber the community personal property evidenced by a document or certificate in the name of that spouse alone or described in a written agreement to which only that spouse is a party.

C. Both spouses must join to manage, control, dispose of or encumber community personal property which is evidenced by a document of title in the name of both spouses where the names of the spouses are joined by the word "and."

An explanation for the presumption contained in Section 57-4A-7.1 is found in Section 57-4A-1.1 as follows:

57-4A-1.1. Purpose of act.—The purpose of the Community Property Act of 1973 [57-4A-1 to 57-4A-11] is to comply with the provisions of section 18 of article 2 of the Constitution of New Mexico, as it was amended in 1972 and as it will be effective on July 1, 1973, in so far as it affects the equal rights of persons regardless of sex. The purpose of the statutory presumption contained herein, that the husband shall be the sole manager of community personal property unless there is an agreement to the contrary, or unless the wife has exercised her option to assume her rights of management of the community personal property, is to provide temporary procedures by which the four hundred year tradition of husband-management can be maintained in those families where the desires of the wife are not made known by either an agreement or by filing a document claiming that right.

Is this a valid reason for permitting husbands to manage and control commercial or business community property? What problems inhere in placing the burden for changing this arrangement upon the wife? Does the statute comport with the command of the state's Equal Rights Amendment?

Another statutory change made to implement the New Mexico Equal Rights Amendment was in the area of testamentary powers. Thus, § 29-1-8 has been repealed, and § 29-1-9 revised to read:

29-1-9. Death of spouse—Community property.—Upon the death of a spouse, the entire community property goes to the surviving spouse, subject to the deceased's power of testamentary disposition over one-half of the community property. In the case of the dissolution of the community by the death of a spouse, the entire community property is subject to the community debts, and the family allowance. The deceased spouse's separate debts and funeral expenses and the charge and expenses of administration are to be satisfied first from his separate property, excluding property held in joint tenancy. Should such property be insufficient, then the deceased spouse's undivided one-half interest in the community property shall be liable.

Page 218. Before California Probate Code, insert:

See text of revised N.M. Rev. Stats. § 29-1-9, above, under which both spouses now have equal rights to dispose of one-half of the community property by will.

Page 257. To note 1, add:

New Mexico has now repealed the "unwritten law defense" in furtherance of the policy expressed in the state's own recent Equal Rights Amendment.

Page 274. To note 3, add:

Compare In re Marriage of Walton, 28 Cal. App. 3d, 104 Cal. Rptr. 472 (1972), in which the respondent wife "asserted that elimination of the fault concept in dissolution proceedings is unjust and unfair because it permits a spouse guilty of morally reprehensible conduct to take advantage of that conduct in terminating marriage against the wishes of an entirely unoffending spouse." 104 Cal. Rptr. at 481. To which the court replied: "While this may be true and while such a result may be offensive to those steeped in the tradition of personal responsibility based upon fault, this contention presents no issue cognizable in the courts. . . . 'It is not the province of the courts to inquire into the wisdom of legislative enactments.' " *Id.* The same case also held that the statutory phrase "irreconcilable differences which have caused the irremediable breakdown of the marriage" was not unconstitutionally vague or ambiguous; and that allowing a marriage to be dissolved for such reasons neither unconstitutionally impaired the obligations of a contract nor deprived the wife of property without due process of law.

Page 282. Following note 1, add:

2. Fla. Stat. § 61.08 (1967), at issue in *Pacheco,* was amended in 1971 to read as follows:

(1) In a proceeding for dissolution of marriage, the court may grant alimony to either party, which alimony may be rehabilitative or permanent in nature. In any award of alimony, the court may order periodic payments or payments in lump sum or both. The court may consider the adultery of a spouse and the circumstances thereof in determining whether alimony shall be awarded to such spouse and the amount of alimony, if any, to be awarded to such spouse.

(2) In determining a proper award of alimony, the court may consider any factor necessary to do equity and justice between the parties.

In Lefler v. Lefler, 264 So. 2d 112 (1972), a husband, having procured a default judgment in a marriage dissolution proceeding, had been awarded by the trial court, pursuant to the above statute, as lump sum alimony the wife's interest in the marital domicile which had been held as a tenancy by the entirety. This was reversed by the appellate court, on the ground that the evidence "clearly could not sustain a finding that" the husband did not have the ability to provide for his necessities. That the husband "had never received any money from his wife and had been paying the bills and 'keeping things going' " was regarded as irrelevant to the alimony decision in the appellate court's view, since the husband's entitlement to alimony, like the wife's under former law, "depends upon a showing of his need and the wife's ability to pay." 264 So. 2d at 114.

Page 284. Following note, add:

2. In Wiegand v. Wiegand, 42 U.S.L.W. 2183 (1973), a Pennsylvania Superior Court, basing its ruling on the Equal Rights of that state's constitution, Pa. Const., Art. I, § 27, held invalid Pennsylvania law permitting a wife, but not a husband, to get a divorce from bed and board, alimony pendente lite, and attendant counsel fees and costs. By contrast, the Virginia Supreme Court found no reversible error in a lower court ruling that neither equal protection nor due process are denied by Virginia statutes affording remedies to wives and women that are not afforded to

husbands. Lilly v. Lilly,   S.E.2d   (Oct. 23, 1973), review denied by United
States Supreme Court, Docket No. 73-1130, N.Y. Times, May 14, 1974, p. 18, col.
3.

Page 284. Before L, insert:

KK. PROPERTY DISTRIBUTION FOLLOWING
MARRIAGE DISSOLUTION

In re Marriage of Cary
California Court of Appeals, First District, Div. 1, 1973
34 Cal. App.3d 345, 109 Cal. Rptr. 862

ELKINGTON, J.—The principal issue presented by this appeal concerns California's
Family Law Act (Civ. Code, § § 4000-5138, inclusive, sometimes hereafter the
"Act"), effective January 1, 1970, which provides among other things that the concept of individual "fault," or "guilt," or "punishment" for such human error, shall
not be considered in determining *family property rights.*

Paul Cary and Janet Forbes, never married to each other, lived together for more
than eight years. During that time they held themselves out to their friends and
parents, and to the world generally, as a married couple; she always used the name
of Cary. They purchased a home and other property, borrowed money, obtained
credit, filed joint income tax returns and otherwise conducted all business as husband and wife. Both knew that they were not married; they had talked several
times about a wedding ceremony, but somehow they never got around to it. Four
children were born to Paul and Janet; they were supported by Paul who always
acknowledged them as his own. Their birth certificates and school registration re-
corded the parents as Paul and Janet Cary. While Paul worked Janet generally
stayed at home taking care of the children and the house.

The relationship between Paul, Janet, and their children must reasonably be
deemed that of a *family,* coming within the broad purview of the Family Law Act.
Paul makes no contention to the contrary.

While living together the parties accumulated some real and personal property
through the earnings of Paul. Had they been married it would have been community property, a fact conceded by the parties.

In 1971 Paul petitioned the superior court for "Nullity of the marriage pursuant
to Civil Code section 4001." A principal trial issue was the question of Janet's
rights in the property acquired with Paul's earnings. The trial court's determination
that this property should be equally divided resulted in the instant appeal by Paul.

An early day, but nevertheless still valid, rationale of California's community
property law is found in *Meyer* v. *Kinzer* (1859) 12 Cal. 247, 251-252, where the
state's Supreme Court said: "The [community property law] proceeds upon the
theory that the marriage, in respect to property acquired during its existence, is a

community of which each spouse is a member, equally contributing by his or her industry to its prosperity, and possessing an equal right to succeed to the property after dissolution, in case of surviving the other. To the community all acquisitions by either, whether made jointly or separately, belong. . . . All property is common property, except that owned previous to marriage or subsequently acquired in a particular way. . . ."

This principle is given present day expression by Civil Code section 687 which, with exceptions here inapplicable, provides: "Community property is property acquired by husband and wife, *or either,* during marriage, . . ." (Italics added.)

While ordinarily applying only to those legally wed, the community property principle has frequently been applied where one or both of the parties mistakenly, *but in good faith,* believed themselves married. . . .

In such situations the property has been treated in substantially the same manner as if the parties had been validly married. No inquiry into the respective property "contributions" was permitted. Speaking of the claim of one who in good faith, but mistakenly, believed her marriage valid, the court in *Coats* v. *Coats* (1911) 160 Cal. 671, 678-679 [118 P. 441], stated:

"[I] t is entirely immaterial that the bulk of the property was acquired between the years 1900 and 1906, and that the plaintiff's services in its accumulation were 'of no monetary value.' She is not suing to recover for services rendered under a contract for labor, nor to establish the value of her interest in a business partnership. What she did, she did as a wife, and her share of the joint accumulations must be measured by what a wife would receive out of community property on the termination of the marriage. 'The law will not inquire . . . whether the acquisition was by the joint efforts of the husband and wife, or attempt to adjust their respective rights in proportion to the amount each contributed thereto. The law will not concern itself with such an inquiry, but will leave the parties to share in the property in the same proportion as though the marriage contract was what the wife had every reason to believe it to be, i.e., a valid marriage. . . .' "

But where unmarried persons knowingly lived together in a "meretricious" or "sinful" relationship the law of California had consistently shown no concern for vindication of property rights, which under a valid marriage would have been legally established. . . . "Equitable considerations" were not present, the courts held, because of the "guilt" of both the parties. . . . The parties were denied any relief and " 'the law would leave them in the position in which they placed themselves. . . .' " often to the profit of one (usually the man) and to the prejudice of the other . . .

Even where a marriage had been solemnized, upon its dissolution and where some moral disparity between the parties was found to exist, it was the judicial practice " 'to visit punishment upon the erring spouse in the apportionment of the community property. . . .' " . . . This punishment might even result in the award of all of the community property to the "innocent" marital partner. . . . In such cases a trial court's failure to punish the errant spouse was an abuse of discretion, requiring reversal of the judgment.

Recognizing the harshness of the rule of punishment for spousal "guilt" some courts announced that, although it continued as law, it ranked lower than many other considerations "in the scale of importance" as a determinant for division of community property. . . .

The "punishment and reward" concept of California's family law was widely criticized. Many believe that it was "tacit recognition of the developing public opinion that resulted in enactment of the new law [the Family Law Act] ." (See Attorney's Guide to Family Law Practice (Cont. Ed.Bar (2d ed. 1972) p. 251.)

"The basic substantive change in the law [brought about by the Family Law Act] is *the elimination of fault or guilt as grounds for* granting or denying divorce and for refusing alimony and *making unequal division of community property. . . .*" (Italics added; *In re Marriage of McKim* (1972) 6 Cal.3d 673, 678 [100 Cal.Rptr. 140, 493 P.2d 868]; and see Civ. Code, § 4800.) It is said that "by far the most significant provision . . . is the mandatory requirement of an equal division of community property. . . ." (Grant, 23 Hastings L.J. (1971-1972) p. 249.) The equal division of community property was one of the ways "of advancing [the Act's primary no-fault philosophy." *(In re Marriage of Juick* (1971) 21 Cal. App.3d 421, 427 [98 Cal.Rptr. 324] .) So strong is the policy behind the Act that in family law proceedings relating to property rights, any pleading or proof relating to misconduct, or "guilt," or "innocence" of a party *"shall be improper* and inadmissible, . . ." (Italics added; see Civ. Code, § 4509.)

In a summary of the Act, and particularly its section 4800 calling for equal property division, respected writers have said:

"The basic theory of the new law is that, in disposing of the property, a dissolution of marriage should be treated much like the dissolution of a business partnership. Regardless of the economic circumstances of business partners or of their moral conduct during the existence of the partnership, on dissolution the partners receive a portion of the assets commensurate with their respective partnership interests." (Attorney's Guide to Family Law Practice (Cont.Ed.Bar (2d ed. 1972) p. 250.)

The Family Law Act applies not only to valid marriages. It expressly covers a family relationship based on a void or voidable marriage where "either party or both parties believed in good faith that the marriage was valid, . . ." (See Civ. Code, § 4452.)[1]

An analysis of section 4452 discloses that where a party to a non-marital family relationship in bad faith knew of the marriage's infirmity or nonexistence, and the other did not, the Act neither penalizes nor rewards the respective parties upon a judicial division of their accumulated property. The party who in bad faith brought

---

1. Civil Code section 4452: "Whenever a determination is made that a marriage is void or voidable and the court finds that either party or parties believed in good faith that the marriage was valid, the court shall declare such party or parties to have the status of a putative spouse, and, if the division of property is in issue, shall divide, in accordance with Section 4800, that property acquired during the union which would have been community property or quasi-community property if the union had not been void or voidable. Such property shall be termed 'quasi-marital property.' If the court expressly reserves jurisdiction, it may make the property division at a time subsequent to the judgment."

about the pseudomarriage is not for the reason left where found by the court. Nor may any "guilt" or "innocence" of the parties in their relationship after entering the illegitimate union be considered by the court. Sections 4452, 4509 and 4800 assure that the parties, without "punishment" or "reward" to either, shall receive an equal division of that which would have been community property had they been validly married.

But in the case before us *both parties* appear "guilty"; each was aware of the lack of a marital ceremony. Paul urges that since the Act does not expressly cover such a situation, the pre-1970 notion that the law must leave the parties where it finds them is the applicable rule.

We disagree.

Giving effect to such an argument would lead to an unreasonable result and frustrate the obvious objective of the Act. We should be obliged to presume a legislative intent that a person, who by deceit leads another to believe a valid marriage exists between them, shall be legally guaranteed half of the property they acquire even though most, or all, may have resulted from the earnings of the blameless partner. At the same time we must infer an inconsistent legislative intent that two persons who, candidly with each other, enter upon an unmarried family relationship, shall be denied any judicial aid whatever in the assertion of otherwise valid property rights.

Statutes must be given a reasonable interpretation; . . . absurd results are to be avoided if possible; . . . and it must be presumed that the Legislature did not use "inconsistent provisions on the same subject. . . ." Above all, the intention of the Legislature must be ascertained; . . . and "regard is to be had not so much to the exact phraseology in which the intent has been expressed as to *the general tenor and scope of the entire scheme embodied in the enactments. . . .*"

By the Family Law Act the Legislature has announced it to be the public policy of this state that concepts of "guilt" (and punishment therefor) and "innocence" (and reward therefor) are no longer relevant in the determination of family property rights, whether there be a legal marriage or not, and if not, regardless of whether the deficiency is known to one, or both, or neither of the parties.

"It is for the Legislature . . . to choose between conflicting policies, . . ." *"The declaration of public policy is essentially a legislative function and although the courts occasionally invade that field, a declaration by the Legislature is paramount. . . ."*

It therefore becomes our duty to give expression to the public policy expressed by the Family Law Act. We hold, as to the issue before us, that the Act supersedes contrary pre-1970 judicial authority.

It follows that the trial court properly disregarded evidence of the "guilt" of the parties to the instant action. Having done so, it was obliged to divide their property evenly, according to the dictate of Civil Code section 4800.

It is argued that our holding would tend to discourage the unemployed family partner from entering into a marital union, since that party without marriage would nevertheless have the marriage's property benefits. But with equal or greater force the point might be made that the pre-1970 rule was calculated to cause the income-producing partner to avoid marriage and thus retain the benefit of all of his or her accumulated earnings.

As we have pointed out, under application of equitable principles a result contrary to our holding was consistently reached prior to the Family Law Act. But our holding in no way conflicts with those high principles.

" 'The jurisdiction of courts of equity is not . . . diminished when by statutory changes some rights cease to exist and certain cases which courts of equity once entertained can no longer arise. [The equity power of courts] was not intended as a limitation upon the power to legislate upon the rights of persons. . . .' "

It should be pointed out that the criteria for application of the rule we apply to the case before us is much more than that of an unmarried living arrangement between a man and woman. The Family Law Act obviously requires that there be established not only an ostensible marital relationship but also an actual family relationship, with cohabitation and mutual recognition and assumption of the usual rights, duties, and obligations attending marriage. . . .

[T]he judgment is affirmed. . . .

Page 285. Before Juri v. Juri, add:

NOTE

Cal. Civ. C. § 4600(a) has been amended so as to delete the language reading: "but, other things being equal, custody should be given to the mother if the child is of tender years." Cal. Stats. 1972, Ch. 1007, § 1. An appeal from a decision of the California District Court of Appeal of March 21, 1974, upholding—as against a constitutional attack—this statute as it stood prior to amendment, has been dismissed by the United States Supreme Court. Stuart v. Stuart, 42 U.S.L.W. 3625 (May 14, 1974).

Page 287. Following note 2, add:

3. In State ex rel Watts v. Watts, 350 N.Y.S.2d 285 (1973), the New York City Family Court held that any presumption favoring a mother over a father as a custodian of children of "tender years" violated state law and the equal-protection guarantee of the federal constitution. Noted the court:

> The "tender years presumption" is actually a blanket judicial finding of fact, a statement by a court that, until proven otherwise by the weight of substantial evidence, mothers are always better suited to care for young children than fathers. This flies in the face of the legislative finding of fact underlying the explicit command of section 240 and section 70 of the Domestic Relations Law, that the best interests of the child are served by the court's

approaching the facts of the particular case before it without sex preconceptions of any kind.

However, the trend in legislation, legal commentary, and judicial decisions is away from the "tender years presumption."

Recent amendments of the Domestic Relations Law of several other states have codified as explicitly as New York the view that the child's best interest requires that neither parent have preference. In Florida, for example, the relevant provision, effective July 1, 1971, states:

> "The court shall award custody and visitation rights of minor children of the parties as a part of proceeding for dissolution of marriage in accordance with the best interests of the child. Upon considering all relevant factors, the father of the child shall be given the same consideration as the mother in determining custody." Fla.Stat. 61.13(2), F.S.A. (1971).

Wisconsin's law also revised in 1971, provides in relevant part:

> "In determining the parent with whom a child shall remain, the court shall consider all facts in the best interest of the child and shall not prefer one parent over the other solely on the basis of the sex of the parent." Wis.Stat. 247.24(3) (1971).

Colorado Rev.Stats. 46-1-5(7) provides:

> "No party shall be presumed to be able to serve the best interests of the child better than any other party because of sex."

Legal scholars advocate this evenhanded approach with near virtual unanimity. See e.g., Podell, Peck and First, Custody to Which Parent? 56 Marquette Univ.L.Rev. Fall 1972; Foster and Freed, Child Custody, 39 N.Y.U.L.Rev. 422, 411, 1964; Polow, Child Custody—The Law and Changing Social Attitudes; ABA Family Law Newsletter, November 1972. Evidence that the courts are taking long strides toward abandoning the "tender years presumption" in favor of an unbiased consideration of the best interests of the children solely on the basis of the individual characteristics and relationships of the parents and children involved is found in the large number of recent custody cases in which the parents were treated equally and the father prevailed. (See the 48 cases collected in Footnote 23, Podell, Peck and First, supra.)

Apart from the question of legality, the "tender years presumption" should be discarded because it is based on outdated social stereotypes rather than on rational and up-to-date consideration of the welfare of the children involved.

The simple fact of being a mother does not, by itself, indicate a capacity or willingness to render a quality of care different from that which the father can provide. The traditional and romantic view, at least since the turn of the century, has been that nothing can be an adequate substitute for mother love.

"For a boy of such tender years nothing can be an adequate substitute for mother love—for that constant ministration required during the period of nurture [she] can give because ... in her alone is service expressed in terms of love. She alone has the patience and sympathy required to mold and soothe the infant mind in its adjustment to its environment. The difference between fatherhood and motherhood in this respect is fundamental, and the law should recognize it unless off-set by undesirable traits in the mother." (Jenkins v. Jenkins, 173 Wis. 592, 181 N.W. 826, 827, 1921).

Later decisions have recognized that this view is inconsistent with informed application of the best interests of the child doctrine and out of touch with contemporary thought about child development and male and female stereotypes.

In Garrett v. Garrett (464 S.W.2d 740, 742, Mo.App., 1971), the court stated:

"The rule giving the mother preferential right to custody is considerably softened by the realization that 'all things never are exactly equal' and is predicted upon the acts of motherhood—not *the fact of motherhood.* Likewise, the rule will yield if the welfare of the children demands it, because this is not a presumption of law but a simple fact of life gleaned from human experience, and the courts are not timid in entrusting children into their father's care and custody when their best interests will be served thereby." (Citations omitted and emphasis added.)

Eminent psychologists and anthropologists, including Margaret Mead, have also acknowledged and asserted that both female and male parents are equally able to provide care and perform child-rearing functions.

"At present, the specific biological situation of the continuing relationship of the child to the biological mother and its need for care by human beings are being hopelessly confused in the ... insistence that the child and mother or mother surrogate must never be separated; that all separation even for a few days is ultimately damaging and that if long enough it does irreversible damage. This is a mere and subtle form of anti-feminism which men—under the guise of exalting the importance of maternity—are tying women more tightly to their children than has been thought necessary since the invention of bottle feeding and baby carriages." Margaret Mead, *Some Theoretical Considerations of the Problems of Mother-Child Separation,* 24 Amer.Jrl. of Orthopsychiatry 24 (1954).

Studies of maternal deprivation have shown that the essential experience for the child is that of mothering—the warmth, consistency and continuity of the relationship rather than the sex of the individual who is performing the mothering function. (See, e.g., R. A. Spitz and Katherine Wolf, *"Anaclitic Depression"*, *Psychoanalytic Study of the Child,* 1946, pages 313-342; Leon J. Yarrow, *Maternal Deprivation: Toward an Empirical and Conceptual Reevaluation,* Psychological Bull., 58, 1961.)

Chapter 5

Sex Roles and Employment

Page 314. Following note, add:

CC. GENERAL PROBLEMS IN PROVING EMPLOYMENT DISCRIMINATION

Griggs v. Duke Power Co.
United States Supreme Court, 1971
401 U.S. 424, 91 S.Ct. 849, 28 L.Ed.2d 158

MR. CHIEF JUSTICE BURGER delivered the opinion of the Court.

We granted the writ in this case to resolve the question whether an employer is prohibited by the Civil Rights Act of 1964, Title VII, from requiring a high school education or passing of a standardized general intelligence test as a condition of employment in or transfer to jobs when (a) neither standard is shown to be significantly related to successful job performance, (b) both requirements operate to disqualify Negroes at a substantially higher rate than white applicants, and (c) the jobs in question formerly had been filled only by white employees as part of a longstanding practice of giving preference to whites.[1]

Congress provided in Title VII of the Civil Rights Act of 1964, for class actions for enforcement of provisions of the Act and this proceeding was brought by a

---

1. The Act provides:

"Sec. 703. (a) It shall be an unlawful employment practice for an employer—

"(2) to limit, segregate, or classify his employees in any way which would deprive or tend to deprive any individual of employment opportunities or otherwise adversely affect his status as an employee, because of such individual's race, color, religion, sex, or national origin.

"(h) Notwithstanding any other provision of this title, it shall not be an unlawful employment practice for an employer . . . to give and to act upon the results of any professionally developed ability test provided that such test, its administration or action upon the results is not designed, intended or used to discriminate because of race, color, religion, sex or national origin. . . ." 78 Stat. 255, 42 U.S.C. § 2000e-2.

group of incumbent Negro employees against Duke Power Company. All the petitioners are employed at the Company's Dan River Steam Station, a power generat-
ing facility located at Draper, North Carolina. At the time this action was instituted, the Company had 95 employees at the Dan River Station, 14 of whom were
Negroes; 13 of these are petitioners here.

The District Court found that prior to July 2, 1965, the effective date of the
Civil Rights Act of 1964, the Company openly discriminated on the basis of race in
the hiring and assigning of employees at its Dan River plant. The plant was organized into five operating departments: (1) Labor, (2) Coal Handling, (3) Operations,
(4) Maintenance, and (5) Laboratory and Test. Negroes were employed only in the
Labor Department where the highest paying jobs paid less than the lowest paying
jobs in the other four "operating" departments in which only whites were employed.[2] Promotions were normally made within each department on the basis of
job seniority. Transferees into a department usually began in the lowest position.

In 1955 the Company instituted a policy of requiring a high school education for
initial assignment to any department except Labor, and for transfer from the Coal
Handling to any "inside" department (Operations, Maintenance, or Laboratory).
When the Company abandoned its policy of restricting Negroes to the Labor Department in 1965, completion of high school also was made a prerequisite to transfer from Labor to any other department. From the time the high school requirement was instituted to the time of trial, however, white employees hired before the
time of the high school education requirement continued to perform satisfactorily
and achieve promotions in the "operating" departments. Findings on this score are
not challenged.

The Company added a further requirement for new employees on July 2, 1965,
the date on which Title VII became effective. To qualify for placement in any but
the Labor Department it became necessary to register satisfactory scores on two
professionally prepared aptitude tests, as well as to have a high school education.
Completion of high school alone continued to render employees eligible for transfer
to the four desirable departments from which Negroes had been excluded if the
incumbent had been employed prior to the time of the new requirement. In September 1965 the Company began to permit incumbent employees who lacked a
high school education to qualify for transfer from Labor or Coal Handling to an
"inside" job by passing two tests—the Wonderlic Personnel Test, which purports to
measure general intelligence, and the Bennett Mechanical Comprehension Test.
Neither was directed or intended to measure the ability to learn to perform a particular job or category of jobs. The requisite scores used for both initial hiring and
transfer approximated the national median for high school graduates.[3]

The District Court had found that while the Company previously followed a policy of overt racial discrimination in a period prior to the Act, such conduct had

2. A Negro was first assigned a job in an
operating department in August 1966, five
months after charges had been filed with the
Equal Employment Opportunity Commission.
The employee, a high school graduate who
had begun in the Labor Department in 1953,
was promoted to a job in the Coal Handling
Department.
3. The test standards are thus more stringent than the high school requirement, since
they would screen out approximately half of
all high school graduates.

ceased. The District Court also concluded that Title VII was intended to be prospective only and, consequently, the impact of prior inequities was beyond the reach of corrective action authorized by the Act.

The Court of Appeals was confronted with a question of first impression, as are we, concerning the meaning of Title VII. After careful analysis a majority of that court concluded that a subjective test of the employer's intent should govern, particularly in a close case, and that in this case there was no showing of a discriminatory purpose in the adoption of the diploma and test requirements. On this basis, the Court of Appeals concluded there was no violation of the Act.

The Court of Appeals reversed the District Court in part, rejecting the holding that residual discrimination arising from prior employment practices was insulated from remedial action.[4] The Court of Appeals noted, however, that the District Court was correct in its conclusion that there was no showing of a racial purpose or invidious intent in the adoption of the high school diploma requirement or general intelligence test and that these standards had been applied fairly to whites and Negroes alike. It held that, in the absence of a discriminatory purpose, use of such requirements was permitted by the Act. In so doing, the Court of Appeals rejected the claim that because these two requirements operated to render ineligible a markedly disproportionate number of Negroes, they were unlawful under Title VII unless shown to be job related.[5] We granted the writ on these claims. 399 U.S. 926.

The objective of Congress in the enactment of Title VII is plain from the language of the statute. It was to achieve equality of employment opportunities and remove barriers that have operated in the past to favor an identifiable group of white employees over other employees. Under the Act, practices, procedures, or tests neutral on their face, and even neutral in terms of intent, cannot be maintained if they operate to "freeze" the status quo of prior discriminatory employment practices.

The Court of Appeals' opinion, and the partial dissent, agreed that, on the record in the present case, "whites register far better on the Company's alternative requirements" than Negroes.[6] 420 F.2d 1225, 1239 n. 6. This consequence would appear to be directly traceable to race. Basic intelligence must have the means of articula-

---

4. The Court of Appeals ruled that Negroes employed in the Labor Department at a time when there was no high school or test requirement for entrance into the higher paying departments could not now be made subject to those requirements, since whites hired contemporaneously into those departments were never subject to them. The Court of Appeals also required that the seniority rights of those Negroes be measured on a plantwide, rather than a departmental, basis. However, the Court of Appeals denied relief to the Negro employees without a high school education or its equivalent who were hired into the Labor Department after institution of the educational requirement.

5. One member of that court disagreed with this aspect of the decision, maintaining, as do the petitioners in this Court, that Title VII prohibits the use of employment criteria that operate in a racially exclusionary fashion

and do not measure skills or abilities necessary to performance of the jobs for which those criteria are used.

6. In North Carolina, 1960 census statistics show that, while 34% of white males had completed high school, only 12% of Negro males had done so. U.S. Bureau of the Census, U.S. Census of Population: 1960, Vol. 1, Characteristics of the Population, pt. 35, Table 47.

Similarly, with respect to standardized tests, the EEOC in one case found that use of a battery of tests, including the Wonderlic and Bennett tests used by the Company in the instant case, resulted in 58% of whites passing the tests, as compared with only 6% of the blacks. Decision of EEOC, CCH Empl. Prac. Guide, ¶ 17,304.53 (Dec. 2, 1966). See also Decision of EEOC 70-552, CCH Empl. Prac. Guide, ¶ 6139 (Feb. 19, 1970).

tion to manifest itself fairly in a testing process. Because they are Negroes, petitioners have long received inferior education in segregated schools and this Court expressly recognized these differences in *Gaston County* v. *United States,* 395 U.S. 285 (1969). There, because of the inferior education received by Negroes in North Carolina, this Court barred the institution of a literacy test for voter registration on the ground that the test would abridge the right to vote indirectly on account of race. Congress did not intend by Title VII, however, to guarantee a job to every person regardless of qualifications. In short, the Act does not command that any person be hired simply because he was formerly the subject of discrimination, or because he is a member of a minority group. Discriminatory preference for any group, minority or majority, is precisely and only what Congress has proscribed. What is required by Congress is the removal of artificial, arbitrary, and unnecessary barriers to employment when the barriers operate invidiously to discriminate on the basis of racial or other impermissible classification.

Congress has now provided that tests or criteria for employment or promotion may not provide equality of opportunity merely in the sense of the fabled offer of milk to the stork and the fox. On the contrary, Congress has now required that the posture and condition of the job-seeker be taken into account. It has—to resort again to the fable—provided that the vessel in which the milk is proffered be one all seekers can use. The Act proscribes not only overt discrimination but also practices that are fair in form, but discriminatory in operation. The touchstone is business necessity. If an employment practice which operates to exclude Negroes cannot be shown to be related to job performance, the practice is prohibited.

On the record before us, neither the high school completion requirement nor the general intelligence test is shown to bear a demonstrable relationship to successful performance of the jobs for which it was used. Both were adopted, as the Court of Appeals noted, without meaningful study of their relationship to job-performance ability. Rather, a vice president of the Company testified, the requirements were instituted on the Company's judgment that they generally would improve the overall quality of the work force.

The evidence, however, shows that employees who have not completed high school or taken the tests have continued to perform statisfactorily and make progress in departments for which the high school and test criteria are now used.[7] The promotion record of present employees who would not be able to meet the new criteria thus suggests the possibility that the requirements may not be needed even for the limited purpose of preserving the avowed policy of advancement within the Company. In the context of this case, it is unnecessary to reach the question whether testing requirements that take into account capability for the next succeeding position or related future promotion might be utilized upon a showing that such long-range requirements fulfill a genuine business need. In the present case the Company has made no such showing.

The Court of Appeals held that the Company had adopted the diploma and test

7. For example, between July 2, 1965, and November 14, 1966, the percentage of white employees who were promoted but who were not high school graduates was nearly identical to the percentage of nongraduates in the entire white work force.

requirements without any "intention to discriminate against Negro employees." 420 F.2d, at 1232. We do not suggest that either the District Court or the Court of Appeals erred in examining the employer's intent; but good intent or absence of discriminatory intent does not redeem employment procedures or testing mechanisms that operate as "built-in headwinds" for minority groups and are unrelated to measuring job capability.

The Company's lack of discriminatory intent is suggested by special efforts to help the undereducated employees through Company financing of two-thirds the cost of tuition for high school training. But Congress directed the thrust of the Act to the *consequences* of employment practices, not simply the motivation. More than that, Congress has placed on the employer the burden of showing that any given requirement must have a manifest relationship to the employment in question.

The facts of this case demonstrate the inadequacy of broad and general testing devices as well as the infirmity of using diplomas or degrees as fixed measures of capability. History is filled with examples of men and women who rendered highly effective performance without the conventional badges of accomplishment in terms of certificates, diplomas, or degrees. Diplomas and tests are useful servants, but Congress has mandated the commonsense proposition that they are not to become masters of reality.

The Company contends that its general intelligence tests are specifically permitted by § 703(h) of the Act.[8] That section authorizes the use of "any professionally developed ability test" that is not "designed, intended *or used* to discriminate because of race . . . ." (Emphasis added.)

The Equal Employment Opportunity Commission, having enforcement responsibility, has issued guidelines interpreting § 703(h) to permit only the use of job-related tests.[9] The administrative interpretation of the Act by the enforcing agency is entitled to great deference. See, *e.g., United States* v. *City of Chicago*, 400 U.S. 8 (1970); *Udall* v. *Tallman*, 380 U.S. 1 (1965); *Power Reactor Co.* v. *Electricians*, 367 U.S. 396 (1961). Since the Act and its legislative history support the Commission's construction, this affords good reason to treat the guidelines as expressing the will of Congress.

Section 703(h) was not contained in the House version of the Civil Rights Act but was added in the Senate during extended debate. For a period, debate revolved around claims that the bill as proposed would prohibit all testing and force employ-

---

8. Section 703(h) applies only to tests. It has no applicability to the high school diploma requirement.

9. EEOC Guidelines on Employment Testing Procedures; issued August 24, 1966, provide:

"The Commission accordingly interprets 'professionally developed ability test' to mean a test which fairly measures the knowledge or skills required by the particular job or class of jobs which the applicant seeks, or which fairly affords the employer a chance to measure the applicant's ability to perform a particular job or class of jobs. The fact that a test was prepared by an individual or organization claiming expertise in test preparation does not, without more, justify its use within the meaning of Title VII."

The EEOC position has been elaborated in the new Guidelines on Employee Selection Procedures, 29 CFR § 1607, 35 Fed. Reg. 12333 (Aug. 1, 1970). These guidelines demand that employers using tests have available "data demonstrating that the test is predictive of or significantly correlated with important elements of work behavior which comprise or are relevant to the job or jobs for which candidates are being evaluated." *Id.*, at § 1607.4(c).

ers to hire unqualified persons simply because they were part of a group formerly subject to job discrimination.[10] Proponents of Title VII sought throughout the debate to assure the critics that the Act would have no effect on job-related tests. Senators Case of New Jersey and Clark of Pennsylvania, comanagers of the bill on the Senate floor, issued a memorandum explaining that the proposed Title VII "expressly protects the employer's right to insist that any prospective applicant, Negro or white, *must meet the applicable job qualifications.* Indeed, the very purpose of Title VII is to promote hiring on the basis of job qualifications, rather than on the basis of race or color." 110 Cong. Rec. 7247.[11] (Emphasis added.) Despite these assurances, Senator Tower of Texas introduced an amendment authorizing "professionally developed ability tests." Proponents of Title VII opposed the amendment because, as written, it would permit an employer to give any test, "whether it was a good test or not, so long as it was professionally designed. Discrimination could actually exist under the guise of compliance with the statute." 110 Cong. Rec. 13504 (remarks of Sen. Case).

The amendment was defeated and two days later Senator Tower offered a substitute amendment which was adopted verbatim and is now the testing provision of § 703(h). Speaking for the supporters of Title VII, Senator Humphrey, who had vigorously opposed the first amendment, endorsed the substitute amendment, stating: "Senators on both sides of the aisle who were deeply interested in title VII have examined the text of this amendment and have found it to be in accord with the intent and purpose of that title." 110 Cong. Rec. 13724. The amendment was then adopted.[12] From the sum of the legislative history relevant in this case, the

10. The congressional discussion was prompted by the decision of a hearing examiner for the Illinois Fair Employment Commission in *Myart* v. *Motorola Co.* (The decision is reprinted at 110 Cong. Rec. 5662.) That case suggested that standardized tests on which whites performed better than Negroes could never be used. The decision was taken to mean that such tests could never be justified even if the needs of the business required them. A number of Senators feared that Title VII might produce a similar result. See remarks of Senators Ervin, 110 Cong. Rec. 5614-5616; Smathers, *id.,* at 5999-6000; Holland, *id.,* at 7012-7013; Hill, *id.,* at 8447; Tower, *id.,* at 9024; Talmadge, *id.,* at 9025-9026; Fulbright, *id.,* at 9599-9600; and Ellender, *id.,* at 9600.

11. The Court of Appeals majority, in finding no requirement in Title VII that employment tests be job related, relied in part on a quotation from an earlier Clark-Case interpretative memorandum addressed to the question of the constitutionality of Title VII. The Senators said in that memorandum:

"There is no requirement in title VII that employers abandon bona fide qualification tests where, because of differences in background and education, members of some groups are able to perform better on these tests than members of other groups. An employer may set his qualifications as high as he likes, he may test to determine which applicants have these qualifications, and he may hire, assign, and promote on the basis of test performance." 110 Cong. Rec. 7213.

However, nothing there stated conflicts with the later memorandum dealing specifically with the debate over employer testing, 110 Cong. Rec. 747 (quoted from in the text above), in which Senators Clark and Case explained that tests which measure "applicable job qualifications" are permissible under Title VII. In the earlier memorandum Clark and Case assured the Senate that employers were not to be prohibited from using tests that determine *qualifications.* Certainly a reasonable interpretation of what the Senators meant, in light of the subsequent memorandum directed specifically at employer testing, was that nothing in the Act prevents employers from requiring that applicants be fit for the job.

12. Senator Tower's original amendment provided in part that a test would be permissible "if . . . in the case of any individual who is seeking employment with such employer, such test is designed to determine or predict whether such individual is suitable or trainable with respect to his employment in the particular business or enterprise involved . . . ." 100 Cong. Rec. 13492. This language indicates that Senator Tower's aim was simply to make certain that job-related tests would be permitted. The opposition to the amendment was based on its loose wording which the proponents of Title VII feared would be susceptible of misinterpretation. The final amendment, which was acceptable to all sides, could hardly have required less of a job relation than the first.

conclusion is inescapable that the EEOC's construction of § 703(h) to require that employment tests be job related comports with congressional intent.

Nothing in the Act precludes the use of testing or measuring procedures; obviously they are useful. What Congress has forbidden is giving these devices and mechanisms controlling force unless they are demonstrably a reasonable measure of job performance. Congress has not commanded that the less qualified be preferred over the better qualified simply because of minority origins. Far from disparaging job qualifications as such, Congress has made such qualifications the controlling factor, so that race, religion, nationality, and sex become irrelevant. What Congress has commanded is that any tests used must measure the person for the job and not the person in the abstract.

The judgment of the Court of Appeals is, as to that portion of the judgment appealed from, reversed.

NOTE

An excellent discussion of the use of statistical evidence to prove a markedly disproportionate impact of a seemingly sex-neutral or racially neutral employment policy appears in Note, Height Standards in Police Employment and the Question of Sex Discrimination, 475 So. Cal. L. Rev. 585, 595-602 (1974).

McDonnell Douglas Corporation v. Green
United States Supreme Court, 1973
−U.S.−, 86 S.Ct. 1817, 36 L.Ed.2d 668

Mr. Justice POWELL delivered the opinion of the Court.

The case before us raises significant questions as to the proper order and nature of proof in action under Title VII of the Civil Rights Act of 1964.

Petitioner, McDonnell Douglas Corporation, is an aerospace and aircraft manufacturer headquartered in St. Louis, Missouri, where it employs over 30,000 people. Respondent, a black citizen of St. Louis, worked for petitioner as a mechanic and laboratory technician from 1956 until August 28, 1964 when he was laid off in the course of a general reduction in petitioner's work force.

Respondent, a long-time activist in the civil rights movement, protested vigorously that his discharge and the general hiring practices of petitioner were racially motivated. As part of this protest, respondent and other members of the Congress on Racial Equality illegally stalled their cars on the main road leading to petitioner's plant for the purpose of blocking access to it at the time of the morning shift change. The District Judge described the plan for, and respondent's participation in, the "stall-in" as follows:

> ". . . five teams, each consisting of four cars would 'tie up' five main access roads into McDonnell at the time of the morning rush hour. The drivers of the cars were instructed to line up next to each other completely blocking the intersections or roads. The drivers were also instructed to stop their cars, turn off the engines, pull the emergency brake, raise all windows, lock the doors,

and remain in their cars until the police arrived. The plan was to have the cars remain in position for one hour.

"Acting under the 'stall in' plan, plaintiff [respondent in the present action] drove his car onto Brown Road, a McDonnell access road, at approximately 7:00 a.m., at the start of the morning rush hour. Plaintiff was aware of the traffic problems that would result. He stopped his car with the intent to block traffic. The police arrived shortly and requested plaintiff to move his car. He refused to move his car voluntarily. Plaintiff's car was towed away by the police, and he was arrested for obstructing traffic. Plaintiff pleaded guilty to the charge of obstructing traffice and was fined." 318 F.Supp. 846.

On July 2, 1965, a "lock-in" took place wherein a chain and padlock were placed on the front door of a building to prevent the occupants, certain of petitioner's employees, from leaving. Though respondent apparently knew beforehand of the "lock-in," the full extent of his involvement remains uncertain.

Some three weeks following the "lock-in," on July 25, 1965, petitioner publicly advertised for qualified mechanics, respondent's trade, and respondent promptly applied for re-employment. Petitioner turned down respondent, basing its rejection on respondent's participation in the "stall-in" and "lock-in." Shortly thereafter, respondent filed a formal complaint with the Equal Employment Opportunity Commission, claiming that petitioner had refused to rehire him because of his race and persistent involvement in the civil rights movement, in violation of §§ 703(a)(1) and 704(a) of the Civil Rights Act of 1964, 42 U.S.C. §§ 2000e-2(a)(1) and 2000e-3(a). The former section generally prohibits racial discrimination in any employment decision while the latter forbids discrimination against applicants or employees for attempting to protest or correct allegedly discriminatory conditions of employment.

The Commission made no finding on respondent's allegation of racial bias under § 703(a)(1), but it did find reasonable cause to believe petitioner had violated § 704(a) by refusing to rehire respondent because of his civil rights activity. After the Commission unsuccessfully attempted to conciliate the dispute, it advised respondent in March 1968, of his right to institute a civil action in federal court within 30 days.

On April 15, 1968, respondent brought the present action, claiming initially a violation of § 704(a) and, in an amended complaint, a violation of §703(a)(1) as well. The District Court, 299 F.Supp. 1100, dismissed the latter claim of racial discrimination in petitioner's hiring procedures on the ground that the Commission had failed to make a determination of reasonable cause to believe that a violation of that section had been committed. The District Court also found that petitioner's refusal to rehire respondent was based solely on his participation in the illegal demonstrations and not on his legitimate civil rights activities. The court concluded that nothing in Title VII or § 704 protected "such activity as employed by the plaintiff in the 'stall in' and 'lock in' demonstrations." 318 F.Supp., at 850.

On appeal, the Eighth Circuit affirmed that unlawful protests were not protected activities under §704(a), but reversed the dismissal of respondent's § 703(a)(1) claim relating to racially discriminatory hiring practices, holding that a prior Commission determination of reasonable cause was not a jurisdictional prerequisite to raising a claim under that section in federal court. The court ordered the case remanded for trial of respondent's claim under § 703(a)(1).

In remanding, the Court of Appeals attempted to set forth standards to govern the consideration of respondent's claim. The majority noted that respondent had established a prima facie case of racial discrimination; that petitioner's refusal to rehire respondent rested on "subjective" criteria which carried little weight in rebutting charges of discrimination; that though respondent's participation in the unlawful demonstrations might indicate a lack of a responsible attitude toward performing work for that employer, respondent should be given the opportunity to demonstrate that petitioner's reasons for refusing to rehire him were merely pretextual. In order to clarify the standards governing the disposition of an action challenging employment discrimination, we granted certiorari, . . .

I

We agree with the Court of Appeals that absence of a Commission finding of reasonable cause cannot bar suit under an appropriate section of Title VII and that the District Judge erred in dismissing respondent's claim of racial discrimination under § 703(a)(1). Respondent satisfied the jurisdictional prerequisites to a federal action (i) by filing timely charges of employment discrimination with the Commission and (ii) by receiving and acting upon the Commission's statutory notice of the right to sue, 42 U.S.C. §§ 2000e-5(a) and 2000e-5(e). The Act does not restrict a complainant's right to sue to those charges as to which the Commission has made findings of reasonable cause, and we will not engraft on the statute a requirement which may inhibit the review of claims of employment discrimination in the federal courts. The Commission itself does not consider the absence of a "reasonable cause" determination as providing employer immunity from similar charges in a federal court, 29 CFR § 1601.30, and the courts of appeal have held that, in view of the large volume of complaints before the Commission and the nonadversary character of many of its proceedings, "court actions under Title VII are *de novo* proceedings and . . . a Commission['s] 'no reasonable cause' finding does not bar a lawsuit in the case."

Petitioner argues, as it did below, that respondent sustained no prejudice from the trial court's erroneous ruling because in fact the issue of racial discrimination in the refusal to re-employ "was tried thoroughly" in a trial lasting four days with "at least 80%" of the questions relating to the issue of "race." Petitioner therefore requests that the judgment below be vacated and the cause remanded with instructions that the judgment of the District Court be affirmed. We cannot agree that the dismissal of respondent's § 703(a)(1) claim was harmless error. It is not clear that the District Court's findings as to respondent's § 704(a) contentions involved the identical issues raised by his claim under § 703(a)(1). The former section relates solely to discrimination against an applicant or employee on account of his participation in legitimate civil rights activities or protests, while the latter section deals with the broader and centrally important question under the Act of whether for any reason, a racially discriminatory employment decision has been made. Moreover, respondent should have been accorded the right to prepare his case and plan the strategy of trial with the knowledge that § 703(a)(1) cause of action was properly before the District Court. Accordingly, we remand the case for trial of respondent's claim of racial discrimination consistent with the views set forth below.

II

The critical issue before us concerns the order and allocation of proof in a private, single-plaintiff action challenging employment discrimination. The language of Title VII makes plain the purpose of Congress to assure equality of employment opportunities and to eliminate those discriminatory practices and devices which have fostered racially stratified job environments to the disadvantage of minority citizens. Griggs v. Duke Power Co., 401 U.S. 424, 429, 91 S.Ct. 849, 852, 28 L.Ed.2d 158 (1971); . . . As noted in *Griggs, supra:*

> "Congress did not intend by Title VII, however, to guarantee a job to every person regardless of qualifications. In short, the Act does not command that any person be hired simply because he was formerly the subject of discrimination, or because he is a member of a minority group. Discriminatory preference for any group, minority or majority, is precisely and only what Congress has proscribed. What is required by Congress is the removal of artificial, arbitrary, and unnecessary barriers to employment when the barriers operate invidiously to discriminate on the basis of racial or other impermissible classification." *Id.,* 401 U.S., at 430, 91 S.Ct., at 853.

There are societal as well as personal interests on both sides of this equation. The broad, overriding interest, shared by employer, employee, and consumer, is efficient and trustworthy workmanship assured through fair and racially neutral employment and personnel decisions. In the implementation of such decisions, it is abundantly clear that Title VII tolerates no racial discrimination, subtle or otherwise.

In this case respondent, the complainant below, charges that he was denied employment "because of his involvement in civil rights activities" and "because of his race and color." Petitioner denied discrimination of any kind, asserting that its failure to re-employ respondent was based upon and justified by his participation in the unlawful conduct against it. Thus, the issue at the trial on remand is framed by those opposing factual contentions. The two opinions of the Court of Appeals and the several opinions of the three judges of the court attempted, with a notable lack of harmony, to state the applicable rules as to burden of proof and how this shifts upon the making of a prima facie case. We now address this problem.

The complainant in a Title VII trial must carry the initial burden under the statute of establishing a prima facie case of racial discrimination. This may be done by showing (i) that he belongs to a racial minority; (ii) that he applied and was qualified for a job for which the employer was seeking applicants; (iii) that, despite his qualifications, he was rejected; and (iv) that, after his rejection, the position remained open and the employer continued to seek applicants from persons of complainant's qualifications.[13] In the instant case, we agree with the Court of Appeals that respondent proved a prima facie case. 463 F.2d, at 353. Petitioner sought mechanics, respondent's trade, and continued to do so after respondent's rejection. Petitioner, moreover, does not dispute respondent's qualifications[14] and acknowledges that his past work performance in petitioner's employ was "satisfactory."

The burden then must shift to the employer to articulate some legitimate, non-discriminatory reason for respondent's rejection. We need not attempt in the instant case to detail every matter which fairly could be recognized as a reasonable basis for a refusal to hire. Here petitioner has assigned respondent's participation in unlawful conduct against it as the cause for his rejection. We think that this suffices to discharge petitioner's burden of proof at this stage and to meet respondent's prima facie case of discrimination.

The Court of Appeals intimated, however, that petitioner's stated reason for refusing to rehire respondent was a "subjective" rather than objective criterion which "carr[ies] little weight in rebutting charges of discrimination," 463 F.2d, at 343. This was among the statements which caused the dissenting judge to read the opinion as taking "the position that such unlawful acts as Green committed against McDonnell would not legally entitle McDonnell to refuse to rehire him, even though no racial motivation was involved. . . ." 463 F.2d, at 355. Regardless of whether this was the intended import of the opinion, we think the court below seriously underestimated the rebuttal weight to which petitioner's reasons were entitled. Respondent admittedly had taken part in a carefully planned "stall-in," designed to tie up access and egress to petitioner's plant at a peak traffic hour. Nothing in Title VII compels an employer to absolve and rehire one who has engaged in such deliberate, unlawful activity against it.[17] In upholding, under the National Labor Relations Act, the discharge of employees who had seized and forcibly retained an employer's factory buildings in an illegal sit-down strike, the Court noted pertinently:

> "We are unable to conclude that Congress intended to compel employers to retain persons in their employ regardless of their unlawful conduct,—to invest those who go on strike with an immunity from discharge for acts of trespass or violence against the employer's property, . . . Apart from the question of

---

13. The facts necessarily will vary in Title VII cases, and the specification above of the prima facie proof required from the complainant in this case is not necessarily applicable in every respect to differing factual situations.

14. We note that the issue of what may properly be used to test qualifications for employment is not present in this case. Where employers have instituted employment tests and qualifications with an exclusionary effect on minority applicants, such requirements must be "shown to bear a demonstrable relationship to successful performance of the jobs" for which they were used. *Griggs, supra*, at 431, 91 S.Ct., at 853.

17. The unlawful activity in this case was directed specifically against petitioner. We need not consider or decide here whether, or under what circumstances, unlawful activity not directed against the particular employer may be a legitimate justification for refusing to hire.

the constitutional validity of an enactment of that sort, it is enough to say that such a legislative intention should be found in some definite and unmistakable expression." NLRB v. Fansteel Corp., 306 U.S. 240, 255, 59 S.Ct. 490, 496, 83 L.Ed. 627 (1939).

Petitioner's reason for rejection thus suffices to meet the prima facie case, but the inquiry must not end here. While Title VII does not, without more, compel rehiring of respondent, neither does it permit petitioner to use respondent's conduct as a pretext for the sort of discrimination prohibited by § 703(a)(1). On remand, respondent must, as the Court of Appeals recognized, be afforded a fair opportunity to show that petitioner's stated reason for respondent's rejection was in fact pretextual. Especially relevant to such a showing would be evidence that white employees involved in acts against petitioner of comparable seriousness to the "stall-in" were nevertheless retained or rehired. Petitioner may justifiably refuse to rehire one who was engaged in unlawful, disruptive acts against it, but only if this criterion is applied alike to members of all races.

Other evidence that may be relevant to any showing of pretextuality includes facts as to the petitioner's treatment of respondent during his prior term of employment, petitioner's reaction, if any, to respondent's legitimate civil rights activities, and petitioner's general policy and practice with respect to minority employment.[18] On the latter point, statistics as to petitioner's employment policy and practice may be helpful to a determination of whether petitioner's refusal to rehire respondent in this case conformed to a general pattern of discrimination against blacks. Jones v. Lee Way Motor Freight, Inc., 431 F.2d 245 (CA10 1970); Blumrosen, Strangers in Paradise: Griggs v. Duke Power Co., and the Concept of Employment Discrimination, 71 Mich.L.Rev. 59, 91-94 (1972).[19] In short, on the retrial respondent must be given a full and fair opportunity to demonstrate by competent evidence that the presumptively valid reasons for his rejection were in fact a coverup for a racially discriminatory decision.

The court below appeared to rely upon Griggs v. Duke Powers Co., *supra*, in which the Court stated: "If an employment practice which operates to exclude Negroes cannot be shown to be related to job performance, the practice is prohibited." *Id.*, 401 U.S., at 431, 91 S.Ct., at 853, 28 L.Ed.2d 158. But *Griggs* differs from the instant case in important respects. It dealt with standardized testing devices which, however neutral on their face, operated to exclude many blacks who

---

18. We are aware that some of the above factors were indeed considered by the District Judge in finding under § 704(a), that "defendant's [here petitioner's] reasons for refusing to rehire the plaintiff were motivated solely and simply by the plaintiff's participation in the 'stall in' and 'lock in' demonstration. 318 F.Supp., at 850. We do not intimate that this finding must be overturned after consideration on remand of respondent's § 703(a)(1) claim. We do, however, insist that respondent under § 703(a)(1) must be given a full and fair opportunity to demonstrate by competent evidence that whatever the stated reasons for his rejection, the decision was in reality

racially premised.

19. The District Court may, for example, determine, after reasonable discovery that "the [racial] composition of defendant's labor force is itself reflective of restrictive or exclusionary practices." See Blumrosen, *supra*, at 92. We caution that such general determinations, while helpful, may not be in and of themselves controlling as to an individualized hiring decision, particularly in the presence of an otherwise justifiable reason for refusing to rehire. See generally, United States v. Bethlehem Steel Corporation, 312 F.Supp. 977, 992 (WDNY 1970), aff'd, 446 F.2d 652 (CA2 1971). Blumrosen, *supra*, at 93.

were capable of performing effectively in the desired positions. *Griggs* was rightly concerned that childhood deficiencies in the education and background of minority citizens, resulting from forces beyond their control, not be allowed to work a cumulative and invidious burden on such citizens for the remainder of their lives. *Id.,* at 430, 91 S.Ct., at 853. Respondent, however, appears in different clothing. He had engaged in a seriously disruptive act against the very one from whom he now seeks employment. And petitioner does not seek his exclusion on the basis of a testing device which overstates what is necessary for competent performance, or through some sweeping disqualification of all those with any past record of unlawful behavior, however remote, insubstantial or unrelated to applicant's personal qualifications as an employee. Petitioner assertedly rejected respondent for unlawful conduct against it and, in the absence of proof of pretextual or discriminatory application of such a reason, this cannot be thought the kind of "artificial, arbitrary, and unnecessary barrier[s] to employment" which the Court found to be the intention of Congress to remove. *Griggs,* p. 431, 91 S.Ct., at 853.[21]

III

In sum, respondent should have been allowed to amend his complaint to include a claim under § 703(a)(1). If the evidence on retrial is substantially in accord with that before us in this case, we think that respondent carried his burden of establishing a prima facie case of racial discrimination and that petitioner successfully rebutted that case. But this does not end the matter. On retrial respondent must be afforded a fair opportunity to demonstrate that petitioner's assigned reason for refusing to reemploy was pretextual or discriminatory in its application. If the District Judge so finds, he must order a prompt and appropriate remedy. In the absence of such a finding, petitioner's refusal to rehire must stand.

The cause is hereby remanded to the District Court for reconsideration in accordance with this opinion.

Remanded.

Page 338. Following note, add:

2. California Unemployment Insurance Code § 2626, prior to January 1, 1974, exempted pregnancy-related work loss from coverage of the state disability insurance program until twenty-eight days after the termination of pregnancy. In Rentzer v. California Unemployment Insurance Appeals Board, 32 Cal. App. 3d 604 (1973),

---

21. It is, of course, a predictive evaluation, resistant to empirical proof, whether "an applicant's past participation in unlawful conduct directed at his prospective employer might indicate the applicant's lack of a responsible attitude toward performing work for that employer." 463 F.2d 353. But in this case, given the seriousness and harmful potential of respondent's participation in the "stall-in" and the accompanying inconvenience to other employees, it cannot be said that petitioner's refusal to employ lacked a rational and neutral business justification. As the Court has noted elsewhere:

"Past conduct may well relate to present fitness; past loyalty may have a reasonable relationship to present and future trust." Garner v. Board of Public Works of Los Angeles, 341 U.S. 716, 720, 71 S.Ct. 909, 912, 95 L.Ed. 1317 (1951).

the California Court of Appeal held that this statute did not bar the payment of benefits on account of disability resulting from medical complications that arise during pregnancy. In Aiello v. Hansen, 359 F. Supp. 792 (1973), a three-judge federal court, apparently without having had the *Rentzer* case called to its attention, held this provision to be in violation of the federal equal-protection clause because it was not based on a classification having a rational and substantial relation to a legitimate state purpose. The *Aiello* decision was reversed, however, by the United States Supreme Court on June 17, 1974, under the name of Geduldig v. Aiello,   U.S.   , 94 S.Ct. 2485, 41 L.Ed.2d 256, 42 U.S.L.W. 4905 (1974). In *Geduldig,* the Supreme Court held: (1) that the *Rentzer* decision and administrative guidelines had mooted the case insofar as the appellees who had abnormal pregnancies were concerned; (2) that California's decision not to insure the risk of disability resulting from normal pregnancy does not constitute an invidious discrimination violative of the Equal Protection Clause. The text of *Geduldig v. Aiello* appears on page 110 *infra.*

Page 346. Erratum:

Change name and citation of principal case from Thompson v. Lambert Point Docks, etc., to Roberts v. General Mills, Inc., 337 F. Supp. 1055 (1971).

Page 385. Note 3, erratum:

Change name and citation of Thompson v. Lambert Point Docks, etc., to Roberts v. General Mills, Inc. 337 F. Supp. 1055 (1971).

Page 389. Following Burns v. Rohr, add:

NOTES

2. A result similar to that in *Burns v. Rohr* was reached in Homemakers, Inc., L.A. v. Division of Industrial Welfare, 356 F. Supp. 1111 (1973). That case held certain protective labor laws in California in conflict with Title VII because they applied to women only. That conflict could not, in the court's opinion, be reconciled by extending the benefits of those laws to men—for the following reasons:

> While this Court may question the motives of plaintiff and sympathize with its women employees, nevertheless it refuses to exercise the legislative power which belongs solely to the California Legislature. This is particularly so where, as here, a bill which would have expressly extended to all employees the Labor Code statutes regulating working conditions of women and minors was passed by the California State Legislature in its 1972 regular

session (A.B. 1710) but was vetoed by the Governor at the close of that session.

Are such reasons sufficient for refusing to extend to men benefits previously conferred on women only by the California legislature and now held, for that reason alone, to be in conflict with Title VII?

3. Compare *Kahn v. Shevin,* page 104 *infra.* What does the result in that case portend for the extension-versus-abrogation question in *Potlatch, Burns,* and *Homemakers?*

Page 406. Following note 2, add:

3. In affirming the decision of the Pennsylvania Supreme Court in the principal case, a 5-4 majority of the United States Supreme Court held that the Pittsburgh ordinance did not violate the newspaper's First Amendment rights since the help-wanted advertisements were "purely commercial advertising," which is not protected by the First Amendment. Pittsburgh Press Co. v. Human Relations Commission, 413 U.S. 376, 93 S.Ct. 2553, 37 L.Ed.2d 699 (1973).

Page 410. To note 2, add:

By contrast, 42 U.S.C. § 1983 (the text of which appears in footnote 1, on page 556 of the main volume), another of the post-Civil War civil rights statutes, permits suit for damages or injunctive relief against a state agency's sex-discriminatory employment practices that violate federal constitutional guarantees. See, e.g., *Cohen v. Chesterfield County School Board,* page 520 of main volume.

Page 410. Following note 2, add:

Alexander v. Gardner-Denver Company
United States Supreme Court, 1974
—U.S.—, 94 S.Ct. 1011, 39 L.Ed.2d 147

MR. JUSTICE POWELL delivered the opinion of the Court.

This case concerns the proper relationship between federal courts and the grievance-arbitration machinery of collective-bargaining agreements in the resolution and enforcement of an individual's rights to equal employment opportunities under Title VII of the Civil Rights Act of 1964, 42 U.S.C. § 2000e *et seq.* Specifically, we must decide under what circumstances, if any, an employee's statutory right to a trial *de novo* under Title VII may be foreclosed by prior submission of his claim to final arbitration under the nondiscrimination clause of a collective-bargaining agreement.

■

I

In May 1966, petitioner Harrell Alexander, Sr., a black, was hired by respondent Gardner-Denver Company (the "company") to perform maintenance work at the company's plant in Denver, Colorado. In June 1968, petitioner was awarded a trainee position as a drill operator. He remained at that job until his discharge from employment on September 29, 1969. The company informed petitioner that he was being discharged for producing too many defective or unusable parts that had to be scrapped.

On October 1, 1969, petitioner filed a grievance under the collective-bargaining agreement in force between the company and petitioner's union, Local No. 3029 of the United Steelworkers of America (the "union"). The grievance stated: "I feel I have been unjustly discharged and ask that I be reinstated with full seniority and pay." No explicit claim of racial discrimination was made.

Under Art. 4 of the collective-bargaining agreement, the company retained "the right to hire, suspend or discharge [employees] for proper cause." Art. 5, § 2 provided, however, that "there shall be no discrimination against any employee on account of race, color, religion, sex, national origin, or ancestry," and Art. 23, § 6(a) stated that "[n]o employee will be discharged, suspended or given a written warning notice except for just cause." The agreement also contained a broad arbitration clause covering "differences aris[ing] between the Company and the Union as to the meaning and application of the provisions of this Agreement" and "any trouble aris[ing] in the plant." Disputes were to be submitted to a multi-step grievance procedure, the first four steps of which involved negotiations between the company and the union. If the dispute remained unresolved, it was to be remitted to compulsory arbitration. The company and the union were to select and pay the arbitrator, and his decision was to be "final and binding upon the Company, the Union, and any employee or employees involved." The agreement further provided that "[t]he arbitrator shall not amend, take away, add to, or change any of the provisions of this Agreement, and the arbitrator's decision must be based solely on an interpretation of the provisions of this Agreement." The parties also agreed that there "shall be no suspension of work" over disputes covered by the grievance-arbitration clause.

The union processed petitioner's grievance through the above machinery. In the final prearbitration step, petitioner raised, apparently for the first time, the claim that his discharge resulted from racial discrimination. The company rejected all of petitioner's claims, and the grievance proceeded to arbitration. Prior to the arbitration hearing, however, petitioner filed a charge of racial discrimination with the Colorado Civil Rights Commission, which referred the complaint to the Equal Employment Opportunity Commission on November 5, 1969.

At the arbitration hearing on November 20, 1969, petitioner testified that his discharge was the result of racial discrimination and informed the arbitrator that he had filed a charge with the Colorado Commission because he "could not rely on the union." The union introduced a letter in which petitioner stated that he was "knowledgeable that in the same plant others have scrapped an equal amount and sometimes in excess, but by all logical reasoning I . . . have been the target of preferential discriminatory treatment." The union representative also testified that the company's usual practice was to transfer unsatisfactory trainee drill operators back to their former positions.

On December 30, 1969, the arbitrator ruled that petitioner had been "discharged for just cause." He made no reference to petitioner's claim of racial discrimination. The arbitrator stated that the union had failed to produce evidence of a practice of transferring rather than discharging trainee drill operators who accumulated excessive scrap, but he suggested that the company and the union confer on whether such an arrangement was feasible in the present case.

On July 25, 1970, the Equal Employment Opportunity Commission determined that there was not reasonable cause to believe that a violation of Title VII of the Civil Rights Act of 1964, 42 U.S.C. § 2000e *et seq.,* had occurred. The Commission later notified petitioner of his right to institute a civil action in federal court within 30 days. Petitioner then filed the present action in the United States District Court for the District of Colorado, alleging that his discharge resulted from a racially discriminatory employment practice in violation of § 703(a)(1) of the Act. See 42 U.S.C. § 2000e-2(a)(1).

The District Court granted respondent's motion for summary judgment and dismissed the action. 346 F. Supp. 1012 (1971). The court found that the claim of racial discrimination had been submitted to the arbitrator and resolved adversely to petitioner.[4] It then held that petitioner, having voluntarily elected to pursue his grievance to final arbitration under the nondiscrimination clause of the collective-bargaining agreement, was bound by the arbitral decision and thereby precluded from suing his employer under Title VII. The Court of Appeals for the Tenth Circuit affirmed *per curiam* on the basis of the District Court's opinion. 466 F.2d 1209 (1972).

We granted petitioner's application for certiorari. 410 U.S. 925 (1973) We reverse.

II

Congress enacted Title VII of the Civil Rights Act of 1964, 42 U.S.C. § 2000e *et seq.,* to assure equality of employment opportunities by eliminating those practices and devices that discriminate on the basis of race, color, religion, sex, or national origin. *McDonnell Douglas Corp.* v. *Green,* 411 U.S. 792, 800 (1973); *Griggs* v. *Duke Power Co.,* 401 U.S. 424 429-430 (1971). Cooperation and voluntary compliance were selected as the preferred means for achieving this goal. To this end, Congress created the Equal Employment Opportunity Commission and established a procedure whereby existing State and local equal employment opportunity agencies, as well as the Commission, would have an opportunity to settle disputes through conference, conciliation, and persuasion before the aggrieved party was permitted to file a lawsuit. In the Equal Employment Opportunity Act of 1972, Pub. L. 92-261, 86 Stat. 103, Congress amended Title VII to provide the Commis-

---

4. In reaching this conclusion, the District Court relied on petitioner's deposition acknowledging that he had raised the racial discrimination claim during the arbitration hearing. 346 F. Supp. 1012, 1014.

sion with further authority to investigate individual charges of discrimination, to promote voluntary compliance with the requirements of Title VII, and to institute civil actions against employers or unions named in a discrimination charge.

Even in its amended form, however, Title VII does not provide the Commission with direct powers of enforcement. The Commission cannot adjudicate claims or impose administrative sanctions. Rather, final responsibility for enforcement of Title VII is vested with federal courts. The Act authorizes courts to issue injunctive relief and to order such affirmative action as may be appropriate to remedy the effects of unlawful employment practices. 42 U.S.C. § 2000e-5(f) and (g). Courts retain these broad remedial powers despite a Commission finding of no reasonable cause to believe that the Act has been violated. *McDonnell Douglas Corp.* v. *Green, supra,* 411 U.S., at 798-799. Taken together, these provisions make plain that federal courts have been assigned plenary powers to secure compliance with Title VII.

In addition to reposing ultimate authority in federal courts, Congress gave private individuals a significant role in the enforcement process of Title VII. Individual grievants usually initiate the Commission's investigatory and conciliatory procedures. And although the 1972 amendment to Title VII empowers the Commission to bring its own actions, the private right of action remains an essential means of obtaining judicial enforcement of Title VII. 42 U.S.C. § 2000e-5(f)(1). In such cases, the private litigant not only redresses his own injury but also vindicates the important congressional policy against discriminatory employment practices. *Hutchings* v. *United States Industries, Inc.,* 428 F.2d 303, 310 (CA5 1970); *Bowe* v. *Colgate-Palmolive Co.,* 416 F.2d 711, 715 (CA7 1969); *Jenkins* v. *United Gas Corporation,* 400 F.2d 28, 33 (CA5 1968). See also *Newman* v. *Piggie Park Enterprises, Inc.,* 390 U.S. 400, 402 (1968).

Pursuant to this statutory scheme, petitioner initiated the present action for judicial consideration of his rights under Title VII. The District Court and the Court of Appeals held, however, that petitioner was bound by the prior arbitral decision and had no right to sue under Title VII. Both courts evidently thought that this result was dictated by notions of election of remedies and waiver and by the federal policy favoring arbitration of labor disputes, as enunciated by this Court in *Textile Workers Union* v. *Lincoln Mills,* 353 U.S. 448 (1957), and the *Steelworkers Trilogy.*[6] See also *Boys Markets, Inc.* v. *Retail Clerks Union,* 398 U.S. 235 (1970); *Gateway Coal Co.* v. *United Mine Workers of America, et al.,*–U.S.–(1974). We disagree.

---

6. *United Steelworkers of America* v. *American Mfg. Co.,* 363 U.S. 564 (1960); *United Steelworkers of America* v. *Warrior & Gulf Navigation Co.,* 363 U.S. 574 (1960); *United Steelworkers of America* v. *Enterprise Wheel & Car Corp.,* 363 U.S. 593 (1960). In *Textile Workers Union* v. *Lincoln Mills, supra,* this Court held that a grievance-arbitration provision of a collective-bargaining agreement could be enforced against unions and employers under § 301 of the Labor Management Relations Act, 29 U.S.C. § 185. The Court noted that the congressional policy, as embodied in § 203(d) of the LMRA, 29 U.S.C. § 173(d), was to promote industrial peace and that the grievance-arbitration provision of a collective agreement was a major factor in achieving this goal. *Id.,* at 455. In the *Steelworkers Trilogy,* the Court further advanced this policy by declaring that an order to arbitrate will not be denied "unless it may be said with positive assurance that the arbitration clause is not susceptible of an interpretation that covers the asserted dispute." *United Steelworkers of America* v. *Warrior Gulf Navigation Co.,* 363 U.S. 564, 582-583 (1960). The Court also stated that "so far as the arbitrator's decision concerns construc-

III

Title VII does not speak expressly to the relationship between federal courts and the grievance-arbitration machinery of collective-bargaining agreements. It does, however, vest federal courts with plenary powers to enforce the statutory requirements; and it specifies with precision the jurisdictional prerequisites that an individual must satisfy before he is entitled to institute a lawsuit. In the present case, these prerequisites were met when petitioner (1) filed timely a charge of employment discrimination with the Commission, and (2) received and acted upon the Commission's statutory notice of the right to sue. 42 U.S.C. §§ 2000e-5(b),(e), and (f). See *McDonnell Douglas Corp.* v. *Green, supra,* 411 U.S., at 798. There is no suggestion in the statutory scheme that a prior arbitral decision either forecloses an individual's right to sue or divests federal courts of jurisdiction.

In addition, legislative enactments in this area have long evinced a general intent to accord parallel or overlapping remedies against discrimination.[7] In the Civil Rights Act of 1964, 42 U.S.C. § 2000a *et seq.,* Congress indicated that it considered the policy against discrimination to be of the "highest priority." *Newman* v. *Piggie Park Enterprises, Inc., supra,* 390 U.S., at 402. Consistent with this view, Title VII provides for consideration of employment-discrimination claims in several forums. See 42 U.S.C. § 2000e-5(b) (EEOC); 42 U.S.C. § 2000e-5(c) (State and local agencies); 42 U.S.C. § 2000e-5(f) (federal courts). And, in general, submission of a claim to one forum does not preclude a later submission to another.[8] See 42 U.S.C. §§ 2000e-5(b) and (f); *McDonnell Douglas Corp.* v. *Green, supra.* Moreover, the legislative history of Title VII manifests a congressional intent to allow an individual to pursue independently his rights under both Title VII and other applicable state and federal statutes.[9] The clear inference is that Title VII was de-

tion of the contract, the courts have no business overruling him because their interpretation of the contract is different from his." *United Steelworkers of America* v. *Enterprise Wheel & Car Corp.,* 363 U.S. 593, 599 (1960). And in *Republic Steel Co.* v. *Maddox,* 379 U.S. 650 (1965), the Court held that grievance-arbitration procedures of a collective bargaining agreement must be exhausted before an employee may file suit to enforce contractual rights.

For the reasons stated in Parts III, IV, and V of this opinion, we hold that the federal policy favoring arbitration does not establish that an arbitrator's resolution of a contractual claim is dispositive of a statutory claim under Title VII.

7. See, *e.g.,* 42 U.S.C. § 1981 (Civil Rights Act of 1866); 42 U.S.C. § 1983 (Civil Rights Act of 1871).

8. For example, Commission action is not barred by "findings and orders" of state or local agencies. See 42 U.S.C. § 2000e-5(b). Similarly, an individual's cause of action is not barred by a Commission finding of no reasonable cause to believe that the Act has been violated. See 42 U.S.C. § 2000e-5(f); *McDonnell Douglas Corp.* v. *Green, supra.*

9. For example, Senator Joseph Clark, one of the sponsors of the bill, introduced an interpretive memorandum which stated: "Nothing in Title VII or anywhere else in this bill affects the rights and obligations under the NLRA or the Railway Labor Act . . . . Title VII is not intended to and does not deny to any individual, rights and remedies which he may pursue under other federal and state statutes. If a given action should violate both Title VII and the National Labor Relations Act, the National Relations Board [*sic*] would not be deprived of jurisdiction." 110 Cong. Rec. 7207 (1964). Moreover, the Senate defeated an amendment which would have made Title VII the exclusive federal remedy for most unlawful employment practices. 110 Cong. Rec. 13650-13652 (1964). And a similar amendment was rejected in connection with the Equal Employment Opportunity Act of 1972. See H. R. 9247, 92d Cong., 1st Sess. (1971). See also 2 U.S. Code Cong. & Admin. News, 92d Cong., 2d Sess. (1972), pp. 2137, 2179, 2181-2182. The report of the Senate Committee responsible for the 1972 Act explained that the "provisions regarding the individual's right to sue under Title VII, nor any of the provisions of this bill, are meant to affect existing rights granted under other laws." S. Rep. No. 415, at 24, 92d Cong., 1st Sess. (1971). For a detailed discussion of the legislative history of the 1972 Act, see Sape and Hart, Title VII Reconsidered: The Equal Opportunity Act of 1972, 40 Geo. Wash. L. Rev. 824 (1972).

signed to supplement, rather than supplant, existing laws and institutions relating to employment discrimination. In sum, Title VII's purpose and procedures strongly suggest that an individual does not forfeit his private cause of action if he first pursues his grievance to final arbitration under the nondiscrimination clause of a collective-bargaining agreement.

In reaching the opposite conclusion, the District Court relied in part on the doctrine of election of remedies.[10] That doctrine, which refers to situations where an individual pursues remedies that are legally or factually inconsistent, has no application in the present context. In submitting his grievance to arbitration, an employee seeks to vindicate his contractual right under a collective-bargaining agreement. By contrast, in filing a lawsuit under Title VII, an employee asserts independent statutory rights accorded by Congress. The distinctly separate nature of these contractual and statutory rights is not vitiated merely because both were violated as a result of the same factual occurrence. And certainly no inconsistency results from permitting both rights to be enforced in their respectively appropriate forums. The resulting scheme is somewhat analogous to the procedure under the National Labor Relations Act, as amended,[12] where disputed transactions may implicate both contractual and statutory rights. Where the statutory right underlying a particular claim may not be abridged by contractual agreement, the Court has recognized that consideration of the claim by the arbitrator as a contractual dispute under the collective-bargaining agreement does not preclude subsequent consideration of the claim by the National Labor Relations Board as an unfair labor practice charge or as a petition for clarification of the union's representation certificate under the Act. *Carey* v. *Westinghouse Corp.*, 375 U.S. 261 (1964).[13] Cf. *Smith* v. *Evening News Assn.*, 371 U.S. 195 (1962). There, as here, the relationship between the forums is complementary since consideration of the claim by both forums may promote the policies underlying each. Thus, the rationale behind the election of remedies doctrine cannot support the decision below.[14]

We are also unable to accept the proposition that petitioner waived his cause of action under Title VII. To begin, we think it clear that there can be no prospective

10. The District Court adopted the reasoning of the Sixth Circuit in *Dewey* v. *Reynolds Metals Co.*, 429 F.2d 324, 332 (1970), affirmed by an equally divided Court, 402 U.S. 689 (1971), which was apparently based in part on the doctrine of election of remedies. See n. 5, *supra.* The Sixth Circuit, however, later described *Dewey* as resting instead on the doctrine of equitable estoppel and on "themes of *res judicata* and collateral estoppel." *Newman* v. *Avco Corp.*, 451 F.2d 743, 746 n. 1 (CA6 1971). Whatever doctrinal label is used, the essence of these holdings remains the same. The policy reasons for rejecting the doctrines of election of remedies and waiver in the context of Title VII are equally applicable to the doctrines of *res judicata* and collateral estoppel.
12. 61 Stat. 136, 29 U.S.C. § 151 *et seq.*
13. As the Court noted in *Carey:*
"By allowing the dispute to go to arbitration . . . those conciliatory measures which Congress deemed vital to 'industrial peace' . . . and which may be dispositive of the entire dispute, are encouraged. The superior authority of the Board may be invoked at any time. Meanwhile the therapy of arbitration is brought to bear in a complicated and troubled area." 375 U.S., at 272.
Should disagreements arise between the Board and the arbitrator, the Board's ruling would, of course, take precedence as to those issues within its jurisdiction. *Ibid.*
14. Nor can it be maintained that election of remedies is required by the possibility of unjust enrichment through duplicative recoveries. Where, as here, the employer has prevailed at arbitration, there of course can be no duplicative recovery. But even in cases where the employee has first prevailed, judicial relief can be structured to avoid such windfall gains. See, *e.g., Oubichon* v. *North American Rockwell Corp.*, 482 F.2d 569 (CA9 1973); *Bowe* v. *Colgate-Palmolive Co.*, 416 F.2d 711 (CA7 1971). Furthermore, if the relief obtained by the employee at arbitration were fully equivalent to that obtainable under Title VII, there would be no further relief for the court to grant and hence no need for the employee to institute suit.

waiver of an employee's rights under Title VII. It is true, of course, that a union may waive certain statutory rights related to collective activity, such as the right to strike. *Mastro Plastics Corp.* v. *NLRB,* 350 U.S. 270 (1956); *Boys Markets, Inc.* v. *Retail Clerks Union,* 398 U.S. 235 (1970). These rights are conferred on employees collectively to foster the processes of bargaining and properly may be exercised or relinquished by the union as collective-bargaining agent to obtain economic benefits for unit members. Title VII, on the other hand, stands on plainly different ground; it concerns not majoritarian processes, but an individual's right to equal employment opportunities. Title VII's strictures are absolute and represent a congressional command that each employee be free from discriminatory practices. Of necessity, the rights conferred can form no part of the collective-bargaining process since waiver of these rights would defeat the paramount congressional purpose behind Title VII. In these circumstances, an employee's rights under Title VII are not susceptible to prospective waiver. See *Wilko* v. *Swan,* 346 U.S. 427 (1953).

The actual submission of petitioner's grievance to arbitration in the present case does not alter the situation. Although presumably an employee may waive his cause of action under Title VII as part of a voluntary settlement,[15] mere resort to the arbitral forum to enforce contractual rights constitutes no such waiver. Since an employee's rights under Title VII may not be waived prospectively, existing contractual rights and remedies against discrimination must result from other concessions already made by the union as part of the economic bargain struck with the employer. It is settled law that no additional concession may be exacted from any employee as the price for enforcing those rights. *J. I. Case Co.* v. *Labor Board,* 321 U.S. 332, 338-339 (1944).

Moreover, a contractual right to submit a claim to arbitration is not displaced simply because Congress also has provided a statutory right against discrimination. Both rights have legally independent origins and are equally available to the aggrieved employee. This point becomes apparent through consideration of the role of the arbitrator in the system of industrial self-government.[16] As the proctor of the bargain, the arbitrator's task is to effectuate the intent of the parties. His source of authority is the collective-bargaining agreement, and he must interpret and apply that agreement in accordance with the "industrial common law of the shop" and the various needs and desires of the parties. The arbitrator, however, has no general authority to invoke public laws that conflict with the bargain between the parties:

15. In this case petitioner and respondent did not enter into a voluntary settlement expressly conditioned on a waiver of petitioner's cause of action under Title VII. In determining the effectiveness of any such waiver, a court would have to determine at the outset that the employee's consent to the settlement was voluntary and knowing. In no event can the submission to arbitration of a claim under the nondiscrimination clause of a collective-bargaining agreement constitute a binding waiver with respect to an employee's rights under Title VII.

16. See Meltzer, Labor Arbitration and Overlapping and Conflicting Remedies for Employment Discrimination, 39 U. Chi. L. Rev. 30, 32-35 (1971); Meltzer, Ruminations About Ideology, Law, and Arbitration, 34 U. Chi. L. Rev. 545 (1967). As the late Dean Shulman stated:

"A proper conception of the arbitrator's function is basic. He is not a public tribunal imposed upon the parties by superior authority which the parties are obliged to accept. He has no general charter to administer justice for a community which transcends the parties. He is rather part of a system of industrial self-government created by and confined to the parties. He serves their pleasure only, to administer the rule of law established by their collective agreement." Shulman, Reason, Contracts and Law in Labor Relations, 68 Harv. L. Rev. 999, 1016 (1955).

"[A]n arbitrator is confined to interpretation and application of the collective bargaining agreement; he does not sit to dispense his own brand of industrial justice. He may of course look for guidance from many sources, yet his award is legitimate only so long as it draws its essence from the collective bargaining agreement. When the arbitrator's words manifest an infidelity to this obligation, courts have no choice but to refuse enforcement of the award." *United Steelworkers of America* v. *Enterprise Wheel & Car Corp.,* 363 U.S., at 597.

If an arbitral decision is based "solely on the arbitrator's view of the requirements of enacted legislation," rather than on an interpretation of the collective-bargaining agreement, the arbitrator has "exceeded the scope of his submission," and the award will not be enforced. *Ibid.* Thus the arbitrator has authority to resolve only questions of contractual rights, and this authority remains regardless whether certain contractual rights are similar to, or duplicative of, the substantive rights secured by Title VII.

IV

The District Court and the Court of Appeals reasoned that to permit an employee to have his claim considered in both the arbitral and judicial forums would be unfair since this would mean that the employer, but not the employee, was bound by the arbitral award. In the District Court's words, it could not "accept a philosophy which gives the employee two strings to his bow when the employer has only one." 346 F.Supp., at 1019. This argument mistakes the effect of Title VII. Under the *Steelworker's Trilogy,* an arbitral decision is final and binding on the employer and employee, and judicial review is limited as to both. But in instituting an action under Title VII, the employee is not seeking review of the arbitrator's decision. Rather, he is asserting a statutory right independent of the arbitration process. An employer does not have "two strings to his bow" wtih respect to an arbitral decision for the simple reason that Title VII does not provide employers with a cause of action against employees. An employer cannot be the victim of discriminatory employment practices. *Oubichon* v. *North American Rockwell Corp.,* 482 F.2d 569, 573 (CA9 1973).

The District Court and the Court of Appeals also thought that to permit a later resort to the judicial forum would undermine substantially the employer's incentive to arbitrate and would "sound the death knell for arbitration clauses in labor contracts." 346 F. Supp., at 1019. Again, we disagree. The primary incentive for an employer to enter into an arbitration agreement is the union's reciprocal promise not to strike. As the Court stated in *Boys Markets, Inc.* v. *Retail Clerks Union,* 398 U.S. 235, 248 (1970), "a no strike obligation, express or implied, is the *quid pro quo* for an undertaking by an employer to submit grievance disputes to the process of arbitration." It is not unreasonable to assume that most employers will regard the benefits derived from a no-strike pledge as outweighing whatever costs may result from according employees an arbitral remedy against discrimination in addition to their judicial remedy under Title VII. Indeed, the severe consequences of a strike may make an arbitration clause almost essential from both the employee's and the employer's perspective. Moreover, the grievance-arbitration machinery of the collective-bargaining agreement remains a relatively inexpensive and expeditious means for resolving a wide range of disputes, including claims of discriminatory employment practices. Where the collective-bargaining agreement contains a nondiscrimination clause similar to Title VII, and where arbitral procedures are fair and regular, arbitration may well produce a settlement satisfactory to both employer and employee. An employer thus has an incentive to make available the conciliatory and therapeutic processes of arbitration which may satisfy an employee's perceived need to resort to the judicial forum, thus saving the employer the expense and aggravation associated with a lawsuit. For similar reasons, the employee also has a strong incentive to arbitrate grievances, and arbitration may often eliminate those misunderstandings or discriminatory practices that might otherwise precipitate resort to the judicial forum.

V

Respondent contends that even if a preclusion rule is not adopted, federal courts should defer to arbitral decisions on discrimination claims where: (i) the claim was before the arbitrator; (ii) the collective-bargaining agreement prohibited the form of discrimination charged in the suit under Title VII; and (iii) the arbitrator has authority to rule on the claim and to fashion a remedy.[17] Under respondent's proposed rule, a court would grant summary judgment and dismiss the employee's action if the above conditions were met. The rule's obvious consequence in the present case would be to deprive the petitioner of his statutory right to attempt to establish his claim in a federal court.

At the outset, it is apparent that a deferral rule would be subject to many of the objections applicable to a preclusion rule. The purpose and procedures of Title VII indicate that Congress intended federal courts to exercise final responsibility for enforcement of Title VII; deferral to arbitral decisions would be inconsistent with that goal. Furthermore, we have long recognized that "the choice of forums inevitably affects the scope of the substantive right to be vindicated." *U.S. Bulk Carriers* v. *Arguelles,* 400 U.S. 358, 359-360 (1971) (Harlan, J., concurring). Respondent's deferral rule is necessarily premised on the assumption that arbitral processes are commensurate with judicial processes and that Congress impliedly intended federal courts to defer to arbitral decisions on Title VII issues. We deem this supposition unlikely.

Arbitral procedures, while well suited to the resolution of contractual disputes, make arbitration a comparatively inappropriate forum for the final resolution of rights created by Title VII. This conclusion rests first on the special role of the arbitrator, whose task is to effectuate the intent of the parties rather than the

---

17. Brief of Respondent, at 37. Respondent's proposed rule is analogous to the NLRB's policy of deferring to arbitral decisions on statutory issues in certain cases. See *Spielberg Manufacturing Co.,* 112 N.L.R.B. 1080, 1082 (1955).

requirements of enacted legislation. Where the collective-bargaining agreement conflicts with Title VII, the arbitration must follow the agreement. To be sure, the tension between contractual and statutory objectives may be mitigated where a collective-bargaining agreement contains provisions facially similar to those of Title VII. But other facts may still render arbitral processes comparatively inferior to judicial processes in the protection of Title VII rights. Among these is the fact that the specialized competence of arbitrators pertains primarily to the law of the shop, not the law of the land. *United Steelworkers of America* v. *Warrior & Gulf Navigation Co.,* 363 U.S. 574, at 581-583.[18] Parties usually choose an arbitrator because they trust his knowledge and judgment concerning the demands and norms of industrial relations. On the other hand, the resolution of statutory or constitutional issues is a primary responsibility of courts, and judicial construction has proven especially necessary with respect to Title VII, whose broad language frequently can be given meaning only by reference to public law concepts.

Moreover, the fact-finding process in arbitration usually is not equivalent to judicial fact-finding. The record of the arbitration proceedings is not as complete; the usual rules of evidence do not apply; and rights and procedures common to civil trials, such as discovery, compulsory process, cross-examination, and testimony under oath, are often severely limited or unavailable. See *Bernhardt* v. *Polygraphic Co.,* 350 U.S. 198, 203 (1956); *Wilko* v. *Swan,* 346 U.S. 427, 435-437 (1953). And as this Court has recognized, "[a]rbitrators have no obligation to the court to give their reasons for an award." *United Steelworkers of America* v. *Enterprise Wheel & Car Corp.,* 363 U.S. 593, at 598. Indeed, it is the informality of arbitral procedure that enables it to function as an efficient, inexpensive, and expeditious means for dispute resolution. This same characteristic, however, makes arbitration a less appropriate forum for final resolution of Title VII issues than the federal courts.[19]

It is evident that respondents' proposed rule would not allay these concerns. Nor are we convinced that the solution lies in applying a more demanding deferral standard, such as that adopted by the Fifth Circuit in *Rios* v. *Reynolds Metals Co.,* 467 F.2d 54 (1972).[20] As respondent points out, a standard that adequately in-

18. See also Gould, Labor Arbitration of Grievances Involving Racial Discrimination, 118 U. Pa. L. Rev. 40, 47-48 (1969); Platt, The Relationship between Arbitration and Title VII of the Civil Rights Act of 1964, 3 Ga. L. Rev. 398 (1969). Significantly, a substantial proportion of labor arbitrators are not lawyers. See Note, The NLRB and Deference to Arbitration, 77 Yale L.J. 1191, 1194, n. 28 (1968). This is not to suggest, of course, that arbitrators do not possess a high degree of competence with respect to the vital role in implementing the federal policy favoring arbitration of labor disputes.

19. A further concern is the union's exclusive control over the manner and extent to which an individual grievance is presented. See *Vaca* v. *Sipes,* 386 U.S. 171 (1967); *Republic Steel Co.* v. *Maddox,* 379 U.S. 650 (1965). In arbitration, as in the collective-bargaining process, the interests of the individual employee may be subordinated to the collective interests of all employees in the bargain-

ing unit. See *J. I. Case Co.* v. *Labor Board,* 321 U.S. 332 (1944). Moreover, harmony of interest between the union and the individual employee cannot always be presumed, especially where a claim of racial discrimination is made. See, *e.g., Steele* v. *Louisville & N. R. Co.,* 323 U.S. 192 (1944); *Tunstall* v. *Brotherhood of Locomotive Firemen,* 323 U.S. 210 (1944). And a breach of the union's duty of fair representation may prove difficult to establish. See *Vaca* v. *Sipes, supra; Humphrey* v. *Moore,* 375 U.S. 335, 342, 348-351. In this respect, it is noteworthy that Congress thought it necessary to afford the protections of Title VII against unions as well as employers. See 52 U.S.C. § 2000e-2(c).

20. In *Rios,* the court set forth the following deferral standard: "First, there may be no deference to the decision of the arbitrator unless the contractual right coincides with rights under Title VII. Second, it must be plain that the arbitrator's decision is in no way violative of the private rights guaranteed by Title VII,

sured effectuation of Title VII rights in the arbitral forum would tend to make arbitration a procedurally complex, expensive, and time-consuming process. And judicial enforcement of such a standard would almost require courts to make *de novo* determinations of the employees' claims. It is uncertain whether any minimal savings in judicial time and expense would justify the risk to vindication of Title VII rights.

A deferral rule also might adversely affect the arbitration system as well as the enforcement scheme of Title VII. Fearing that the arbitral forum cannot adequately protect their rights under Title VII, some employees may elect to bypass arbitration and institute a lawsuit. The possibility of voluntary compliance or settlement of Title VII claims would thus be reduced, and the result could well be more litigation, not less.

We think, therefore, that the federal policy favoring arbitration of labor disputes and the federal policy against discriminatory employment practices can best be accommodated by permitting an employee to pursue fully both his remedy under the grievance-arbitration clause of a collective-bargaining agreement and his cause of action under Title VII. The federal court should consider the employee's claim *de novo*. The arbitral decision may be admitted as evidence and accorded such weight as the court deems appropriate.[21]

NOTES

1. To what extent does the last sentence in the principal case undercut the balance of the opinion?

2. If a collective bargaining agreement in an enterprise employing substantial numbers of women employees provides: "Promotions shall be made on the basis of seniority, but in no event shall women employees be promoted from their entering positions," and also contains an arbitration clause, would *Gardner-Denver* permit the arbitrator to ignore the latter part of the provision on grounds of its conflict with Title VII?

3. Would *Gardner-Denver* prevent the N.L.R.B. from deferring to arbitral settle-

nor of the public policy which inheres in Title VII. In addition, before deferring, the district court must be satisfied that (1) the factual issues before it are identical to those decided by the arbitrator; (2) the arbitrator had power under the collective agreement to decide the ultimate issue of discrimination; (3) the evidence presented at the arbitral hearing dealt adequately with all factual issues; (4) the arbitrator actually decided the factual issues presented to the court; (5) the arbitration proceeding was fair and regular and free of procedural infirmities. The burden of proof in establishing these conditions of limitation will be upon the respondent as distinguished from the claimant." 467 F.2d, at 58. For a discussion of the problems posed by application of the *Rios* standard, see Note, Judicial Deference to Arbitrators' Decisions in Title VII Cases, 26 Stan. L. Rev. 421 (1974).

21. We adopt no standards as to the weight to be accorded an arbitral decision, since this must be determined in the court's discretion with regard to the facts and circumstances of each case. Relevant factors include the existence of provisions in the collective-bargaining agreement that conform substantially with Title VII, the degree of procedural fairness in the arbitral forum, adequacy of the record with respect to the issue of discrimination, and the special competence of particular arbitrators. Where an arbitral determination gives full consideration to an employee's Title VII rights, a court may properly accord it great weight. This is especially true where the issue is solely one of fact, specifically addressed by the parties and decided by the arbitrator on the basis of an adequate record. But courts should ever be mindful that Congress, in enacting Title VII, thought it necessary to provide a judicial forum for the ultimate resolution of discriminatory employment claims. It is the duty of courts to assure the full availability of this forum.

ment of a dispute within its jurisdiction? *Cf.* Collyer Insulated Wire, 192 NLRB No. 150, 1971 CCH NLRB ¶ 23,385.

Page 431. At end of note 3, add:

On appeal, the United States Court of Appeals, Third Circuit, reversed the trial court's decision in *Robert Hall* as to part-time personnel and affirmed as to full-time personnel—thus holding that Robert Hall had not violated the Equal Pay Act in either instance. Observed the court:

> The overwhelming evidence which showed that the men's department was more profitable than the women's was sufficient to justify the differences in base salary. These statistics proved that Robert Hall's wage differentials were not based on sex but instead fully supported the reasoned business judgment that the sellers of women's clothing could not be paid as much as the sellers of men's clothing. Robert Hall's executives testified that it was their practice to base their wage rates on these departmental figures.
>
> While no business reason could justify a practice clearly prohibited by the act, the legislative history set forth above indicates a Congressional intent to allow reasonable business judgments to stand. It would be too great an economic and accounting hardship to impose upon Robert Hall the requirement that it correlate the wages of each individual with his or her performance. This could force it toward a system based totally upon commissions, and it seems unwise to read such a result into § 206(d)(1)(iv). Robert Hall's method of determining salaries does not show the "clear pattern of discrimination," (Rep. Goodell, 109 Cong.Rec. 9203), that would be necessary for us to make it correlate more precisely the salary of each of its employees to the economic benefit which it receives from them. Robert Hall introduced substantial evidence. This is not a case where if we sustain the proof as justification for a wage differential "the exception will swallow the rule." Shultz v. First Victoria National Bank, 420 F.2d 648, 656, 657 (5th Cir. 1969).
>
> The Secretary contends that our decision in Shultz v. Wheaton Glass Company, supra, supports the district court's decision not to rely on group averages to justify the wage differential. Cf. Hodgson v. Brookhaven General Hospital, 436 F.2d 719, 725 (5th Cir. 1970) and Shultz v. American Can Co., 424 F.2d 356, 358, 360-61 (8th Cir. 1970). We do not agree that *Wheaton* supports the district court. In that case the question, in part, was whether additional duties allegedly performed by certain males would justify paying males more than females. The courts held that the employers had failed to show that all of the males performed the additional duties. Here all of the salesmen perform the same duties. One could analogize to *Wheaton Glass* and say that as the alleged justification there was the additional duties, the alleged justification here is the economic benefits. And as the employer there did not

prove that each individual performed the duties here Robert Hall did not prove that each individual provided economic benefits. However, the nature of the proof required distinguishes the two cases. It would not have been difficult in *Wheaton* for the employer to have proved that each or most male workers performed the additional duties. That is not the case here.

Also, in *Wheaton Glass,* the court relied on the fact that there had been no finding that the women workers could not perform the additional duties allegedly performed by the men. Here there was a specific finding by the district court, unchallenged by the Secretary, that the women could not perform the work done by the men.

Hodgson v. Robert Hall Clothes, Inc., 473 F.2d 589 (1973), cert. denied U.S. , 94 S.Ct. 50, 38 L.Ed.2d 85 (1973).

Corning Glass Works v. Brennan
United States Supreme Court, 1974
—U.S.—, 94 S.Ct. 2223, 41 L.Ed.2d 1

MR. JUSTICE MARSHALL delivered the opinion of the Court.

These cases arise under the Equal Pay Act of 1963, 29 U. S. C. § 206 (d)(1), which added to the Fair Labor Standards Act the principle of equal pay for equal work regardless of sex. The principal question posed is whether Corning Glass Works violated the Act by paying a higher base wage to male night shift inspectors than it paid to female inspectors performing the same tasks on the day shift, where the higher wage was paid in addition to a separate night shift differential paid to all employees for night work. In No. 73-29, the Court of Appeals for the Second Circuit, in a case involving several Corning plants in Corning, New York, held that this practice violated the Act. 474 F. 2d 226 (1973). In No. 73-695, the Court of Appeals for the Third Circuit, in a case involving a Corning plant in Wellsboro, Pennsylvania, reached the opposite conclusion. 480 F. 2d 1254 (1973). We granted certiorari and consolidated the cases to resolve this unusually direct conflict between two circuits. —U. S.—. Finding ourselves in substantial agreement with the analysis of the Second Circuit, we affirm in No. 73-29 and reverse in No. 73-695.

I

Prior to 1925, Corning operated its plants in Wellsboro and Corning only during the day, and all inspection work was performed by women. Between 1925 and 1930, the company began to introduce automatic production equipment which made it desirable to institute a night shift. During this period, however, both New York and Pennsylvania law prohibited women from working at night.[2] As a result,

2. New York prohibited the employment of women between 10 p. m. and 6 a. m. See 1927 N. Y. Laws, c. 453; 1930 N. Y. Laws, c. 868. Pennsylvania prohibited them from working between midnight and 6 a. m. See Act of July 25, 1913, Pub. L. 1024.

in order to fill inspector positions on the new night shift, the company had to recruit male employees from among its male day workers. The male employees so transferred demanded and received wages substantially higher than those paid to women inspectors engaged on the two day shifts.[3] During this same period, however, no plant-wide shift differential existed and male employees working at night, other than inspectors, received the same wages as their day shift counterparts. Thus a situation developed where the night inspectors were all male,[4] the day inspectors all female, and the male inspectors received significantly higher wages.

In 1944, Corning plants at both locations were organized by a labor union and a collective-bargaining agreement was negotiated for all production and maintenance employees. This agreement for the first time established a plant-wide shift differential,[5] but this change did not eliminate the higher base wage paid to male night inspectors. Rather, the shift differential was superimposed on the existing difference in base wages between male night inspectors and female day inspectors.

Prior to the June 11, 1964, effective date of the Equal Pay Act,[6] the law in both Pennsylvania and New York was amended to permit women to work at night.[7] It was not until some time after the effective date of the Act, however, that Corning initiated efforts to eliminate the differential rates for male and female inspectors.

3. Higher wages were demanded in part because the men had been earning more money on their day shift jobs than women were paid for inspection work. Thus, at the time of the creation of the new night shift, female day shift inspectors received wages ranging from 20 to 30 cents per hour. Most of the men designated to fill the newly created night shift positions had been working in the blowing room where the lowest wage rate was 48 cents per hour and where additional incentive pay could be earned. As night shift inspectors these men received 53 cents per hour. There is also some evidence in the record that additional compensation was necessary because the men viewed inspection jobs as "demeaning" and as "women's work."

4. A temporary exception was made during World War II when manpower shortages caused Corning to be permitted to employ women on the steady night shift inspection jobs at both locations. It appears that women night inspectors during this period were paid the same higher night shift wages earned by the men.

5. The shift differential was originally three cents an hour for the afternoon shift and five cents an hour for the night shift. It has been increased to 10 and 16 cents per hour respectively.

6. Section 4 of the Equal Pay Act provided that the Act would take effect upon the expiration of one year from June 10, 1963, the date of its enactment, except that in the case of employees covered by a bona fide collective-bargaining agreement in effect at least 30 days prior to the date of enactment, the Act would take effect upon the termination of such collective-bargaining agreement. It is conceded that the Act became effective with respect to the Corning, New York plants on June 11, 1964, though it is also stipulated that the statute of limitations barred all claims for backpay prior to November 1,

1964. With respect to the Wellsboro plant, there is apparently some dispute between the company and the Secretary as to when the Act took effect. Corning evidently believes the Act took effect on January 20, 1965, because of an outstanding collective-bargaining agreement. The Secretary claims that this agreement was reopened on January 24, 1964, and that the plant therefore became subject to the Act's requirements on June 11, 1964, one year after enactment. We see no need to resolve this question as it appears that, in any event, the parties agree the statute of limitations bars recovery of back wages for any violation prior to October 1966.

7. In New York, a 1953 amendment allowed females over the age of 21 to work after midnight in factories operating multiple shifts where the Industrial Commissioner found transportation and safety conditions to be satisfactory and granted approval. See 1953 N. Y. Laws, c. 708, amending N. Y. Labor Law § 172, now codified at N. Y. Labor Law § 173 (3)(a)(1) (McKinney 1965). In Pennsylvania, the law was amended in 1947 to permit women to work at night conditioned upon the approval of the State Department of Labor, but State regulations required that, in order to obtain approval to employ women at night, an employer was required to furnish transportation where public transportation was not available. The District Court in No. 73-695 found that public transportation was not available in Wellsboro and that it was not economically feasible for Corning to furnish transportation for its female employees. In July 1965, however, the Pennsylvania regulations were amended to permit employers to hire women at night where regular private transportation is available. See 2 CCH Lab. L. Rept., ¶ 44,501, at 56,781 (1970).

Beginning in June 1966, Corning started to open up jobs on the night shift to women. Previously separate male and female seniority lists were consolidated and women became eligible to exercise their seniority, on the same basis as men, to bid for the higher paid night inspection jobs as vacancies occurred.

On January 20, 1969, a new collective-bargaining agreement went into effect, establishing a new "job evaluation" system for setting wage rates. The new agreement abolished for the future the separate base wages for day and night shift inspectors and imposed a uniform base wage for inspectors exceeding the wage rate for the night shift previously in effect. All inspectors hired after January 20, 1969, were to receive the same base wage, whatever their sex or shift. The collective-bargaining agreement further provided, however, for a higher "red circle" rate for employees hired prior to January 20, 1969, when working as inspectors on the night shift. This "red circle" rate served essentially to perpetuate the differential in base wages between day and night inspectors.

The Secretary of Labor brought these cases to enjoin Corning from violating the Equal Pay Act[8] and to collect back wages allegedly due female employees because of past violations. Three distinct questions are presented: (1) Did Corning ever violate the Equal Pay Act by paying male night shift inspectors more than female day shift inspectors? (2) If so, did Corning cure its violation of the Act in 1966 by permitting women to work as night shift inspectors? (3) Finally, if the violation was not remedied in 1966, did Corning cure its violation in 1969 by equalizing day and night inspector wage rates but establishing higher "red circle" rates for existing employees working on the night shift?

II

Congress' purpose in enacting the Equal Pay Act was to remedy what was perceived to be a serious and endemic problem of employment discrimination in private industry—the fact that the wage structure of "many segments of American industry has been based on an ancient but outmoded belief that a man, because of his role in society, should be paid more than a woman, even though his duties are the same." S. Rept. No. 176, 88th Cong., 1st Sess. (1963), at 1. The solution adopted was quite simple in principle: to require that "equal work be rewarded by equal wages." *Ibid.*

The Act's basic structure and operation are similarly straightforward. In order to make out a case under the Act, the Secretary must show that an employer pays different wages to employees of opposite sexes "for equal work on jobs the performance of which requires equal skill, effort, and responsibility, and which are performed under similar working conditions." Although the Act is silent on this

---

8. The District Court in No. 73-29 issued a broadly worded injunction against all future violations of the Act. The Court of Appeals modified the injunction by limiting it to inspectors at the three plants at issue in that case, largely because of that Court's belief that "Corning had been endeavoring since 1966—sincerely, if ineffectively—to bring itself into compliance." 474 F. 2d, at 236. Since the Government did not seek certiorari from this aspect of the Second Circuit's judgment, we have no occasion to consider this question.

point, its legislative history makes plain that the Secretary has the burden of proof on this issue, as both of the courts below recognized.

The Act also establishes four exceptions—three specific and one a general catch-all provision—where different payment to employees of opposite sexes "is made pursuant to (i) a seniority system; (ii) a merit system; (iii) a system which measures earnings by quantity or quality of production; or (iv) a differential based on any other factor other than sex." Again, while the Act is silent on this question, its structure and history also suggest that once the Secretary has carried his burden of showing that the employer pays workers of one sex more than workers of the opposite sex for equal work, the burden shifts to the employer to show that the differential is justified under one of the Act's four exceptions. All of the many lower courts that have considered this question have so held, and this view is consistent with the general rule that the application of an exemption under the Fair Labor Standards Act is a matter of affirmative defense on which the employer has the burden of proof.

The contentions of the parties in this case reflect the Act's underlying framework. Corning argues that the Secretary has failed to prove that Corning ever violated the Act because day shift work is not "performed under similar working conditions" as night shift work. The Secretary maintains that day shift and night shift work are performed under "similar working conditions" within the meaning of the Act.[13] Although the Secretary recognizes that higher wages may be paid for night shift work, the Secretary contends that such a shift differential would be based upon a "factor other than sex" within the catch-all exception to the Act and that Corning has failed to carry its burden of proof that its higher base wage for male night inspectors was in fact based on any factor other than sex.

The courts below relied in part on conflicting statements in the legislative history having some bearing on this question of statutory construction. The Third Circuit found particularly significant a statement of Congressman Goodell, a sponsor of the Equal Pay bill, who, in the course of explaining the bill on the floor of the House, commented that "standing as opposed to sitting, pleasantness or unpleasantness of surroundings, periodic rest periods, hours of work, *differences in shift,* all would logically fall within the working conditions factor." 109 Cong. Rec. 9209 (1973) (emphasis added). The Second Circuit, in contrast, relied on a statement from the House Committee Report which, in describing the broad general exception for differentials "based on any other factor other than sex," stated: "Thus, among other things, shift differentials . . . would also be excluded. . . ." H. R. Rep. No. 309, 88th Cong., 1st Sess. (1963), at 3.

---

13. The Secretary also advances an argument that even if night and day inspection work is assumed not to be performed under similar working conditions, the differential in base wages is nevertheless unlawful under the Act. The additional burden of working at night, the argument goes, was already fully reflected in the plant-wide shift differential, and the shifts were made "similar" by payment of the shift differential. This argument does not appear to have been presented to either the Second or the Third Circuit, as the opinions in both cases reflect an assumption on the part of all concerned that the Secretary's case would fail unless night and day inspection work was found to be performed under similar working conditions. For this reason, and in view of our resolution or the "working condition" issue, we have no occasion to consider and intimate no views on this aspect of the Secretary's argument.

We agree with Judge Friendly, however, that in this case a better understanding of the phrase "performed under similar working conditions" can be obtained from a consideration of the way in which Congress arrived at the statutory language than from trying to reconcile or establish preferences between the conflicting interpretations of the Act by individual legislators or the committee reports. As Mr. Justice Frankfurter remarked in an earlier case involving interpretation of the Fair Labor Standards Act, "regard for the specific history of the legislative process that culminated in the Act now before us affords more solid ground for giving it appropriate meaning." *United States* v. *Universal C. I. T. Credit Corp.*, 344 U. S. 218, 222 (1952).

The most notable feature of the history of the Equal Pay Act is that Congress recognized early in the legislative process that the concept of equal pay for equal work was more readily stated in principle than reduced to statutory language which would be meaningful to employers and workable across the broad range of industries covered by the Act. As originally introduced, the Equal Pay bills required equal pay for "equal work on jobs the performance of which requires equal skills." There were only two exceptions—for differentials "made pursuant to a seniority or merit increase system which does not discriminate on the basis of sex. . . ."

In both the House and Senate committee hearings, witnesses were highly critical of the Act's definition of equal work and of its exemptions. Many noted that most of American industry used formal, systematic job evaluation plans to establish equitable wage structures in their plants. Such systems, as explained coincidentally by a representative of Corning Glass Works who testified at both hearings, took into consideration four separate factors in determining job value—skill, effort, responsibility and working conditions— and each of these four components was further systematically divided into various subcomponents. Under a job evaluation plan, point values are assigned to each of the subcomponents of a given job, resulting in a total point figure representing a relatively objective measure of the job's value.

In comparison to the rather complex job evaluation plans used by industry, the definition of equal work used in the first drafts of the Equal Pay Act was criticized as unduly vague and incomplete. Industry representatives feared that as a result of the Act's definition of equal work, the Secretary of Labor would be cast in the position of second-guessing the validity of a company's job evaluation system. They repeatedly urged that the bill be amended to include an exception for job classification systems, or otherwise to incorporate the language of job evaluation into the bill. Thus Corning's own representative testified:

"Job evaluation is an accepted and tested method of obtaining equity in wage relationship.

"A great part of industry is committed to job evaluation by past practice and by contractual agreement as the basis for wage administration.

" 'Skill' alone, as a criterion, fails to recognize other aspects of the job situation that affect job worth.

"We sincerely hope that this committee in passing language to eliminate wage differences based on sex alone, will recognize in its language the general role of job evaluation in establishing equitable rate relationships."

We think it plain that in amending the Act's definition of equal work to its present form, the Congress acted in direct response to these pleas. Spokesmen for the amended bill stated, for example, during the House debates:

"The concept of equal pay for jobs demanding equal skill has been expanded to require also equal effort, responsibility, and similar working conditions. These factors are the core of all job classification systems. They form a legitimate basis for differentials in pay."

Indeed, the most telling evidence of congressional intent is the fact that the Act's amended definition of equal work incorporated the specific language of the job evaluation plan described at the hearings by Corning's own representative—that is, the concepts of "skill," "effort," "responsibility," and "working conditions."

Congress' intent, as manifested in this history, was to use these terms to incorporate into the new federal act the well-defined and well-accepted principles of job evaluation so as to ensure that wage differentials based upon bona fide job evaluation plans would be outside the purview of the Act. The House Report emphasized:

"This language recognizes there are many factors which may be used to measure the relationships between jobs and which establish a valid basis for a difference in pay. These factors will be found in a majority of the job classification systems. Thus, it is anticipated that a bona fide job classification system that does not discriminate on the basis of sex will serve as a valid defense to a charge of discrimination." H. R. Rep., *supra*, at 3.

It is in this light that the phrase "working conditions" must be understood, for where Congress has used technical words or terms of art, "it [is] proper to explain them by reference to the art or science to which they [are] appropriate." *Greenleaf* v. *Goodrich,* 101 U. S. 278, 284 (1879). See also *National Labor Relations Board* v. *Highland Park Mfg. Co.,* 341 U. S. 322, 326 (1951) (Frankfurter, J., dissenting). This principle is particularly salutary where, as here, the legislative history reveals that Congress incorporated words having a special meaning within the field regulated by the statute so as to overcome objections by industry representatives that statutory definitions were vague and incomplete.

While a layman might well assume that time of day worked reflects one aspect of a job's "working conditions," the term has a different and much more specific meaning in the language of industrial relations. As Corning's own representative testified at the hearings, the element of working conditions encompasses two subfactors: "surroundings" and "hazards." "Surroundings" measure the elements, such as toxic chemicals or fumes, regularly encountered by a worker, their intensity, and their frequency. "Hazards" take into account the physical hazards regularly encountered, their frequency, and the severity of injury they can cause. This definition of "working conditions" is not only manifested in Corning's own job evaluation plans but is also well accepted across a wide range of American industry.

Nowhere in any of these definitions is time of day worked mentioned as a relevant criterion. The fact of the matter is that the concept of "working conditions," as used in the specialized language of job evaluation systems, simply does not encompass shift differentials. Indeed, while Corning now argues that night inspection work is not equal to day inspection work, all of its own job evaluation plans, including the one now in effect, have consistently treated them as equal in all respects, including working conditions. And Corning's Manager of Job Evaluation testified in No. 73-29 that time of day worked was not considered to be a "working condition." Significantly, it is not the Secretary in this case who is trying to look behind Corning's bona fide job evaluation system to require equal pay for jobs which Corning has historically viewed as unequal work. Rather, it is Corning which asks us to differentiate between jobs which the company itself has always equated. We agree with the Second Circuit that the inspection work at issue in this case, whether performed during the day or night, is "equal work" as that term is defined in the Act.[24]

This does not mean, of course, that there is no room in the Equal Pay Act for nondiscriminatory shift differentials. Work on a steady night shift no doubt has psychological and physiological impacts making it less attractive than work on a day shift. The Act contemplates that a male night worker may receive a higher wage than a female day worker, just as it contemplates that a male employee with 20 years seniority can receive a higher wage than a woman with two years seniority. Factors such as these play a role under the Act's four exceptions—the seniority differential under the specific seniority exception, the shift differential under the catch-all exception for differentials "based on any other factor other than sex."[25]

The question remains, however, whether Corning carried its burden of proving that the higher rate paid for night inspection work, until 1966 performed solely by men, was in fact intended to serve as compensation for night work, or rather constituted an added payment based upon sex. We agree that the record amply supported the District Court's conclusion that Corning had not sustained its burden of proof.[26] As its history revealed, "the higher night rate was in large part the product of the generally higher wage level of male workers and the need to compensate them for performing what were regarded as demeaning tasks." 474 F. 2d, at 233. The differential in base wages originated at a time when no other night employees received higher pay than corresponding day workers and it was maintained long after the company instituted a separate plant-wide shift differential

---

24. In No. 73-29, Corning also claimed that the night inspection work was not equal to day shift inspection work because night shift inspectors had to do a certain amount of packing, lifting, and cleaning which was not performed by day shift inspectors. Noting that it is now well settled that jobs need not be identical in every respect before the Equal Pay Act is applicable, the Court of Appeals concluded that the extra work performed by night inspectors was of so little consequence that the jobs remained substantially equal. See 474 F. 2d, at 234. See also *Shultz* v. *Wheaton Glass Co., supra,* n. 11, 421 F. 2d, at 265; *Shultz* v. *American Can Co., supra,* n. 10, 424 F. 2d, at 360; *Hodgson* v. *Fairmont Supply Co., supra,* n. 10, 454 F. 2d, at 493. The company has not pursued this issue here.

25. An administrative interpretation by the Wage and House Administrator recognizes the legitimacy of night shift differentials shown to be a factor other than sex. See 39 CFR § 800.145 (1973).

26. This question, as well as the questions discussed in Part III, *infra,* were considered by the District Court and the Court of Appeals only in No. 73-29, and not in 73-695, since in the latter case the courts below concluded that the Secretary had failed to prove that night and day shift inspection work was performed under similar working conditions. We deal with these issues, then, only on the basis of the record in No. 73-29. To the extent that there are any differences in the records in these two cases on factual matters relating to these questions, we leave it to the District Court and the Court of Appeals in No. 73-695 to resolve these questions, in the first instance, on the basis of the record created in that case.

which was thought to compensate adequately for the additional burdens of night work. The differential arose simply because men would not work at the low rates paid women inspectors, and it reflected a job market in which Corning could pay women less than men for the same work. That the company took advantage of such a situation may be understandable as a matter of economics, but its differential nevertheless became illegal once Congress enacted into law the principle of equal pay for equal work.

III

We now must consider whether Corning continued to remain in violation of the Act after 1966 when, without changing the base wage rates for day and night inspectors, it began to permit women to bid for jobs on the night shift as vacancies occurred. It is evident that this was more than a token gesture to end discrimination, as turnover in the night shift inspection jobs was rapid. The record in No. 73-29 shows, for example, that during the two-year period after June 1, 1966, the date women were first permitted to bid for night inspection jobs, women took 152 of the 278 openings, and women with very little seniority were able to obtain positions on the night shift. Relying on these facts, the company argues that it ceased discriminating against women in 1966, and was no longer in violation of the Equal Pay Act.

But the issue before us is not whether the company, in some abstract sense, can be said to have treated men the same as women after 1966. Rather, the question is whether the company remedied the specific violation of the Act which the Secretary proved. We agree with the Second Circuit, as well as with all other circuits that have had occasion to consider this issue, that the company could not cure its violation except by equalizing the base wages of female day inspectors with the higher rates paid the night inspectors. This result is implicit in the Act's language, its statement of purpose, and its legislative history.

As the Second Circuit noted, Congress enacted the Equal Pay Act "[r] ecognizing the weaker bargaining position of many women and believing that discrimination in wage rates represented unfair employer exploitation of this source of cheap labor." 474 F. 2d, at 234. In response to evidence of the many families dependent on the income of working women, Congress included in the Act's statement of purpose a finding that "the existence . . . of wage differentials based on sex depresses wages and living standards for employees necessary for their health and efficiency." Pub. L. No. 88-36, § 2 (a) (1), 77 Stat. 56 (1963). And Congress declared it to be the policy of the Act to correct this condition. *Id.,* § 2 (b).

To achieve this end, Congress required that employers pay equal pay for equal work and then specified:

> *"Provided,* That an employer who is paying a wage differential in violation of this subsection shall not, in order to comply with the provisions of this subsection, reduce the wage rate of any employee."

The purpose of this proviso was to ensure that to remedy violations of the Act,

"The lower wage rate must be increased to the level of the higher." H.R. Rep. No. 309, *supra,* at 3. Comments of individual legislators are all consistent with this view. Representative Dwyer remarked, for example, "The objective of equal pay legislation ... is not to drag men workers to the wage levels of women, but to raise women to the levels enjoyed by men in cases where discrimination is still practiced." Representative Griffin also thought it clear that "The only way a violation could be remedied under the bill is for the lower wages to be raised to the higher."

By proving that after the effective date of the Equal Pay Act, Corning paid female day inspectors less than male night inspectors for equal work, the Secretary implicitly demonstrated that the wages of female day shift inspectors were unlawfully depressed and that the fair wage for inspection work was the base wage paid to male inspectors on the night shift. The whole purpose of the Act was to require that these depressed wages be raised, in part as a matter of simple justice to the employees themselves, but also as a matter of market economics, since Congress recognized as well that discrimination in wages on the basis of sex "constitutes an unfair method of competition." § 2 (5).

We agree with Judge Friendly that

> "In light of this apparent congressional understanding, we cannot hold that Corning, by allowing some—or even many—women to move into the higher paid night jobs, achieved full compliance with the Act. Corning's action still left the inspectors on the day shift—virtually all women—earning a lower base wage than the night shift inspectors because of a differential initially based on sex and still not justified by any other consideration; in effect, Corning was still taking advantage of the availability of female labor to fill its day shift at a differentially low wage rate not justified by any factor other than sex." 474 F. 2d, at 235.

The Equal Pay Act is broadly remedial, and it should be construed and applied so as to fulfill the underlying purposes which Congress sought to achieve. If, as the Secretary proved, the work performed by women on the day shift was equal to that performed by men on the night shift, the company became obligated to pay the women the same base wage as their male counterparts on the effective date of the Act. To permit the company to escape that obligation by agreeing to allow some women to work on the night shift at a higher rate of pay as vacancies occurred would frustrate, not serve, Congress' ends. See *Shultz* v. *American Can Co.,* 424 F. 2d 356, 359 (CA8 1970); *Hodgson* v. *Miller Brewing Co.,* 457 F. 2d 221, 227 (CA7 1972); *Hodgson* v. *Square D Co.,* 459 F. 2d 805, 808-809 (CA6 1972).

The company's final contention—that it cured its violation of the Act when a new collective-bargaining agreement went into effect on January 20, 1969—need not detain us long. While the new agreement provided for equal base wages for night or day inspectors hired after that date, it continued to provide unequal base wages for employees hired before that date, a discrimination likely to continue for some time into the future because of a large number of laid-off employees who had to be offered re-employment before new inspectors could be hired. After considering the rather complex method in which the new wage rates for employees hired prior to January 1969 were calculated and the company's stated purpose behind the provisions of the new agreement, the District Court in No. 73-29 concluded that the lower base wage for day inspectors was a direct product of the company's failure to equalize the base wages for male and female inspectors as of the effective date of the Act. We agree it is clear from the record that had the company equalized the base wage rates of male and female inspectors on the effective date of the Act, as the law required, the day inspectors in 1969 would have been entitled to the same higher "red circle" rate the company provided for night inspectors. We therefore conclude that on the facts of this case, the company's continued discrimination in base wages between night and day workers, though phrased in terms of a neutral factor other than sex, nevertheless operated to perpetuate the effects of the company's prior illegal practice of paying women less than men for equal work. Cf. *Griggs* v. *Duke Power Co.,* 401 U. S. 424, 430 (1971).

The judgment in No. 73-29 is affirmed. The judgment in No. 73-695 is reversed and the case remanded to the Court of Appeals for further proceedings consistent with this opinion.

It is so ordered.

Page 437. Following note 2, add:

3. For further material on affirmative action programs, see *DeFunis* v. *Odegaard,* p. 120 of Supplement. Though *DeFunis* concerns a preferential admissions policy for students to a state-supported law school, the opinion of the Washington Supreme Court in that case also examines a number of cases that have addressed the affirmative action question, often with conflicting results, in the employment context.

Page 440. To note, add:

More recently, the National Labor Relations Board, in a 3-2 decision involving Teamsters Local 390, Miami, has indicated that it will withhold certification as the exclusive bargaining representative from a union that practices discrimination against minority groups. Albuquerque Journal, June 13, 1974, p. E14, cols. 1-2.

Page 448. Before notes, insert:

Jubilee Mfg. Co. and United Steelworkers, AFL-CIO
National Labor Relations Board, 1973
202 NLRB No. 2, 82 LRRM 1482

... "The complaint alleged that Respondent violated Section 8(a)(1) and (3) of the Act by discriminating in granting wage increases and paying wage rates to male employees based solely on the consideration of sex. In addition, the complaint alleged that Respondent violated Section 8(a)(5) of the Act by insisting to the point of impasse during collective-bargaining negotiations on a contractual provision on which it was relying as the basis for unilaterally granting wage increases and paying wage rates to its employees on a sexually discriminatory basis.

"The Administrative Law Judge concluded that the record does not establish that Respondent has developed and practiced a policy of discrimination based on sex. He therefore found it unnecessary to decide whether an employer's policy and practice of invidious discrimination against its employees on the basis of race, color, religion, sex, or national origin interferes with or restrains the discriminated employees in exercising their Section 7 rights in violation of Section 8(a)(1) and (3) of the Act. In regard to the 8(a)(5) allegation, as he found that Respondent did not discriminate on the basis of sex by the aforesaid practices, he concluded that the matter of minimum rates was not an illegal subject and was instead a mandatory topic which could be bargained on to impasse. He further concluded that an impasse was reached but that the Union, not Respondent, created the impasse. In view of the foregoing, the Administrative Law Judge recommended that the 8(a)(1), (3), and (5) allegations relating to alleged sex discrimination be dismissed in their entirety.

"We agree that these allegations of the complaint should be dismissed but solely for the reasons set forth herein.

"*I. Alleged Sex Discrimination:* While we have serious doubts about the validity of the Administrative Law Judge's finding of nondiscrimination, we find it unnecessary to resolve this question, for, in our view, discrimination based on race, color, religion, sex, or national origin, standing alone, which is all that is alleged herein, is not 'inherently destructive' of the employees' Section 7 rights and therefore is not violative of Section 8(a)(1) and (3) of the Act. There must be actual evidence, as opposed to speculation, of a nexus between the alleged discriminatory conduct and the interference with, or restraint of, employees in the exercise of those rights protected by the Act.

"In United Packinghouse, Food and Allied Workers International Union, AFL-CIO v. N.L.R.B., 416 F.2d 1126, 70 LRRM 2489, 73 LRRM 2095 (C.A.D.C.), cert. denied 396 U.S. 903, 72 LRRM 2658, a panel of the United States Circuit Court for the District of Columbia held that an employer's discrimination against its employees on account of race or national origin is a violation of Section 8(a)(1) of the Act because such discrimination (1) sets up an unjustified clash of interests between groups of workers, thus frustrating the possibility of concerted action; and (2) creates in its victims an apathy or docility which inhibits them from asserting their rights against the employer-perpetrator of the discrimination. With all due respect to the court, we are unable to agree with this legal conclusion.

"Although employer discrimination may have the effect of setting group against group, that result is by no means inevitable. A continued practice of discrimination may in fact cause minority groups to coalesce, and it is possible that this could lead to collective action with nonminority group union members.[2] Furthermore, docil-

---

2. See New Negro Alliance v. Sanitary Grocery Co., 303 U.S. 552, 2 LRRM 592; N.L.R.B. v. Baltimore Luggage Company, 387 F.2d 744, 745-749, 67 LRRM 2209 (C.A. 4).

ity is only one of several possible consequences of an employer's discrimination. In light of the increased militancy of minority groups today, it seems apparent that minority groups in different areas of the country, in different situations and at different times, react dissimilarly to discriminatory practices.

"Nor do we find merit in the contention that a policy and practice of invidious discrimination in the face of a union's ineffective efforts to eliminate such discrimination has the 'foreseeable consequence' of discouraging union membership within the meaning of Section 8(a)(3) of the Act, and discouraging the exercise of Section 7 rights within the meaning of Section 8(a)(1) of the Act. Ineffective efforts in other areas, as for example when a union seeks unsuccessfully to gain a wage increase, may well result in the union's losing face with the employees it represents. Yet, to say that an employer's refusal to give a wage increase violates Section 8(a)(3) or (1) because of this loss of face seems to us beyond the reasonable intent of the Statute.

"This is not to say categorically that discrimination on the basis of race, color, religion, sex, or national origin is necessarily or always beyond the reach of the statute. Such discrimination can be violative of Section 8(a)(1), (3), and (5) in certain contexts, and we have so held. However, in each of these areas in which we have decided issues involving discrimination there has been the necessary direct relationship between the alleged discrimination and our traditional and primary functions of fostering collective bargaining, protecting employees' rights to act concertedly, and conducting elections in which the employees have the opportunity to cast their ballots for or against a union in an atmosphere conducive to the sober and informed exercise of the franchise.

"Thus, in the context of representation elections, we have held that flagrant and irrelevant appeals to racial prejudice which deliberately seek to overemphasize and exacerbate racial feelings will be grounds for setting aside an election.[3] In addition, we have held that when employees band together to protest their employer's discriminatory practices, whether actual or supposed, their concerted effort is the kind of activity which falls within the protection of Section 7 of the Act.[4] The reason such activity is protected is that:

'The desire [for nondiscriminatory employment practices] relates to a condition of employment affecting the entire bargaining unit; it is not personal to [the individual employees involved] .'[5]

"Therefore, while, as we have held above, discrimination on the basis of race, color, religion, sex, or national origin is not per se a violation of the Act, that is not to say that such discrimination does not directly affect terms and conditions of employment. It clearly does, and concerted activity intended to remedy such discrimination is protected under our Act.

---

3. Sewell Manufacturing Company, 138 NLRB 66, 50 LRRM 1532.

4. Tanner Motor Livery, Ltd., 148 NLRB 1402, 1403-04. 57 LRRM 1170, remanded 349 F.2d 1, 59 LRRM 2784 (C.A. 9), original decision affirmed 166 NLRB 551, 65 LRRM 1502, enfd. 419 F.2d 216, 72 LRRM 2866 (C.A. 9); Mason and Hanger-Silas Mason Co., Inc., 179 NLRB 434, 72 LRRM 1372; Washington State Service Employees State Council No. 18, 188 NLRB No. 141, 76 LRRM 1467.

5. N.L.R.B. v. Tanner Motor Livery, Ltd., 419 F.2d 216, 218, 72 LRRM 2866 (C.A. 9).

"Thus, we have found that an employer violates Section 8(a)(5) of the Act by refusing to bargain in good faith concerning the elimination of existing[6] or alleged[7] racial discrimination. Similarly, we have also held that an employer violates Section 8(a)(5) by insisting on bargaining for union acceptance of provisions within a supposed nondiscrimination clause which would prevent the union from fulfilling its duty of fair representation and expose the union to legal liabilities under Title VII of the Civil Rights Act of 1964.[8] In addition, we have found that an employer's unilateral elimination of the female employees in its plant at the very moment that the union was negotiating for equal pay for them was an attempt to bypass bargaining with the union and was an unlawful refusal to bargain in violation of Section 8(a)(5) of the Act.[9]

"Finally, in an 8(a)(3) context, we have found that an employer's discharge of female workers was unlawful when the real reason for their discharge was their union's attempt to negotiate better working standards for female employees as a group or individually.[10]

"*II. Alleged Refusal to Bargain:* While, as mentioned previously, a refusal to bargain over the elimination of actual or suspected discrimination violates Section 8(a)(5) and (1) of the Act, we conclude in the circumstances herein that the evidence does not establish that Respondent refused to bargain about alleged sex discrimination and that, if anything, the evidence shows that it was the Union rather than Respondent who by its intransigence from the beginning of negotiations prevented any meaningful bargaining about this subject. In this regard, we note that Earl Graham, the Union's staff representative, walked out of the initial bargaining session when told the Respondent was firm about retaining the minimum rate provision which the Union alleged was being used to perpetuate sex discrimination. It was also Graham who at the final bargaining meeting did not respond to the Respondent's reclassification proposal with a counterproposal but rather declared the Union had nothing further to offer. Furthermore, at no time did the Union during bargaining request a broad nondiscrimination clause, ask Respondent to post the material handler jobs, or suggest that Respondent institute an affirmative anti-discrimination policy.

"In view of the foregoing, we shall order that the complaint herein be dismissed in its entirety."

Complaint is dismissed.

FANNING, Member, concurring:

"I agree with the majority that the complaint in this case should be dismissed. However, I reach this conclusion, as did the Administrative Law Judge, solely on

6. Farmers' Cooperative Compress, 169 NLRB 290, 67 LRRM 1266, enfd. on this ground 416 F.2d 1126, 70 LRRM 2489, 73 LRRM 2095 (C.A.D.C.), cert. denied 396 U.S. 903, 72 LRRM 2658.

7. Farmers' Cooperative Compress, 194 NLRB No. 3, fn. 11, 78 LRRM 1465. Southwestern Pipe, Inc., 179 NLRB 364, 72 LRRM 1377, 73 LRRM 1051, mod. on other grounds 444 F.2d 340, 77 LRRM 2317 (C.A. 5).

8. Southwestern Pipe, Inc., supra at 374-376.

9. Edmund A. Gray Co., Inc., 142 NLRB 590, 53 LRRM 1110.

10. Edmund A. Gray Co., Inc., supra; Bankers Warehouse Company, 146 NLRB 1197, 56 LRRM 1045.

the ground that the General Counsel has not presented sufficient evidence to warrant a finding of discrimination based on sex.

"The record shows that the Employer employs a production and maintenance force of 43 employees, 36 women and 7 men. The jobs in the lower classifications are filled by women. The two top paying jobs are filled by seven men and three women. Of the men, five are classified as material handlers, a job requiring unusual physical strength, including the ability to unload boxes weighing several hundred pounds. For some years the Employer has had a policy of paying these employees more than the minimum contract rate to attract and retain in its employ individuals capable of performing such duties. The testimony of Vice President Lewis that no female employee had ever asked directly or through her Union to be transferred to material handling is uncontradicted on the record. Nor does the General Counsel allege that any female employee has ever been refused consideration to be so employed. No grievance has ever been filed by, or on behalf of, such an employee alleging that the Employer had refused to employ her as a material handler because of her sex. Obviously, the job of material handler is not suited to all persons, male or female. Many men do not have the physical strength to move heavy objects. It would also seem clear to me that most women are poorly equipped to perform such tasks. In the context of these facts I cannot conclude that this Employer has refused to employ women as material handlers simply because they were women and not men.

"Unlike the majority, I have found it necessary to resolve the question of discrimination before attempting to answer the more complex and difficult legal question of sexual discrimination under our Statute. Having found no such discrimination, it seems to me that this record is an inadequate vehicle to present my views in this important area of labor-management relations. Without a factual setting to support a finding of illegality I am reluctant to state a legal conclusion which would be, at best, mere dicta. I therefore adopt as my own the findings of fact and legal conclusions of the Administrative Law Judge."

JENKINS, Member, dissenting:

"Unlike my colleagues, I would find that Respondent engaged in a practice of unlawful sex discrimination and that the foreseeable consequences of this practice were an interference with employee rights and the discouragement of union membership in violation of Section 8(a)(1) and (3) of the Act we administer. Also, unlike my colleagues, I would find that Respondent violated Section 8(a)(5) of our Act by insisting to the point of impasse on retaining contractual authority to continue this unlawful discriminatory practice.

"The relevant facts are simply stated. Respondent employs approximately 43 unit employees, 36 of whom are women. Under Respondent's collective-bargaining agreement with the Union, the jobs held by members of the bargaining unit are divided into 10 classifications—Groups I through X—although, in current practice only the classifications in Groups I through V are used. The higher the group classification, the higher the wage scale for those employees.

"Since 1959, all employees in the three lowest paid groups have been females. In the second highest paid group, Group IV, all the permanent employees are men; while in the highest paid classification, Group V, both male and female have been employed.

"Specifically, as of the dates of the hearing, of the 10 top paying jobs (Groups IV and V), seven were filled by males and three by females. Of the male employees (seven out of seven) 100 percent occupy the two top paying groups (IV and V) and only 8.3 percent of the female employees (3 of 36) hold positions in these two groups. As previously noted, no female employees occupy jobs in Group IV. In Group V, three of the five jobs are held by females; however, these three women all earn substantially less than their male counterparts even though two of the females have greater seniority than the two males. In fact, the senior male employee in Group IV earns the same or more than the two most senior females in Group V.

"Further evidence of Respondent's employment practices can be gleaned from the manner in which Respondent interpreted and applied the contractual wage scale to attract and retain male employees. Thus, the collective-bargaining agreement provides minimum rates for each of these group classifications and a 4-cent-per-hour increase for employees who have worked over 30 days. It is undisputed that, for more than five years, Respondent has been paying the material handlers in Group IV (who are all males), starting rates in excess of the contract's minimum rate for this classification and, in most instances, it exceeded the wage rate to be effective after 30 days' employment.[11] A similar practice was being followed when Respondent gave a 10-cent-an-hour increase to the two male employees in Group V making their wage rates substantially higher than those of two more senior female employees in the same group. These wage increases were granted for the avowed purpose of bringing the wages of these employees in line with the rates paid to material handlers in Group IV and preventing the Group V males from seeking employment elsewhere.

"From the foregoing, there can be no doubt of Respondent's preference for males in the position of material handler in Group IV and of its policy of granting higher wage rates to male employees similarly situated. Of course with regard to Group IV, we have no females similarly situated because Respondent ignored contractual procedures and filled these positions from the outside. The contract provides that job vacancies are to be filled in order of departmental seniority and if no one suitable is available, the jobs are to be posted plantwide and bid upon by any employee. It is only after this procedure has been exhausted, that the Respondent is authorized to hire from the outside. In practice, however, no female employee was ever offered the job of material handler even though females in the plant generally have more seniority than male employees. Also, Respondent conceded that with respect to material handler jobs it ignored the posting requirements set forth in the contract and filled these vacancies exclusively from the outside and that this constituted a departure from the manner in which the jobs in other classifications were filled.

"Merely on the basis of the statistical evidence showing the breakdown in em-

11. Respondent sought to justify this practice on the ground that men were generally "breadwinners" and that this was the only way it could attract and retain them.

ployment and job classifications for male and female employees at Respondent's plant, one must conclude that at least a prima facie case of sex discrimination has been established.[12] Of course, as I have indicated above, the evidence presented here encompasses more than just statistics. In filling vacancies for the material handlers' classification, Respondent completely ignored the bid procedures established in the collective-bargaining agreement and hired exclusively from the outside. Furthermore, it hired only male employees for this classification and started them at a wage rate which exceeded the minimum rate provided for in the contract. As might be expected, no female employee was ever hired at a starting rate higher than her classification's minimum wage rate. The preferential wage policy for male employees was completed when Respondent chose to raise the wage rates of male employees in Group V to bring them in line with the rates being paid to the male material handlers.

"In order to properly determine the effects of Respondent's employment practices under the provisions of our Act, we should first look for guidance in that broad field of law which constitutes our national labor policy. The National Labor Relations Act as a piece of social legislation was not meant to be read and interpreted in a vacuum. Rather, as I indicated in an earlier dissent,[13] the Act we administer must be read consistently with other Federal statutes which are a part of this national labor policy.[14]

"The starting point in examining our national policy concerning discrimination in employment based on race or sex must, of course, be the United States Supreme Court's landmark decision in Steele v. Louisville & Nashville Railroad Co.[15] There, the Court, in defining a union's obligations under the doctrine of fair representation, stated that discriminations based on race alone are obviously irrelevant and invidious and Congress plainly did not undertake to authorize the employees' bargaining representative to make such discriminations. Since Steele, racial discrimination in employment whether by unions or employers, has been unlawful and there is no reason to believe that the principles established in Steele would not apply with equal force to situations where the discrimination in employment has been on the basis of sex, rather than race. It is also well settled that the Court in Steele was not promulgating a doctrine which had application only to situations arising under the Railway Labor Act, but rather it intended that the principles enunciated in Steele would apply with equal force in cases arising under the National Labor Relations Act.[16] This judicial concept received further recognition with the legislative embodiment of the Steele principles in Title VII of the Civil Rights Act of 1964 which specifically prohibits discrimination in employment based on race, color, religion, sex, or national origin.

12. "In cases concerning racial discrimination, statistics often tell much and courts listen." Parham v. Southwestern Bill Telephone Co., 433 F.2d 421, 2 FEP Cases 1017 (C.A. 8). Obviously, the same observation may be made with respect to cases involving sex discrimination. See also Griggs v. Duke Power Co., 401 U.S. 424, 3 FEP Cases 175.
13. The Emporium, 192 NLRB No. 19, 77 LRRM 1669.

14. Textile Workers Union of America, AFL-CIO v. Lincoln Mills. 353 U.S. 448, 40 LRRM 2113.
15. 323 U.S. 192, 15 LRRM 708.
16. Wallace Corporation v. N.L.R.B., 323 U.S. 248, 15 LRRM 697; Ford Motor Co. v. Huffman, 345 U.S. 330, 31 LRRM 2548; Humphrey v. Moore, 375 U.S. 335, 55 LRRM 2031.

"Although, the fair representation doctrine has been a part of our national labor policy since the Court's 1944 decision in the Steele case,[18] the National Labor Relations Board has been extremely slow in giving effect to these principles. Although the Board has had jurisdiction over a union's unfair labor practices since the 1947 Taft-Hartley amendments[19] to our Act, it was not until its 1962 decision in Miranda Fuel[20] that the Board found an unfair labor practice in a union's breach of its duty of fair representation. In Miranda Fuel, a majority of the Board held that Section 7 of our Act gives employees the right to be free from unfair or irrelevant or invidious treatment by their exclusive bargaining agent in matters affecting their employment and that Section 8(b)(1)(A) of the Act prohibits labor organizations, when acting in a statutory representative capacity, from taking action against any employee upon considerations or classifications which are irrelevant, invidious, or unfair.[21] The Board majority also held that an employer who participates in such arbitrary union conduct violates Section 8(a)(1) and the employer and the union may violate Section 8(a)(3) and 8(b)(2), respectively, when, for arbitrary or irrelevant reasons or upon the basis of an unfair classification, the union attempts to cause or does cause an employer to derogate the employment status of an employee.[22]

"Although the Board's Miranda Fuel decision was denied enforcement by the United States Court of Appeals for the Second Circuit,[23] the doctrine was later upheld by the United States Court of Appeals for the Fifth Circuit.[24] Any further doubts concerning the viability of the doctrine were resolved by the United States Supreme Court's decision in Vaca v. Sipes, when the Court seemingly gave full recognition and approval to the Board's Miranda Fuel doctrine and, in fact, criticized the Board for its 'tardy' assumption of jurisdiction in these cases.[25]

"As indicated, under our Miranda Fuel doctrine, an employer may itself be guilty of unfair labor practices under our Act when it joins the statutory representative in acting against employees on invidious or irrelevant considerations. But what of situations where the employer is alone responsible for establishing and maintaining employment practices which are based on invidious or irrelevant considerations? Are not such practices just as inherently destructive of employees' Section 7 rights as those engaged in by a union and, if so, has not the employer interfered with these employee rights in violation of Section 8(a)(1) of our Act? In United Packinghouse, Food and Allied Workers International Union, AFL-CIO v. N.L.R.B., the United States Court of Appeals for the District of Columbia gave us its answers to these vexing problems. There the court, in remanding the case to us, held that an employer's maintenance of racial discrimination in his employment practices violates Section 8(a)(1) of our Act because it creates an 'unjustified clash of inter-

18. The applicability of this doctrine to cases arising under the National Labor Relations Act was announced by the United States Supreme Court on the very day it handed down its historic decision in the Steele case. See Wallace Corp. v. N.L.R.B., supra.

19. Labor Management Relations Act of 1947, 29 U.S.C. § 158(b).

20. Miranda Fuel Company, Inc., 140 NLRB 181, 51 LRRM 1584.

21. Id. at 185.

22. Id. at 185-186.

23. N.L.R.B. v. Miranda Fuel Co., Inc., 326 F.2d 172, 54 LRRM 2715 (1963).

24. Local Union No. 12, United Rubber Workers [Goodyear Tire & Rubber Co.] v. N.L.R.B., 368 F.2d 12, 63 LRRM 2395, cert. denied 329 U.S. 837, 66 LRRM 2306.

25. 386 U.S. 171, 183, 64 LRRM 2369.

ests' among the employees which tends to reduce their ability to work in concert toward their legitimate goals, and because it creates among its victims 'an apathy or docility' which inhibits them from asserting their rights in the employment relation. On remand, of course, the Board was obligated to accept the court's rationale as 'the law of the case.' However, in resolving the issues open to the Board on the remand, my colleagues concluded that the evidence did not support a finding that the employer had maintained a policy and practice of invidious racial discrimination against its employees on account of their race or national origin. As a consequence of this determination, my colleagues were not required to apply the court's rationale and, in fact, expressed no opinion on it.[27] I dissented because, in my view, the evidence established that the employer was discriminating on racial and ethnic grounds in its employment practices and policies and, under the principles laid down by the court, such conduct constitutes a violation of Section 8(a)(1) of our Act. As I indicated in my dissent:

'It is the divisiveness, induced and fostered among the employees by the "clash of interests" which the employer's racial discrimination creates, which is the source of the unlawful restraint and interference with the employees' exercise of their concerted rights. The employees are forced to expend their time, effort, and money to eliminate a condition of employment based on indivdious differentiation (race) which is unlawful and thus should never have existed.'

"If one were to accept guidance from the principles I have discussed, above, we would of necessity be constrained to conclude on the basis of the evidence before us that Respondent's employment practices were violative of our Act. Certainly, the fact that we are involved here with discrimination based on sex rather than race is of no significance. The same principles apply to all such forms of discrimination as my colleagues readily admit. Unfortunately, my colleagues in the majority are, in my judgment, willing to give only limited application and effect to our national labor policy and they specifically reject the court's interpretation of that policy in the United Packinghouse Workers case, supra. Member Fanning, on the other hand, finds insufficient evidence to establish that Respondent discriminated on the basis of sex and, consequently, he finds it unnecessary, at this time, to pass upon the court's rationale in United Packinghouse Workers.

"As I understand Member Fanning's concurrence, he accepts Respondent's representation that the job of material handler requires unusual physical strength, including the ability to unload boxes weighing several hundred pounds and, from this, he concludes that the job is one which most women are poorly equipped to perform. While I am willing to concede that in certain employment situations the sex of the individual is a bona fide occupational qualification for the position,[28] I do not think it proper to engage in broad generalizations which are too often based on stereotyped characterizations of the capabilities of men and women. In other

27. Farmers' Cooperative Compress, 194 NLRB No. 3, 78 LRRM 1465.
    28. It is significant that, under Title VII of the Civil Rights Act of 1964, an exception to the overall proscriptions is provided in cir-cumstances where sex is a bona fide occupational qualification reasonably necessary to the normal operation of that particular business or enterprise. See 42 U.S.C. § 2000e-2(e).

words, the mere fact that a job involves the use of physical strength does not automatically remove members of the female sex from consideration. Rather, it must be demonstrated that women as a class have been unable to meet the physical requirements of the job and the burden of establishing that sex is a bona fide occupational qualification is upon the party raising it.

"The principal difficulty I have with Member Fanning's conclusion is that it is based on testimony which is purely conclusionary in nature and drawn from an examination of job classifications which were prepared some 20 to 25 years ago. Perhaps today, the job requirements for material handlers at Respondent's plant are the same as they were some 20 years ago, but it is just as likely that significant changes have occurred over the years. More important, in point of fact, we know nothing about the present day job requirements for material handlers at Respondent's plant. Nor do we know whether, or not the physical qualifications for employees in one group classification differ in any way from those in another classification. Simply stated the record before us contains no specific evidence concerning the physical requirements for the different job classifications at Respondent's plant. What we are left with then is Respondent's undocumented and unsupported assertion that, at present, the job of material handler requires great physical ability and that this consideration necessitates and justifies the hiring of only males for this position. Furthermore, Respondent seems to ask us to assume that the necessary physical characteristics are to be found in all males, because there is no evidence that Respondent evaluates the physical attributes or abilities of the males it selects. I think Respondent has clearly failed to meet its burden of establishing that its prima facie discriminatory employment practices are justifiable in light of the special requirements of the job of material handler.

"Moreover, even if I have to accept Respondent's representation that this position requires great physical strength, which on this record I cannot, I would be unwilling to conclude on the basis of this evidence alone that females, as a class, do not possess the necessary qualifications to perform the work. Such a conclusion would be valid only if Respondent's hiring experience demonstrated that females generally failed to possess the physical qualifications necessary to perform this work. However, no such characterization can be made here because Respondent's practice has been systematically to exclude females from consideration for the position of material handler. This also, in large part, explains the failure of the female employees to grieve over Respondent's total disregard of the bid procedures established in the collective-bargaining agreement. When, as here, the discriminatory practice is of longstanding duration and total in its application, employees may well conclude that it would be a futile gesture to insist upon being considered for jobs which Respondent believes they are not qualified to perform. In any event, the absence of any acts of discrimination against any specific individual proves nothing when it has already been established that Respondent's practices constitute and result in discrimination against individuals as a class. Nor does it matter that Respondent may not have intentionally sought to produce such a result. The unlawfulness of the practice is determined by the consequence it produces, rather than by the motivation behind it.[29] In sum, then I feel constrained to conclude that Respondent discriminated on the basis of sex with regard to its employment practices and policies and that such conduct is contrary to our national labor policy.

"Turning now to the arguments raised in the majority opinion, I note, at the outset, that my majority colleagues agree that discrimination on the basis of sex is on an equal footing with discrimination based on race. Also, unlike Member Fanning, they are willing to concede that the evidence before us may very well establish that Respondent's employment practices resulted in discrimination on the basis of sex.[30] The majority's unwillingness to find a violation under our Act is based on the theory that there is no direct relationship between the discriminatory practices, which have been described, and the fundamental rights accorded to employees under the provisions of the National Labor Relations Act. In short, they reject the view that employment practices which are discriminatory and unquestionably illegal under Federal law have, of necessity, the inherent effect of interfering with employee rights under our Act. To the "show how he or she was hurt" argument, I readily admit there is very little I can say except to answer that this only proves how widespread and successful were the illegal practices. Such a position rejects the Supreme Court's rationale in Griggs, supra, and the court of appeals rationale in United Packinghouse Workers, supra.

"The majority believes it is by no means inevitable that such discriminatory practices will result in the destruction of employee rights under our Act. To the argument that such practices produce an unjustified clash of interests among groups of employees, they reply that it is just as likely that the effect may be one of causing minority groups to coalesce and unite in common purpose with non-minority group members. That is, they expect the beneficiaries of the unlawful practice to join hands with the victims.

"Such arguments were made when Congress was considering the enactment of legislation which is now the Civil Rights Act of 1964. The claim was then made that no additional safeguards or protections were necessary because of a general awareness on the part of blacks and other minority groups of their fundamental rights as American citizens and their increasing involvement and willingness to act in concert in defense of these rights. However, the Civil Rights Act of 1964 was enacted into law because of the overwhelming evidence that large segments of our population were being denied fundamental rights that this legislation was designed to protect. The individuals discriminated against cannot and should not be expected to take the steps necessary to establish that Respondent specifically discriminated against each and every one of them.[31]

"For reasons stated, I would find that Respondent's illegal employment practices

29. Griggs v. Duke Power Co., 401 U.S. 424, 3 FEP Cases 175.

30. In reaching their conclusions, my majority colleagues find it unnecessary to determine whether or not Respondent's employment practices, in fact, constituted sexual discrimination.

31. In other situations, arising under our Act, we presume that an employer's restrictive practices are inherently destructive of employees' Sec. 7 rights without requiring specific evidence as to the effects on individuals of the restrictive practice. For example, we will find unlawful and strike down an overly broad no-solicitation rule without regard to its actual application or enforcement, simply because such a rule has a general inhibiting effect on employees in the exercise of their Sec. 7 rights. See Joseph Horne Co., 186 NLRB No. 104, 75 LRRM 1426.

and policies were inherently destructive of employee rights under Section 7 of our Act and, further, that Respondent by engaging in such practices unlawfully discriminated against its female employees.[32] Accordingly, I conclude, contrary to my majority colleagues, that, by such conduct, Respondent has violated Section 8(a)(1) and (3) of our Act.

"Consistent with the foregoing, I would also find, contrary to my majority colleagues,[33] that during contract negotiations Respondent insisted to the point of impasse upon retaining contractual authorization to continue its discriminatory practices and by so doing engaged in conduct violative of Section 8(a)(5) of the Act. As the record clearly shows, Respondent interpreted the word 'minimum' in the wage clause of the existing contract as permitting it to pay higher wages and grant special increases above the contract rate in order to attract and keep male employees. In other words, Respondent interpreted the wage clause as permitting the payment of whatever rates it chose, over and above the minimum rates spelled out in the contract. When the Union learned that certain male employees were being paid rates of pay higher than those called for in the contract, it asked Respondent to explain its justification for such action. Respondent replied by offering its interpretation of the word "minimum" in the wage provision of the existing contract.

"When the existing contract expired, the Union proposed at the first negotiating session that the word 'minimum' be deleted from all future contracts. Respondent refused and indicated it intended to continue the practice because it felt that it had to pay more money 'to attract the men off the street in the first place,' and because it felt the 'men' were the 'breadwinners' in the family. To the Union's accusation that this action was in violation of Federal and state law, Respondent replied 'that if there was a law against giving merit raises it was a funny law.'

"The parties had three bargaining sessions, the last two of which were held under the auspices of Federal mediators, but they remained deadlocked over the issue of whether the word 'minimum' should be deleted from the contract. Following these meetings, Respondent, at one point, offered to adhere to the minimum rates for a year, but with the added proviso that it would inform the Union if it needed to exceed the rates. This proposal was correctly characterized by the Administrative Law Judge as not a real change of position and the Union made no effort to respond to this proposal. However, the Union did on several occasions attempt to get together with Respondent, but to no avail. Finally during a chance encounter between Union Representative Graham and Respondent's vice president, Lewis, about a month and a half after the last bargaining session, Graham proposed to Lewis that the parties meet again to resolve the issues. Lewis replied: 'Well, this has

32. My majority colleagues' comparison of a situation where a union has failed to eliminate a practice of invidious discrimination with one where the union has failed to gain an economic concession from an employer is curious. Of course, both actions may have the foreseeable consequence of discouraging union membership among employees, but the former is the product of an unlawful activity, whereas the latter is based on legal and legitimate considerations.

33. Member Fanning does not reach this precise issue because of his conclusion that the evidence does not establish that Respondent engaged in discriminatory employment practices.

went [sic] too far now, I don't see how we possibly could, we have to have the right to give the men more money so that we can get men in the plant.'

"I have already described in detail Respondent's discriminatory employment practices, and it will suffice to point out here that it was through Respondent's interpretation and implementation of the wage provision in its contract that it was able to effectuate these discriminatory policies. Therefore, when, during negotiations, Respondent adamantly insisted upon the retention of the minimum wage clause, it was in fact insisting upon the right to continue its discriminatory practices. To such a condition, the Union could not legally agree because the Union would itself then be equally responsible for perpetrating sex discrimination.[34] Moreover, by agreeing to such a condition, the Union would be violating its statutory obligation of fair representation toward all unit employees.[35]

"It is not surprising, then, that the Union found no legitimate basis on which it could agree to Respondent's proposal. The Union offered no counterproposal, but, again, one would be hard pressed to devise a proposal which would be acceptable to one who insists upon the 'right' to discriminate. In any event, it was at this juncture that the Union abandoned any further formal meetings with the Respondent and my majority colleagues are quick to point to this as the crucial event in the bargaining negotiations. They might be correct if the evidence indicated any softening of its position by Respondent. However, the evidence is quite to the contrary. At the conclusion of the formal negotiations, Respondent was still adamant about retaining the right to continue its illegal practices. Following this, Respondent made only one change in its proposal which the Administrative Law Judge found constituted no real alteration of its position. On the other hand, the Union made several efforts to resume the negotiations only to be rebuffed by the final comment that Respondent considered its interpretation of the minimum wage provision necessary to its continued operations.

"In such circumstances I can only conclude that Respondent insisted to the point of impasse upon retaining the right to continue its discriminatory practices and that it also failed to accord the Union the full recognition to which it is entitled under the Act. Such conduct constitutes a refusal to bargain within the meaning of Section 8(a)(5) of the Act.[36]

"In conclusion then, I would reverse the Administrative Law Judge and find the Section 8(a)(1), (3), and (5) violations which are predicated upon the Respondent's practice of sex discrimination. In all other respects, I would affirm the Administrative Law Judge's dismissal of the allegations of the complaint."

34. Vaca v. Sipes, 386 U.S. 171, 64 LRRM 2369.
35. Steele v. Louisville & Nashville Railroad Co., 323 U.S. 192, 15 LRRM 708; Miranda Fuel Co., 140 NLRB 181, 51 LRRM 1584, enforcement denied 326 F.2d 172, 54 LRRM 2715.
36. Southwestern Pipe, Inc., 179 NLRB 364, 72 LRRM 1377, 73 LRRM 1051, modified on other grounds 444 F.2d 340, 77 LRRM 2317 (C.A. 5).

Chapter 6

Sex Roles and the Constitution

Page 475. To note 2, add:

In Millenson v. New Hotel Monteleone, Inc. 475 F.2d 736 (1973, *cert denied* – U.S.–, 94 S.Ct. 376, 38 L.Ed.2d 250 (1973), *Moose Lodge* was relied upon by the Fifth Circuit Court of Appeals in its holding that, in a situation comparable to the one involved in Seidenberg v. McSorley's Old Ale House, Inc., no state action was present. Stated the court (475 F.2d at 736):

> [T]he dispositive issue in the instant case is whether the issuance of regulatory licenses to a public accommodation by a state will suffice to color the admission policies of the former with the authority and involvement of the latter.
>
> For Millenson to succeed it is necessary for her to show that the state licensing system encourages, mandates, or affirmatively authorizes the admission policies of the grill. A cursory examination of these state licensing statutes manifestly leads one to the conclusion that they are completely unrelated to the admission policies of the licensees.
>
> The impetus for the grills's admission policies originated with the hotel and not with the state. Justice Rehnquist's observations in *Moose Lodge,* are equally applicable and decisive of Millenson's contentions. Justice Rehnquist stated:

> > There is no suggestion in this record that the Pennsylvania Act, either as written or as applied, discriminates against minority groups either in their right to apply for club licenses themselves or in their right to purchase and be served liquor in places of public accommodation.

> > * * * * * *

> > However detailed this type of regulation may be in some particulars, it cannot be said to in any way foster or encourage racial discrimination. Nor can it be said to make the State in any realistic sense a partner or even a joint venturer in the club's enterprise.

Compare the opinion of Chief Justice Burger and Justices Stewart and Rehnquist in Columbia Broadcasting Sys., Inc. v. Democratic Nat. Comm., 412 U.S. 94, 114-121, 93 S.Ct. 2080, 2092-2096, 36 L.Ed.2d 772, 790-794 (1973) that, notwithstanding extensive federal regulation and licensing of the broadcast industry, a broadcast licensee's refusal to accept a paid editorial advertisement does not constitute "governmental action" for First Amendment purposes.

Page 494. Following note 2, add:

3. The question left open in *Costello* was finally decided by the New Jersey Supreme Court in State v. Chambers, 63 N.J. 287, 307 A.2d 78 (1973), holding a violation of equal protection that state's statutory provisions for sentencing a female offender to an indeterminate term where a male offender convicted of the same offense would be sentenced to a state prison for a minimum-maximum term.

Page 513. Following note 6, add:

7. In Locker v. Kirby, 31 Cal. App. 3d 520, 107 Cal. Rptr. 446 (1973), the California Court of Appeal, Second District, was confronted with a challenge by liquor licensees and waitresses to a rule of the Department of Alcoholic Beverage Control prohibiting licensees from employing or using topless waitresses on premises where liquor is sold. Among other issues dealt with by the court was the following (107 Cal. Rptr. 449-451):

> We turn then to one remaining contention. Taking their cue, evidently, from Sail'er Inn, Inc. v. Kirby, 5 Cal.3d 1, 95 Cal.Rptr. 329, 485 P.2d 529, petitioners argue that rule 143.2 is invalid by reason of equal protection concepts and an asserted conflict with the 1964 Civil Rights Act, with section 18, Article XX of California Constitution and with section 1411 of the Labor Code. It is pointed out that the rule does not prohibit display of the naked male chest. We are told that because of this fact there is a discrimination between male and female which is objectionable under the constitutional and statutory provisions mentioned.
>
> *Sail'er Inn* held invalid under these provisions (except the Labor Code section which was not discussed at length) section 25656 of the Business and Professions Code. That section prohibited the employment of women as bartenders except in certain limited circumstances. The case is distinguishable. The California Supreme Court held that a classification based upon sex was within the "suspect" category which requires strict scrutiny to withstand an equal protection attack. In such a situation "the state bears the burden of establishing not only that it has a *compelling* interest which justifies the law but that the distinctions drawn by the law are *necessary* to further its purpose. . . ." After examining various arguments in support of and against section 25656, the court concluded that the state had not only failed to establish a compelling interest but had not shown any interest at all. . . . In reaching this conclusion the court said "The Legislature may, of course, pass laws to prevent 'improprieties' in connection with the sale of alcoholic beverages. . . . Where the evil which the Legislature seeks to prevent can be directly prevented through nondiscriminatory legislation, and where the class singled out by the Legislature has no necessary connection with the evil to be prevented, the statute must be struck down as an invidious discrimination

against that class. . . ." The court recognized that bartending and related jobs, though regulated, are lawful.

The rule challenged here does prohibit a female from working as a waitress while bare-breasted. There are no proven facts before us to establish that it prevents her from pursuing the lawful profession of a waitress, and that state of the record alone would serve to distinguish *Sail'er*. We need not rest on this premise however since it is evident that rule 143.2 was promulgated to prevent " 'improprieties' in connection with the sale of alcoholic beverages" (*Sail'er* at 20, 95 Cal.Rptr. at 342, 485 P.2d at 542) and such laws are proper. (Ibid.) It is not disputed here that rule 143.2 and its companion rules were adopted after hearings in which evidence was produced justifying respondent in so doing.[4] (California v. LaRue, *supra,* 409 U.S. 109, 93 S.Ct. 390, 34 L.Ed.2d 342, 347-348, 350.) The hearings disclosed a connection between sex and alcohol which the respondent determined required regulation.

As was the case with the Supreme Court in *Boreta,* "We decline to probe the metaphysics of toplessness 'as such.' " (2 Cal.3d at 107, 84 Cal.Rptr. at 128, 465 P.2d at 16.)[5] We note, however, the indisputable fact that the naked female breast has for centuries been a symbol of sexuality but that no such generalization can be made about the male chest. Given that fact and the obvious physical differences between mature male and female breasts, and also given the state's interest in regulating the sale of alcoholic beverages and the broad sweep of authority which the states have in this area by virtue of the Twenty-First Amendment[6] we hold that rule 143.2 does not offend equal protection concepts. There is clearly a necessary connection between that which is sought to be prevented and the class to which the rule is directed.

Article XX, section 18 of the California Constitution is not offended by the rule. It proscribes disqualifying a person from entering a lawful vocation because of sex. Rule 143.2 does not have the effect. It does not prevent petitioner Harmon from working as a waitress, nor indeed does it prevent her from doing so in topless dress so long as no alcoholic beverage license is involved on the premises in question. For the same reasons petitioners' attacks on rule 143.2 based upon the 1964 Civil Rights Act[7] and on Labor Code section 1411[8] must fall.

4. Section 25750 of the Business and Professions Code authorizes respondent to make and prescribe reasonable rules. When respondent tried to take disciplinary action against licensees employing topless waitresses simply on the ground that such employment was contrary to public welfare or morals, without a factual showing of the point, our Supreme Court suggested the adoption of factual grounded regulations as a reliable alternative. (Boreta Enterprises, Inc. v. Department of Alcoholic Beverage Control. 2 Cal.3d 85, 106, 84 Cal.Rptr. 113, 465 P.2d 1.)

5. Some discussion of the place of openly exposed female bosom in contemporary society is found in *Boreta* itself (2 Cal.3d at 101-102, 84 Cal.Rptr. 113, 465 P.2d 1.) Those interested in the subject are also referred to Robins v. County of Los Angeles, 248 Cal.App.2d 1, 56 Cal.Rptr. 853 and In re

Davis, 242 Cal.App.2d 645, 51 Cal.Rptr. 702.

6. The authority is not unlimited. (Sail'er Inn, Inc. v. Kirby, *supra,* 5 Cal.3d 1, 95 Cal. Rptr. 329, 485 P.2d 529; Wisconsin v. Constantineau, 400 U.S. 433, 91 S.Ct. 507, 27 L.Ed.2d 515.)

7. The particular part of the act in question, Section 2000e-2, among other things makes it an unlawful employment practice for an employer to discriminate against any individual on account of sex. (42 U.S.C.A. § 2000e-2.)

8. The section declares it to be the public policy of the state to protect and safeguard the right and opportunity of all persons without discrimination on account of sex, *inter alia,* to seek, obtain and hold employment. The right to do so is declared to be a civil right by section 1412 of the Labor Code.

[In the light of Sail'er Inn, was the following case correctly decided?]

People v. Olague
Appellate Department, Superior Court, Los Angeles County, California, 1973
31 Cal. App. 3d Supp. 5, 106 Cal.Rptr. 612.

HOLMES, Judge.

The orders of the municipal court sustaining respondent's demurrer and dismissing the action raise only the question of whether the challenged statute is unconstitutional on its face. We address ourselves to that question only.

Section 270 of the Penal Code has been before the appellate courts many times. It is held to have important public objectives for the support of children. . . . The means prescribed under this statute to further its legitimate objectives is for local law enforcement agencies to initiate a judicial inquiry as to the willingness and ability of a father to support his child. The state must first prove that the accused is the father and that the child has been abandoned or deserted by the father or that the father has omitted to supply necessaries of life to the child. If these elements are proved, it then becomes the father's burden to prove that his default was not wilful or without excuse. If he fails to discharge that burden he is criminally liable. If he meets his burden of proof, like proceedings are authorized to be taken against the mother.

The issue raised in this case is whether the statute is so unreasonable on its face as to create an invidious discrimination between fathers and mothers, thereby denying equal protection of the law to fathers.

In order to decide that issue it is necessary to determine which of the "two level" standards this statute must meet in order to pass the test of legality laid down in equal protection cases. . . .

Ever since the Penal Code was adopted in 1872, section 270 has expressed the policy of the state that both parents are responsible for support of their children. In People v. Sorenson (1968) 68 Cal.2d 280, at page 287, 66 Cal.Rptr. 7, 12, 437 P.2d 495, 500, the court said:

> "Rather than punishment of the neglectful parents, the principal statutory objectives are to secure support of the child and to protect the public from the burden of supporting a child who has a parent able to support him."

The statute is thus seen to reflect a basic state concern for the survival of children. The manner of enforcement is secondary. We, therefore, are dealing only with the narrow issue of the right of the state to enforce the undoubted duty of both parents to support their children (Civ.Code, § 206) by proceeding initially against the father and secondarily against the mother. Stated bluntly, the interest espoused herein by the respondent is his desire to evade a basic legal obligation. We are not dealing with a fundamental personal or political right, such as the right of a parent to the association and comfort of his child (Stanley v. Illinois (1972) 405

U.S. 645, 92 S.Ct. 1208, 31 L.Ed.2d 551), or to engage in gainful employment (Phillips v. Martin Marietta Corporation (1971) 400 U.S. 542, 91 S.Ct. 496, 27 L.Ed.2d 613; Sail'er Inn v. Kirby (1971) 5 Cal.3d 1, 95 Cal.Rptr. 329, 485 P.2d 529), or to exercise equal voting rights (Carrington v. Rash (1965) 380 U.S. 89, 85 S.Ct. 775, 13 L.Ed.2d 675); nor is this a case where no legitimate state objective is involved (Reed v. Reed (1971) 404 U.S. 71, 92 S.Ct. 251, 30 L.Ed.2d 225; In re Antazo, *supra,* 3 Cal.3d 100, 89 Cal.Rptr. 255, 473 P.2d 999).

Neither is this a case of "suspect classification" on the basis of sex. The law imposes the obligation of support on both parents. The challenged statute implies that, in the opinion of the Legislature, it is reasonable, in the enforcement of that law, to differentiate between *mothers* as a class and *fathers* as a class. The classification is not between men, as such and women, as such; it is between two classes of human beings both of which have a common obligation. The question is whether the legislative command that enforcement of that obligation shall proceed first against one of those classes rather than both is supported by articulable reasons.

It follows from the limited and peculiar nature of the interest asserted by the respondent father—i.e., the *desire* to resist and defeat his duty to support his child unless and until the state proceeds against the mother—is not of that "fundamental" kind which invokes "an attitude of active and critical analysis, subjecting the classification to strict scrutiny" by the court and requiring the state to prove that "it has a *compelling* interest" and that the classification is "necessary to further [the state's] purpose. . . ."

The proper test of constitutionality in this case is, rather,

"the conventional standard for reviewing economic and social welfare legislation challenged as a denial of equal protection. The standard upholds the legislature's discretionary choice of differentiated treatment if it bears a rational relationship to a conceivably legitimate state purpose, i.e., if it has a rational basis; it requires the reviewing court to draw a presumption that the facts supply a rational basis and imposes the burden of demonstrating arbitrariness upon the statute's assailant. [citations.] "

This case is before us without any factual record; therefore the respondent has not discharged his burden of "demonstrating arbitrariness" unless such demonstration appears on the face of the statute itself.

Respondent contends that the claimed invidious discrimination is shown on the face of the statute because it impliedly admits that mothers are equally capable, with fathers, of supporting their children since they are subject to prosecution for nonsupport in the event the father fails in his duty. The conclusion does not follow from its premise. The statute is equally consistent with the view that fathers generally are more able, financially, and better situated, economically, to support their children than are mothers.

In determining the need and propriety of classified legislation, where the same does not appear upon the face of the legislative enactment, the court may resort to its judicial knowledge of the contemporaneous conditions and situation of the people, the existing economic, sociological, and civic policy of the state and all other matters of common knowledge. . . .

The court will judicially notice that Penal Code section 270 in substantially its present form was enacted in 1923; that although, during the ensuing 50 years the structure of our society has undergone far-reaching changes of many kinds, the family remains the basic social unit; that children still must be fed and nurtured by their parents; that serious and increasing strains have developed in the family unit due to a variety of causes, including the phenomenon of working mothers and the proliferation of divorce; that these centrifugal forces have resulted, in many cases, in division of the family and establishment of multiple households; that, despite current efforts to minimize the fact, mothers generally do not compete in the labor market on terms of equality with fathers; that the compensation of mothers in employment is generally lower than for fathers and opportunities for advancement and for business independence are less for mothers; that working mothers frequently are required to spend a substantial part of their earnings for care of their children by others; and that, despite the changes in social life during the past half-century, young children still are largely regarded and treated as the special concern of their mothers, who devote a major share of otherwise employable time to the care of children.

These commonly known facts of present day life are sufficient to support the legislative diversification of fathers and mothers in Penal Code section 270.

In conclusion, it bears emphasis that it is the legal duty of both parents to support their children. In our existing state of society fathers generally are better situated to meet this obligation than mothers. It avails nothing to contend that the facts of life should be different; that both parents should be equally able to discharge their parental duty. Perhaps this will come to pass some day, but it is not true today. The fact that there may be exceptions such as indigent or dissolute fathers, or wealthy and independent mothers, does not vitiate the reasonableness of section 270 in our present social environment (People v. Western Fruit Growers (1943) 22 Cal.2d 494, 506-507, 140 P.2d 13; Harriman v. City of Beverly Hills (1969) 275 Cal.App.2d 918, 925, 80 Cal.Rptr. 426).

The judgment is reversed.

NOTES

1. Do you agree with the court's conclusion that: "We are not dealing with a fundamental personal or political right. . . ."? If you don't, which fundamental right of the defendant is dealt with in the case?

2. In stating that "Neither is this a case of 'suspect classification' on the basis of sex," is the court being faithful to the teaching of *Sail'er Inn* under the circumstances?

Page 520. Following notes, add:

Frontiero v. Richardson
United States Supreme Court, 1973
411 U.S. 677, 93 S.Ct. 1764, 36 L.Ed.2d 583

Mr. Justice **Brennan** announced the judgment of the Court and an opinion in which Mr. Justice **Douglas**, Mr. Justice **White**, and Mr. Justice **Marshall** join.

The question before us concerns the right of a female member of the uniformed services[1] to claim her spouse as a "dependent" for the purposes of obtaining increased quarters allowances and medical and dental benefits under 37 USC § § 401, 403 [37 USCS § § 401, 403], and 10 USC § § 1072, 1076 [10 USCS § § 1072, 1076], on an equal footing with male members. Under these statutes, a serviceman may claim his wife as a "dependent" without regard to whether she is in fact dependent upon him for any part of her support. 37 USC § 401(1); 10 USC § 1072(A) [37 USCS § 401(1); 10 USCS § 1072(A)]. A servicewoman, on the other hand, may not claim her husband as a "dependent" under these programs unless he is in fact dependent upon her for over one-half of his support. 37 USC § 401; 10 USC § 1072(2)(C) [37 USCS § 401; 10 USCS § 1072(2)(C)].[2] Thus, the question for decision is whether this difference in treatment constitutes an unconstitutional discrimination against servicewomen in violation of the Due Process Clause of the Fifth Amendment. A three-judge District Court for the Middle District of Alabama, one judge dissenting, rejected this contention and sustained the constitutionality of the provisions of the statutes making this distinction. 341 F Supp 201 (1972). We noted probable jurisdiction. 409 US 840, 34 L Ed 2d 78, 93 S Ct 64 (1972). We reverse.

I

In an effort to attract career personnel through re-enlistment, Congress established, in 37 USC § § 401 et seq. [37 USCS § § 401 et seq.], and 10 USC § § 1071 et seq. [10 USCS § § 1071 et seq.], a scheme for the provision of fringe benefits to members of the uniformed services on a competitive basis with business and industry. Thus, under 37 USC § 403 [37 USCS § 403], a member of the uniformed services with dependents is entitled to an increased "basic allowance for quarters" and, under 10 USC § 1076 [10 USCS § 1076], a member's dependents are provided comprehensive medical and dental care.

1. The "uniformed services" include the Army, Navy, Air Force, Marine Corps, Coast Guard, Environmental Science Services Administration, and Public Health Service. 37 USC § 101(3); 10 USC § 1072(1) [37 USCS § 101(3); 10 USCS § 1072(1)].

2. 37 USC § 401 [37 USCS § 401] provides in pertinent part:

"In this chapter, 'dependent,' with respect to a member of a uniformed service, means—
"(1) his spouse;
* * * * * *

"However, a person is not a dependent of a female member unless he is in fact dependent on her for over one-half of his support. . . ."
10 USC § 1072(2) [10 USCS § 1072(2)] provides in pertinent part:
" 'Dependent,' with respect to a member . . . of a uniformed service, means—
"(A) the wife;
* * * * * *
"(C) the husband, if he is in fact dependent on the member . . . for over one-half of his support. . . ."

Appellant Sharron Frontiero, a lieutenant in the United States Air Force, sought increased quarters allowances, and housing and medical benefits for her husband, appellant Joseph Frontiero, on the ground that he was her "dependent." Although such benefits would automatically have been granted with respect to the wife of a male member of the uniformed services, appellant's application was denied because she failed to demonstrate that her husband was dependent on her for more than one-half of his support.[4] Appellants then commenced this suit, contending that, by making this distinction, the statutes unreasonably discriminate on the basis of sex in violation of the Due Process Clause of the Fifth Amendment.[5] In essence, appellants asserted that the discriminatory impact of the statutes is two-fold: first, as a procedural matter, a female member is required to demonstrate her spouse's dependency, while no such burden is imposed upon male members; and second, as a substantive matter, a male member who does not provide more than one-half of his wife's support receives benefits, while a similarly situated female member is denied such benefits. Appellants therefore sought a permanent injunction against the continued enforcement of these statutes and an order directing the appellees to provide Lieutenant Frontiero with the same housing and medical benefits that a similarly situated male member would receive.

Although the legislative history of these statutes sheds virtually no light on the purposes underlying the differential treatment accorded male and female members, a majority of the three-judge District Court surmised that Congress might reasonably have concluded that, since the husband in our society is generally the "breadwinner" in the family—and the wife typically the "dependent" partner—"it would be more economical to require married female members claiming husbands to prove actual dependency than to extend the presumption of dependency to such members." 341 F Supp, at 207. Indeed, given the fact that approximately 99% of all members of the uniformed services are male, the District Court speculated that such differential treatment might conceivably lead to a "considerable saving of administrative expense and manpower." Ibid.

II

At the outset, appellants contend that classifications based upon sex, like classifications based upon race, alienage, and national origin, are inherently suspect and must therefore be subjected to close judicial scrutiny. We agree and, indeed, find at least implicit support for such an approach in our unanimous decision only last Term in Reed v Reed, 404 US 71, 30 L Ed 2d 225, 92 S Ct 251 (1971).

In Reed, the Court considered the constitutionality of an Idaho statute providing that, when two individuals are otherwise equally entitled to appointment as admin-

---

4. Appellant Joseph Frontiero is a full-time student at Huntingdon College in Montgomery, Alabama. According to the agreed stipulation of facts, his living expenses, including his share of the household expenses, total approximately $354 per month. Since he receives $205 per month in veterans' benefits, it is clear that he is not dependent upon appellant Sharron Frontiero for more than one-half of his support.

5. "[W]hile the Fifth Amendment contains no equal protection clause, it does forbid discrimination that is 'so unjustifiable as to be violative of due process.' " Schneider v. Rusk, 377 US 163, 12 L Ed 2d 218, 84 S Ct 1187, 1190; see Shapiro v Thompson, 394 US 618, 641-642, 22 L Ed 2d 600, 89 S Ct 1322, 1335 (1969); Bolling v Sharpe, 347 US 497, 98 L Ed 2d 884, 74 S Ct 693 (1954).

istrator of an estate, the male applicant must be preferred to the female. Appellant, the mother of the deceased, and appellee, the father, filed competing petitions for appointment as administrator of their son's estate. Since the parties, as parents of the deceased, were members of the same entitlement class, the statutory preference was invoked and the father's petition was therefore granted. Appellant claimed that this statute, by giving a mandatory preference to males over females without regard to their individual qualifications, violated the Equal Protection Clause of the Fourteenth Amendment.

The Court noted that the Idaho statute "provides that different treatment be accorded to the applicants on the basis of their sex; it thus establishes a classification subject to scrutiny under the Equal Protection Clause." 404 US, at 75, 30 L Ed 2d 225. Under "traditional" equal protection analysis, a legislative classification must be sustained unless it is "patently arbitrary" and bears no rational relationship to a legitimate governmental interest. . . .

In an effort to meet this standard, appellee contended that the statutory scheme was a reasonable measure designed to reduce the workload on probate courts by eliminating one class of contests. Moreover, appellee argued that the mandatory preference for male applicants was in itself reasonable since "men [are] as a rule more conversant with business affairs than . . . women."[10] Indeed, appellee maintained that "it is a matter of common knowledge, that women still are not engaged in politics, the professions, business or industry to the extent that men are."[11] And the Idaho Supreme Court, in upholding the constitutionality of this statute, suggested that the Idaho Legislature might reasonably have "concluded that in general men are better qualified to act as an administrator than are women."[12]

Despite these contentions, however, the Court held the statutory preference for male applicants unconstitutional. In reaching this result, the Court implicitly rejected appellee's apparently rational explanation of the statutory scheme, and concluded that, by ignoring the individual qualifications of particular applicants, the challenged statute provided "dissimilar treatment for men and women who are . . . similarly situated." Reed v Reed, supra, at 77, 30 L Ed 2d 225. The Court therefore held that, even though the State's interest in achieving administrative efficiency "is not without some legitimacy," "[t]o give a mandatory preference to members of either sex over members of the other, merely to accomplish the elimination of hearings on the merits, is to make the very kind of arbitrary legislative choice forbidden by the [Constitution]. . . ." Id., at 76, 30 L Ed 2d 225. This departure from "traditional" rational basis analysis with respect to sex-based classifications is clearly justified.

There can be no doubt that our Nation has had a long and unfortunate history of sex discrimination.[13] Traditionally, such discrimination was rationalized by an attitude of "romantic paternalism" which, in practical effect, put women not on a

10. Brief of Appellee, at 12, Reed v Reed, 404 US 71, 30 L Ed 2d 225, 92 S Ct 251 (1971).
11. Id., at 12-13.
12. Reed v Reed, 93 Idaho 511, 514, 465 P2d 635, 638 (1970).
13. Indeed, the position of women in this country at its inception is reflected in the view expressed by Thomas Jefferson that women should be neither seen nor heard in society's decisionmaking councils. See M. Gruberg, Women in American Politics 4 (1968). See also A. de Tocqueville, Democracy in America, pt 2 (Reeves tr 1840), in World's Classic Series 400 (Galaxy ed 1947).

pedestal, but in a cage. Indeed, this paternalistic attitude became so firmly rooted in our national consciousness that, exactly 100 years ago, a distinguished member of this Court was able to proclaim:

> "Man is, or should be, woman's protector and defender. The natural and proper timidity and delicacy which belongs to the female sex evidently unfits it for many of the occupations of civil life. The constitution of the family organization, which is founded in the divine ordinance, as well as in the nature of things, indicates the domestic sphere as that which properly belongs to the domain and functions of womanhood. The harmony, not to say identity, of interests and views which belong, or should belong, to the family institution is repugnant to the ideas of a woman adopting a distinct and independent career from that of her husband. . . .
>
> ". . . The paramount destiny and mission of woman are to fulfill the noble and benign offices of wife and mother. This is the law of the Creator." Bradwell v Illinois, 83 US [16 Wall] 130, 141, 21 L Ed 442 (1873) (Bradley, J., concurring).

As a result of notions such as these, our statute books gradually became laden with gross, stereotypical distinctions between the sexes and, indeed, throughout much of the 19th century the position of women in our society was, in many respects, comparable to that of blacks under the pre-Civil War slave codes. Neither slaves nor women could hold office, serve on juries, or bring suit in their own names, and married women traditionally were denied the legal capacity to hold or convey property or to serve as legal guardians of their own children. See generally, L. Kanowitz, Women and the Law: The Unfinished Revolution 5-6 (1969); G. Myrdal, An American Dilemma 1073 (2d ed 1962). And although blacks were guaranteed the right to vote in 1870, women were denied even that right—which is itself "preservative of other basic civil and political rights"[14]—until adoption of the Nineteenth Amendment half a century later.

It is true, of course, that the position of women in America has improved markedly in recent decades.[15] Nevertheless, it can hardly be doubted that, in part because of the high visibility of the sex characteristic,[16] women still face pervasive, although at times more subtle, discrimination in our educational institutions, on the job market and, perhaps most conspicuously, in the political arena.[17] See generally,

---

14. Reynolds v Sims, 377 US 533, 562, 12 L Ed 2d 506, 84 S Ct 1362 (1964); see Dunn v Blumstein, 405 US 330, 336, 31 L Ed 2d 274, 92 S Ct 995 (1972); Kramer v Union Free School District, 395 US 621, 626, 23 L Ed 2d 583, 89 S Ct 1886 (1969); Yick Wo v Hopkins, 118 US 356, 370, 30 L Ed 220, 6 S Ct 1064 (1886).

15. See generally, The President's Task Force on Women's Rights and Responsibilities, A Matter of Simple Justice (1970); L. Kanowitz, Women and the Law: The Unfinished Revolution (1969); A. Montague, Man's Most Dangerous Myth (4th ed 1964); The President's Commission on the Status of Women, American Women (1963).

16. See, e. g., Note, Sex Discrimination and Equal Protection: Do We Need a Constitutional Amendment?, 84 Harv L Rev 1499, 1507 (1971).

17. It is true, of course, that when viewed in the abstract, women do not constitute a small and powerless minority. Nevertheless, in part because of past discrimination, women are vastly underrepresented in this Nation's decisionmaking councils. There has never been a female President, nor a female member of this Court. Not a single woman presently sits in the United States Senate, and only 14 women hold seats in the House of Representatives. And, as appellants point out, this underrepresentation is present throughout all levels

K. Amundsen, The Silenced Majority: Women and American Democracy (1971); The President's Task Force on Women's Rights and Responsibilities, A Matter of Simple Justice (1970).

Moreover, since sex, like race and national origin, is an immutable characteristic determined solely by the accident of birth, the imposition of special disabilities upon the members of a particular sex because of their sex would seem to violate "the basic concept of our system that legal burdens should bear some relationship to individual responsibility. . . ." Weber v Aetna Casualty & Surety Co., 406 US 164, 175, 31 L Ed 2d 768, 92 S Ct 1400 (1972). And what differentiates sex from such nonsuspect statutes as intelligence or physical disability, and aligns it with the recognized suspect criteria, is that the sex characteristic frequently bears no relation to ability to perform or contribute to society.[18] As a result, statutory distinctions between the sexes often have the effect of invidiously relegating the entire class of females to inferior legal status without regard to the actual capabilities of its individual members.

We might also note that, over the past decade, Congress has itself manifested an increasing sensitivity to sex-based classifications. In Tit VII of the Civil Rights Act of 1964, for example, Congress expressly declared that no employer, labor union, or other organization subject to the provisions of the Act shall discriminate against any individual on the basis of "race, color, religion, *sex,* or national origin."[19] Similarly, the Equal Pay Act of 1963 provides that no employer covered by the Act "shall discriminate . . . between employees on the basis of *sex.*"[20] And § 1 of the Equal Rights Amendment, passed by Congress on March 22, 1972, and submitted to the legislatures of the States for ratification, declares that "[e]quality of rights under the law shall not be denied or abridged by the United States or by any State on account of sex."[21] Thus, Congress has itself concluded that classifications based upon sex are inherently invidious, and this conclusion of a coequal branch of Government is not without significance to the question presently under consideration. Cf. Oregon v Mitchell, 400 US 112, 240, 248-249, 27 L Ed 2d 272, 91 S Ct 260 (1970); Katzenbach v Morgan, 384 US 641, 648-649, 16 L Ed 2d 828, 86 S Ct 1717 (1966).

With these considerations in mind, we can only conclude that classifications based upon sex, like classifications based upon race, alienage, or national origin, are inherently suspect, and must therefore be subjected to strict judicial scrutiny. Ap-

of our State and Federal Government. See Joint Reply Brief of Appellants and American Civil Liberties Union (Amicus Curiae) 9.

18. See, e. g., Developments in the Law—Equal Protection, 82 Harv L Rev 1065, 1173-1174 (1969).

19. 47 USC §§ 2000e-2(a), (b), (c). [47 USCS §§ 2000e-2(a), (b), (c)]. (Emphasis added.) See generally, Sape & Hart, Title VII Reconsidered: The Equal Employment Opportunity Act of 1972, 40 Geo Wash L Rev 824 (1972); Developments in the Law—Employment Discrimination and Title VII of the Civil Rights Act of 1964, 84 Harv L Rev 1109 (1971).

20. 29 USC § 206(d) [29 USCS § 206(d)]. (Emphasis added.) See generally, Murphy, Female Wage Discrimination: A Study of the Equal Pay Act 1963-1970. 39 U Cin L Rev 615 (1970).

21. HJ Res No. 208, 92d Cong, 2d Sess (1972). In conformity with these principles, Congress in recent years has amended various statutory schemes similar to those presently under consideration so as to eliminate the differential treatment of men and women. See 5 USC § 2108 [5 USCS § 2108], as amended, 85 Stat 644; 5 USC § 7152 [5 USCS § 7152], as amended, 85 Stat 644; 5 USC § 8341 [5 USCS § 8341], as amended, 84 Stat 1961; 38 USC § 102(b) [38 USCS § 102(b)], as amended, 86 Stat 1074.

plying the analysis mandated by that stricter standard of review, it is clear that the statutory scheme now before us is constitutionally invalid.

III

The sole basis of the classification established in the challenged statutes is the sex of the individuals involved. Thus, under 37 USC § § 401, 403 [37 USCS § § 401, 403], and 10 USC § § 1072, 1076 [10 USCS § § 1072, 1076], a female member of the uniformed services seeking to obtain housing and medical benefits for her spouse must prove his dependency in fact, whereas no such burden is imposed upon male members. In addition, the statutes operate so as to deny benefits to a female member, such as appellant Sharron Frontiero, who provides less than one-half of her spouse's support, while at the same time granting such benefits to a male member who likewise provides less than one-half of his spouse's support. Thus, to this extent at least, it may fairly be said that these statutes command "dissimilar treatment for men and women who are . . . similarly situated." Reed v Reed, supra, at 77, 30 L Ed 2d 225.

Moreover, the Government concedes that the differential treatment accorded men and women under these statutes serves no purpose other than mere "administrative convenience." In essence, the Government maintains that, as an empirical matter, wives in our society frequently are dependent upon their husbands, while husbands rarely are dependent upon their wives. Thus, the Government argues that Congress might reasonably have concluded that it would be both cheaper and easier simply conclusively to presume that wives of male members are financially dependent upon their husbands, while burdening female members with the task of establishing dependency in fact.[22]

The Government offers no concrete evidence, however, tending to support its view that such differential treatment in fact saves the Government any money. In order to satisfy the demands of strict judicial scrutiny, the Government must demonstrate, for example, that it is actually cheaper to grant increased benefits with respect to *all* male members, than it is to determine which male members are in fact entitled to such benefits and to grant increased benefits only to those members whose wives actually meet the dependency requirement. Here, however, there is substantial evidence that, if put to the test, many of the wives of male members would fail to qualify for benefits.[23] And in light of the fact that the dependency determination with respect to the husbands of female members is

---

22. It should be noted that these statutes are not in any sense designed to rectify the effects of past discrimination against women. See Gruenwald v. Gardner, 390 F2d 591 (CA2 1968), cert denied, 393 US 982, 21 L Ed 2d 445, 89 S Ct 456 (1968); cf. Jones v Alfred H. Mayer Co. 392 US 409, 20 L Ed 2d 1189, 88 S Ct 2186 (1968); South Carolina v Katzenbach, 383 US 301, 15 L Ed 2d 769, 86 S Ct 803 (1966). On the contrary, these statutes seize upon a group—women—who have historically suffered discrimination in

employment, and rely on the effects of this past discrimination as a justification for heaping on additional economic disadvantages. Cf. United States v Gaston County, 395 US 285, 296-297, 23 L Ed 2d 309, 89 S Ct 1720 (1969).

23. In 1971, 43% of all women over the age of 16 were in the labor force, and 18% of all women worked full-time 12 months per year. See U.S. Women's Bureau, Dept. of Labor, Highlights of Women's Employment & Education 1 (W. B. Pub. No. 71-191, March

presently made solely on the basis of affidavits, rather than through the more costly hearing process, the Government's explanation of the statutory scheme is, to say the least, questionable.

In any case, our prior decisions make clear that, although efficacious administration of governmental programs is not without some importance, "the Constitution recognizes higher values than speed and efficiency." Stanley v Illinois, 405 US 645, 656, 31 L Ed 2d 551, 92 S Ct 1208 (1972). And when we enter the realm of "strict judicial scrutiny," there can be no doubt that "administrative convenience" is not a shibboleth, the mere recitation of which dictates constitutionality. . . . On the contrary, any statutory scheme which draws a sharp line between the sexes, *solely* for the purpose of achieving administrative convenience, necessarily commands "dissimilar treatment for men and women who are . . . similarly situated," and therefore involves the "very kind of arbitrary legislative choice forbidden by the [Constitution] . . . ." Reed v Reed, supra, at 77, 76, 30 L Ed 2d 225. We therefore conclude that, by according differential treatment to male and female members of the uniformed services for the sole purpose of achieving administrative convenience, the challenged statutes violate the Due Process Clause of the Fifth Amendment insofar as they require a female member to prove the dependency of her husband.[25]

Reversed.

Mr. Justice **Stewart** concurs in the judgment, agreeing that the statutes before us work an invidious discrimination in violation of the Constitution. Reed v Reed, 404 US 71, 30 L Ed 2d 225, 92 S Ct 251.

Mr. Justice **Rehnquist** dissents for the reasons stated by Judge Rives in his opinion for the District Court, Frontiero v Laird, 341 F Supp 201 (1972).

Mr. Justice **Powell**, with whom The **Chief Justice** and Mr. Justice **Blackmun** join, concurring in the judgment.

I agree that the challenged statutes constitute an unconstitutional discrimination against service women in violation of the Due Process Clause of the Fifth Amendment, but I cannot join the opinion of Mr. Justice Brennan, which would hold that all classifications based upon sex, "like classifications based upon race, alienage, and national origin," are "inherently suspect and must therefore be subjected to close judicial scrutiny." Supra, at 5, 36 L Ed 2d 589. It is unnecessary for the Court in

---

1972). Moreover, 41.5% of all married women are employed. See U. S. Bureau of Labor Statistics, Dept. of Labor, Work Experience of the Population in 1971 4 (Summary Special Labor Force Report, August 1972). It is also noteworthy that, while the median income of a male member of the armed forces is approximately $3,686, see The Report of the President's Commission on an All Volunteer Armed Force 51, 181 (1970), the median income for all women over the age of 14, including those who are not employed, is approximately $2,237. See U.S. Dept. of Commerce, Bureau of the Census, Statistical Abstract of the United States Table No. 535 (1972). Applying the statutory definition of "dependency" to these statistics, it appears that, in the "median" family, the wife of a male member must have personal expenses of approximately $4,474, or about 75% of the total family income, in order to qualify as a "dependent."

25. As noted earlier, the basic purpose of these statutes was to provide fringe benefits to members of the uniformed services in order to establish a compensation pattern which would attract career personnel through re-enlistment. See n 3, supra, and accompanying text. Our conclusion in no wise invalidates the statutory schemes except insofar as they require a female member to prove the dependency of her spouse. See Weber v Aetna Casualty & Surety Co. 406 US 164, 31 L Ed 2d 768, 92 S Ct 1400 (1972); Levy v Louisiana, 391 US 68, 20 L Ed 2d 436, 88 S Ct 1509 (1968); Moritz v Commissioner of Internal Revenue, 469 F2d 466 (CA10 1972). See also 1 USC § 1 [1 USCS § 1].

this case to characterize sex as a suspect classification, with all of the far-reaching implications of such a holding. Reed v Reed, 404 US 71, 30 L Ed 2d 225, 92 S Ct 251 (1971), which abundantly supports our decision today, did not add sex to the narrowly limited group of classifications which are inherently suspect. In my view, we can and should decide this case on the authority of Reed and reserve for the future any expansion of its rationale.

There is another, and I find compelling, reason for deferring a general categorizing of sex classifications as invoking the strictest test of judicial scrutiny. The Equal Rights Amendment, which if adopted will resolve the substance of this precise question, has been approved by the Congress and submitted for ratification by the States. If this Amendment is duly adopted, it will represent the will of the people accomplished in the manner prescribed by the Constitution. By acting prematurely and unnecessarily, as I view it, the Court has assumed a decisional responsibility at the very time when state legislatures, functioning within the traditional democratic process, are debating the proposed Amendment. It seems to me that this reaching out to pre-empt by judicial action a major political decision which is currently in process of resolution does not reflect appropriate respect for duly prescribed legislative processes.

There are times when this Court, under our system, cannot avoid a constitutional decision on issues which normally should be resolved by the elected representatives of the people. But democratic institutions are weakened, and confidence in the restraint of the Court is impaired, when we appear unnecessarily to decide sensitive issues of broad social and political importance at the very time they are under consideration within the prescribed constitutional processes.

NOTES

1. In Robinson v. Board of Regents of Eastern Kentucky University, 475 F.2d 707 (1973), a state-supported university's dormitory curfew restrictions applicable to women students only were upheld under the "any rational basis" test. Stated the court:

> The State's basic justification for the classification system is that of safety. It asserts that women are more likely to be criminally attacked later at night and are physically less capable of defending themselves than men. It concludes that the safety of women will be protected by having them in their dormitories at certain hours of the night. The goal of safety is a legitimate concern of the Board of Regents and this court cannot say that the regulations in question are not rationally related to the effectuation of this reasonable goal.
>
> The appellant claims that the safety justification is undermined by the shifting curfew for different nights of the week asserting that the streets are no safer at 12:30 a.m. on Saturday than they are at 12:30 a.m. on Wednesday. We hold, however, that the State could properly take into consideration the fact that on weekend nights many coeds have dates and ought to be per-

mitted to stay out later than on weekday nights. A classification having some reasonable basis does not offend the equal protection clause merely because it is not drawn with mathematical nicety.

The Robinson case was decided between the United States Supreme Court's decisions in *Reed* and *Frontiero*. Nevertheless, on May 14, 1974, many months after its decision in *Frontiero*, the Court denied certiorari in *Robinson*. 42 U.S.L.W. 3629 (1974). Is the result in *Robinson* reconcilable with *Frontiero?* With *LaFleur*, page 149 *infra?*

2. In Wiesenfeld v. Secretary of Health, Education & Welfare, 367 F. Supp. 981, a widower challenged the constitutionality of 42 U.S.C. § 402(g) on equal-protection grounds because it allowed only widows and not widowers to collect certain social security benefits. Discussing the evolving tests to be applied to sex discrimination challenges under the equal protection clause, the court stated:

> Subsequent to *Frontiero* and *Reed*, some courts and commentator have interpreted these two cases as creating an "intermediate test" for legislative discrimination based upon sex. Eslinger v. Thomas, 476 F.2d 225, 231 (4th Cir. 1972); Wark v. Robbins, 458 F.2d 1295, 1297 n. 4 (1st Cir. 1972) (dictum); *see generally* Gunther, The Supreme Court 1971 Term—Forward: In Search of Evolving Doctrine on a Changing Court, 86 Harv.L.Rev. 1 (1972); Getman, The Emerging Constitutional Principle of Sexual Equality, The Supreme Court Review 157 (1972). Others view this "new test" as a "slightly altered" rational basis standard or as "general shift" from the traditional test to a "slightly, but perceptibly, more rigorous" standard. Green v. Waterford Board of Education, 473 F.2d 629, 633 (2d Cir. 1973); Aiello v. Hansen, 359 F.Supp. 792, 796 (N.D.Cal.1973); Brenden v. Independent School District 742, 477 F.2d 1292, 1300 (8th Cir. 1973).
>
> Apparently this "new test" developed from the language of Chief Justice Burger in *Reed* when, for a unanimous Court he quoted Royster Guano Co. v. Virginia, 253 U.S. 412, 415, 40 S.Ct. 560, 64 L.Ed. 989 (1920) that
>
>> "(a) classification 'must be reasonable, not arbitrary, and must rest upon some ground of difference having a fair and substantial relation to the object of the legislation, so that all persons similarly circumstanced shall be treated alike.' "
>
> 404 U.S. at 76, 92 S.Ct. at 254.

Royster Guano Co. can hardly be considered as a strong foundation for a "new" equal protection standard. In that case a successful attack was made upon a Virginia statute which taxed all income of local corporations derived from business done outside Virginia and business done within it while exempting entirely the income derived from outside Virginia by local corporations which do no local business. It is evident that *Royster Guano Co.* depended upon the "traditional" equal protection standard which evolved during that era of the Supreme Court's history when governmental economic regulations were constantly challenged on equal protection grounds.

In *Reed* and *Frontiero* we do not discern a "new intermediate" equal protection test, and we reject those cases which adopt such standards. We do, however, perceive an expression of deep concern by the Supreme Court to analyze statutory classifications based upon sex in more pragmatic terms of this everyday modern world rather than in the stereotyped generalizations of the Victorian age. At best, all that can be gleaned from *Reed* and *Frontiero* is that until the Supreme Court is faced squarely with the problem of extending *Reed* in a case where a sexual classification could be validly upheld under the "traditional" test but not under "close judicial scrutiny", we cannot be absolutely certain how statutory sex discrimination fits within equal protection doctrine. Up to this time only four members of the Court have been willing to hold that sex is a suspect classification.

The obvious reluctance of the Supreme Court to decide whether or not to categorize sex as "inherently suspect" apparently originates from an unwillingness to intrude into that area while the Equal Rights Amendment is pending ratification by the States. It also arises from the principle that if a statute violates equal protection doctrine under a lesser standard, there is no need to examine that classification by "close judicial scrutiny". *Aiello, supra* 359 F.Supp. at 796; *see also* Eisenstadt v. Baird, 405 U.S. 438, 447 n. 7, 92 S.Ct. 1029, 31 L.Ed.2d 349 (1972). Consequently, we must first proceed to an analysis of whether Section 402(g) is rationally related to some valid public purpose. . . .

When this standard is applied to Section 402(g), we find that this measure is a rational attempt by Congress to protect women and families who have lost the male head of the household. This choice by Congress is not arbitrary because it is very evident that women have been and continue to be unable to earn income equal to that of men even though Congress has clearly indicated that job discrimination on the basis of sex shall be unlawful. . . .

Having determined that Section 402(g) satisfies the "traditional" equal protection standard, we must determine whether the test of "close judicial scrutiny" should be applied and whether sex should be declared as "inherently suspect". We are persuaded by the opinion of Mr. Justice Brennan in *Frontiero* that sex is "inherently suspect." When the higher standard is applied to Section 402(g), that section violates the equal protection component of the Fifth Amendment.

When Section 402(g) is applied to the facts of this case and viewed under "close judicial scrutiny", even though Congress may have intended that this section rectify the effects of past and present discrimination against women, it operates to "heap on" additional economic disadvantages to women wage earners such as Paula Wiesenfeld. *Frontiero supra,* at 689 n. 22, 93 S.Ct. 1764. During her employment as a teacher, maximum social security payments were deducted from her salary. Yet, upon her tragic death, her surviving spouse and child receive less social security benefits than those of a male teacher who earned the same salary and made the same social security payments.

While affirmative legislative or executive action may satisfy a compelling governmental interest to undue [sic] the past discrimination against such suspect groups as racial minorities,[29] such action cannot meet the higher equal protection standard if it discriminates against some of the group which it is designed to protect. Because Section 402(g) discriminates against women such as Paula Wiesenfeld who have successfully gained employment as well as against men and children who have lost their wives and mothers, we find this section violates the Fifth Amendment.

For these reasons we grant summary judgment for the plaintiff.

Will *Wiesenfeld* survive the result in *Kahn v. Shevin,* p. 104 *infra?*

3. The "intermediate test" for equal-protection purposes, rejected by the court in *Wiesenfeld,* is described in Boraas v. Village of Belle Terre, 476 F.2d 806, 814 (1973) as follows:

> Faced recently with the issue under similar circumstances the Supreme Court appears to have moved from this rigid dichotomy, sometimes described as a "two-tiered" formula, toward a more flexible and equitable approach, which permits consideration to be given to evidence of the nature of the unequal classification under attack, the nature of the rights adversely affected, and the governmental interest urged in support of it. Under this approach the test for application of the Equal Protection Clause is whether the legislative classification is *in fact* substantially related to the object of the statute.... If the classification, upon review of facts bearing on the foregoing relevant factors, is shown to have a substantial relationship to a lawful objective and is not void for other reasons, such as overbreadth, it will be upheld. If not, it denies equal protection.

Under this test, the Court of Appeals of the Second Circuit invalidated as an equal-protection violation a New York village ordinance restricting land use to one-family dwellings and defining "family" to mean one or more persons related by blood or marriage, or not more than two unrelated persons, living and cooking together as a single housekeeping unit. This decision has been reversed, however, by the United States Supreme Court in Village of Belle Terre v. Boraas, U.S. , 94 S.Ct. 1536, 39 L.Ed.2d 797 (1974). In the view of Mr. Justice Douglas, writing for the majority, the village ordinance was simply a zoning regulation. As such, it is simply a species of "economic and social legislation where legislatures have historically drawn lines which we respect against the charge of violation of the Equal

---

29. *See, e.g.,* Contractors Ass'n of Eastern Pa. v. Secretary of Labor, 442 F.2d 159, 176-177 (3d Cir. 1971), cert. denied, 404 U.S. 854, 92 S.Ct. 98, 30 L.Ed.2d 95 (1971); Joyce v. McCrane, 320 F.Supp. 1284, 1291-1293 (D.N.J.1970); Carter v. Gallagher, 452 F.2d 315 (8th Cir. 1971) (en banc), cert. denied, 406 U.S. 950, 92 S.Ct. 2045, 32 L.Ed.2d 338 (1972); United States v. Ironworkers Local 86, 443 F.2d 544 (9th Cir. 1971), cert. denied, 404 U.S. 984, 92 S.Ct. 447, 30 L.Ed.2d 367 (1971); United States v. Wood, Wire & Metal Lathers Int. U., L.U., 341 F.Supp 694, 699 (S.D.N.Y.1972), aff'd, 471 F.2d 408, 413 (2d Cir. 1973), cert denied, 412 U.S. 939, 93 S.Ct. 2773, 37 L.Ed.2d 398 (1973); Southern Illinois Builders Association v. Ogilvie, 471 F.2d 680, 685-686 (7th Cir. 1972); United States v. Local Union No. 212, 472 F.2d 634, 636 (6th Cir. 1973).

Protection Clause if the law be 'reasonable not arbitrary' and bears 'a rational relationship to a [permissible] state objective.' " 94 S.Ct. at 1540.

4. Is Mr. Justice Powell correct when he states that for the Court to categorize sex classifications as suspect now would be disruptive to the legislative-ratification debate surrounding the Equal Rights Amendment? Compare Statement of Leo Kanowitz on the ERA, pp. 541-42 of the main volume. Should that statement be regarded as part of the legislative history of the ERA? Does it dispose of Mr. Justice Powell's argument?

E. PREFERENTIAL TREATMENT AND AFFIRMATIVE ACTION

Kahn v. Shevin
United States Supreme Court, 1974
U.S.   , 94 S.Ct. 1734, 40 L.Ed.2d 189

MR. JUSTICE DOUGLAS delivered the opinion of the Court.

Since at least 1885, Florida has provided for some form of property tax exemption for widows.[1] The current law granting all widows an annual $500 exemption, Fla. Stat. § 196.191(7), has been essentially unchanged since 1941.[2] Appellant Kahn is a widower who lives in Florida and applied for exemption to the Dade County Tax Assessor's Office. It was denied because the statute offers no analogous benefit for widowers. Kahn then sought a declaratory judgment in the Circuit Court for Dade County, Florida, and that court held the statute violative of the Equal Protection Clause of the Fourteenth Amendment because the classification "widow" was based upon gender. The Florida Supreme Court reversed, finding the classification valid because it has a "fair and substantial relation to the object of the legislation,"[3] that object being the reduction of the "disparity between the economic capabilities of a man and a woman." Kahn appealed here, 28 U.S.C. § 1257(2), and we noted probable jurisdiction, −U.S.−. We affirm.

There can be no dispute that the financial difficulties confronting the lone woman in Florida or in any other State exceed those facing the man. Whether from overt discrimination or from the socialization process of a male dominated culture, the job market is inhospitable to the woman seeking any but the lowest paid jobs.[4] There are of course efforts underway to remedy this situation. On the federal level

---

1. Article IX, § 9 of the 1885 Florida constitution provided that: "There shall be exempt from taxation property to the value of two hundred dollars to every widow that has a family dependent on her for support, and to every person that has lost a limb or been disabled in war or by misfortune."

2. In 1941 Fla. Stat. § 192.06(7) exempted "[p]roperty to the value of five hundred dollars to every widow . . . ." The current provision, challenged here, provided that: "The following property shall be exempt from taxation:

* * *

"(7) Property to the value of five hundred dollars to every widow and to every person who is a bona fide resident of the state and has lost a limb or been disabled in war or military hostilities or by misfortune."

3. Quoting *Reed* v. *Reed*, 404 U.S. 71, 76.

4. In 1970 while 40% of males in the work force earned over $10,000, and 70% over $7,000, 45% of women working full time earned less than $5,000, and 73.9% earned less than $7,000. U.S. Department of Commerce, Bureau of the Census: Current Population Reports, P-60, No. 80.

Title VII of the Civil Rights Act of 1964 prohibits covered employers and labor unions from discrimination on the basis of sex. 42 U.S.C. § § 2000e-2(a), (b), (c), as does the Equal Pay Act of 1963, 29 U.S.C. § 206(d). But firmly entrenched practices are resistent to such pressures, and indeed, data compiled by the Woman's Bureau of the United States Department of Labor shows that in 1972 woman working full time had a median income which was only 57.9% of the male median —a figure actually six points lower than had been achieved in 1955.[5] Other data points in the same direction.[6] The disparity is likely to be exacerbated for the widow. While the widower can usually continue in the occupation which preceded his spouse's death in many cases the widow will find herself suddenly forced into a job market with which she is unfamiliar, and in which, because of her former economic dependency, she will have fewer skills to offer.[7]

There can be no doubt therefore that Florida's differing treatment of widows and widowers "rest [s] upon some ground of difference having a fair and substantial relation to the object of the legislation." *Reed* v. *Reed,* 404 U.S. 71, 76, quoting *Royster Guano Co.* v. *Virginia,* 253 U.S. 412, 415.

This is not a case like *Frontiero* v. *Richardson,* 411 U.S. 677, where the Government denied its female employees both substantive and procedural benefits granted males *"solely* for administrative convenience." *Id.,* at 690 (emphasis in original).[8] We deal here with a state tax law reasonably designed to further the state policy of cushioning the financial impact of spousal loss upon the sex for whom that loss imposes a disproportionately heavy burden. We have long held that "[w]here taxation is concerned and no specific federal right, apart from equal protection, is imperiled, the States have large leeway in making classifications and drawing lines

5. The Women's Bureau provides the following data:

Year	Median earnings		Women's median earnings as percent of men's
	Women	Men	
1972	$5,903	$10,202	57.9
1971	5,593	9,399	59.5
1970	5,323	8,966	59.4
1969	4.977	8,227	60.5
1968	4,457	7,664	58.2
1967	4,150	7,182	57.8
1966	3,973	6,848	58.0
1965	3,823	6,375	60.0
1964	3,690	6,195	59.6
1963	3,561	5,978	59.6
1962	3,446	5,794	59.5
1961	3,351	5,644	59.4
1960	3,293	5,417	60.8
1959	3,193	5,209	61.3
1958	3,102	4,927	63.0
1957	3,008	4,713	63.8
1956	2,827	4,466	63.3
1955	2,719	4,252	63.9

Note.—Data for 1962-72 are not strictly comparable with those for prior years, which are for wage and salary income only and do not include earnings of self-employed persons.

Source: Table prepared by Women's Bureau, Employment Standards Administration, U.S. Department of Labor, from data published by Bureau of the Census, U.S. Department of Commerce.

6. For example, in 1972 the median income of women with four years of college was $8,736—exactly $100 more than the median income of men who had never even completed one year of high school. Of those employed as managers or administrators, the women's median income was only 53.2% of the men's, and in the professional and technical occupations the figure was 67.5%. Thus the disparity extends even to women occupying jobs usually thought of as well paid. Tables prepared by the Women's Bureau, Employment Standards Aministration, U.S. Department of Labor.

7. It is still the case that in the majority of families where both spouses are present, the woman is not employed. A. Ferris, Indicators of Trends in the Status of American Women 95 (1971).

8. And in *Frontiero* the plurality opinion also noted that the statutes there were "not in any sense designed to rectify the effects of past discrimination against women. On the contrary, these statutes seize upon a group—women—who have historically suffered discrimination in employment, and rely upon the effects of this past discrimination as a justification for heaping on additional economic disadvantages." *Frontiero* v. *Richardson,* 411 U.S. 677, 689 n. 22 (citations omitted).

which in their judgment produce reasonable systems of taxation." *Lehnhausen* v. *Lake Shore Auto Parts Co.*, 410 U.S. 356, 359. A state tax law is not arbitrary although it "discriminate[s] in favor of a certain class . . . if the discrimination is founded upon a reasonable distinction, or difference in state policy," not in conflict with the Federal Constitution. *Allied Stores* v. *Bowers*, 358 U.S. 522, 528. This principle has weathered nearly a century of Supreme Court adjudication,[9] and it applies here as well. The statute before us is well within those limits.[10]

Affirmed.

MR. JUSTICE BRENNAN, with whom MR. JUSTICE MARSHALL joins, dissenting.

The Court rejects widower Kahn's claim of denial of equal protection on the ground that the limitation in § 196.191(7), which provides an annual $500 property tax exemption to widows, is a legislative classification that bears a fair and substantial relation to "the state policy of cushioning the financial impact of spousal loss upon the sex for whom that loss imposes a disproportionately heavy burden." *Ante*, p. 4. In my view, however, a legislative classification that distinguishes potential beneficiaries solely by reference to their gender-based status as widows or widowers, like classifications based upon race,[1] alienage,[2] and national origin,[3] must be subjected to close judicial scrutiny, because it focuses upon generally immutable characteristics over which individuals have little or no control, and also because gender-based classifications too often have been inexcusably utilized to stereotype and stigmatize politically powerless segments of society. See *Frontiero* v. *Richardson*, 411 U.S. 677 (1973). The Court is not therefore free to sustain the

9. See *Bell's Gap R. Co.* v. *Pennsylvania*, 134 U.S. 232, 237; *Madden* v. *Kentucky*, 309 U.S. 83, 87-88; *Lawrence* v. *State Tax Comm'n*, 286 U.S. 276; *Royster Guano* v. *Virginia*, 253 U.S. 412.
10. The dissents argue that the Florida Legislature could have drafted the statute differently, so that its purpose would have been accomplished more precisely. But the issue of course is not whether the statute could have been drafted more wisely, but whether the lines chosen by the Florida Legislature are within constitutional limitations. The dissent would use the Equal Protection Clause as a vehicle for reinstating notions of substantive due process that have been repudiated. "We have returned to the original constitutional proposition that courts do not substitute their social and economic beliefs for the judgment of legislative bodies, who are elected to pass laws." *Ferguson* v. *Skrupa*, 372 U.S. 726, 730.
Gender has never been rejected as an impermissible classification in all instances. Congress has not so far drafted women into the Armed Services, 50 App. U.S.C. § 454. The famous Brandeis Brief in *Muller* v. *Oregon*, 208 U.S. 412, on which the court specifically relied, *id.*, at 419-420, emphasized that the special physical organization of women has a bearing on the "conditions under which she should be permitted to toil." *Id.*, at 420. These instances are pertinent to the problem

in the tax field which is presented by the present case. Mr. Chief Justice Hughes in speaking for the Court said:
"The states, in the exercise of their taxing power, as with respect to the exertion of other powers, are subject to the requirements of the due process and equal protection clauses of the Fourteenth Amendment, but that Amendment imposes no iron rule of equality, prohibiting the flexibility and variety that are appropriate to schemes of taxation. ... In levying such taxes, the State is not required to resort to close distinctions or to maintain a precise, scientific uniformity with reference to composition, use or value. To hold otherwise would be to subject the essential taxing power of the State to an intolerable supervision, hostile to the basic principles of our Government and wholly beyond the protection which the general clause of the Fourteenth Amendment was intended to secure." *Ohio Oil Co.* v. *Conway*, 281 U.S. 146, 159.
1. See *Loving* v. *Virginia*, 388 U.S. 1, 11 (1967); *McLaughlin* v. *Florida*, 379 U.S. 184, 191-192 (1964); *Bolling* v. *Sharpe*, 347 U.S. 497, 499 (1954).
2. See *Graham* v. *Richardson*, 403 U.S. 365, 372 (1971).
3. See *Oyama* v. *California*, 332 U.S. 633, 644-646 (1948); *Korematsu* v. *United States*, 323 U.S. 214, 216 (1944); *Hirabayashi* v. *United States*, 320 U.S. 81, 100 (1943).

statute on the ground that it rationally promotes legitimate governmental interests; rather, such suspect classifications can be sustained only when the State bears the burden of demonstrating that the challenged legislation serves overriding or compelling interests that cannot be achieved either by a more carefully tailored legislative classification or by the use of feasible less drastic means. While, in my view, the statute serves a compelling governmental interest by "cushioning the financial impact of spousal loss upon the sex for whom that loss imposes a disproportionately heavy burden," I think that the statute is invalid because the State's interest can be served equally well by a more narrowly drafted statute.

Gender-based classifications cannot be sustained merely because they promote legitimate governmental interests, such as efficacious administration of government. *Frontiero* v. *Richardson, supra; Reed* v. *Reed,* 404 U.S. 71 (1971). For "when we enter the realm of 'strict judicial scrutiny,' there can be no doubt that 'administrative convenience' is not a shibboleth, the mere recitation of which dictates constitutionality. See *Shapiro* v. *Thompson,* 394 U.S. 618 (1969); *Carrington* v. *Rash,* 380 U.S. 89 (1965). On the contrary, any statutory scheme which draws a sharp line between the sexes, *solely* for the purpose of achieving administrative convenience, necessarily commands 'dissimilar treatment for men and women who are ... similarly situated,' and therefore involves the 'very kind of arbitrary legislative choice forbidden by the [Constitution]. . . .' *Reed* v. *Reed,* 404 U.S., at 77, 76." *Frontiero* v. *Richardson, supra,* 411 U.S., at 690. But Florida's justification of § 196.191(7) is not that it serves administrative convenience or helps to preserve the public fisc. Rather, the asserted justification is that § 196.191(7) is an affirmative step toward alleviating the effects of past economic discrimination against women.[4]

I agree that, in providing special benefits for a needy segment of society long the victim of purposeful discrimination and neglect, the statute serves the compelling state interest of achieving equality for such groups.[5] No one familiar with this country's history of pervasive sex discrimination against women[6] can doubt the need for remedial measures to correct the resulting economic imbalances. Indeed, the extent of the economic disparity between men and women is dramatized by the data cited by the Court, *ante,* pp. 2-4. By providing a property tax exemption for widows, § 196.191(7) assists in reducing that economic disparity for a class of women particularly disadvantaged by the legacy of economic discrimination.[7] In

---

4. Appellee's Brief, pp. 24-25; Oral Tr. pp. 29-31. The State's argument is supported by the Florida Supreme Court which held that the object of § 196.191(7) was to help "reduce the disparity between the economic capabilities of a man and a woman. . . ." 273 So.2d 72, 73 (1973).

5. Significantly, the Florida statute does not compel the beneficiaries to accept the State's aid. The taxpayer must file for the tax exemption. This case, therefore, does not require resolution of the more difficult questions raised by remedial legislation which makes special treatment mandatory. See Note, Developments in the Law—Equal Protection, 82 Harv. L. Rev. 1065, 1113-1117 (1969).

6. See *Frontiero* v. *Richardson,* 411 U.S. 677 (1973); *Sail'er Inn, Inc.* v. *Kirby,* 5 Cal.3d 1, 485 P.2d 529 (1971). See generally The President's Task Force on Women's Rights and Responsibilities, A Matter of Simple Justice (1970); L. Kanowitz, Women and the Law: The Unfinished Revolution (1969).

7. As noted by the Court, *ante,* pp. 2-4:

"[D]ata compiled by the Woman's Bureau of the United States Department of Labor shows that in 1972 a woman working full time had a median income which was only 57.9% of the male median—a figure actually six points lower than had been achieved in 1955 . . . . The disparity is likely to be exacerbated for the widow. While the widower can usually continue in the occupation which preceded

that circumstance, the purpose and effect of the suspect classification is ameliorative; the statute neither stigmatizes nor denigrates widowers not also benefited by the legislation. Moreover, inclusion of needy widowers within the class of beneficiaries would not further the State's overriding interest in remedying the economic effects of past sex discrimination for needy victims of that discrimination. While doubtless some widowers are in financial need, no one suggests that such need results from sex discrimination as in the case of widows.

The statute nevertheless fails to satisfy the requirements of equal protection, since the State has not borne its burden of proving that its compelling interest could not be achieved by a more precisely tailored statute or by use of feasible less drastic means. Section 196.191(7) is plainly overinclusive, for the $500 property tax exemption may be obtained by a financially independent heiress as well as by an unemployed widow with dependent children. The State has offered nothing to explain why inclusion of widows of substantial economic means was necessary to advance the State's interest in ameliorating the effects of past economic discrimination against women.

Moreover, alternative means of classification, narrowing the class of widow beneficiaries, appear readily available. The exemption is granted only to widows who complete and file with the tax assessor a form application establishing their status as widows. By merely redrafting that form to exclude widows who earn annual incomes, or possess assets, in excess of specified amounts, the State could readily narrow the class of beneficiaries to those widows for whom the effects of past economic discrimination against women have been a practical reality.

MR. JUSTICE WHITE, dissenting.

The Florida tax exemption at issue here is available to all widows but not to widowers. The presumption is that all widows are financially more needy and less trained or less ready for the job market than men. It may be that most widows have been occupied as housewife, mother and homemaker and are not immediately prepared for employment. But there are many rich widows who need no largess from the State; many others are highly trained and have held lucrative positions long before the death of their husbands. At the same time, there are many widowers who are needy and who are in more desperate financial straits and have less access to the job market than many widows. Yet none of them qualifies for the exemption.

I find the discrimination invidious and violative of the Equal Protection Clause. There is merit in giving poor widows a tax break, but gender-based classifications are suspect and require more justification than the State has offered.

I perceive no purpose served by the exemption other than to alleviate current economic necessity, but the State extends the exemption to widows who do not need the help and denies it to widowers who do. It may be administratively inconvenient to make individual determinations of entitlement and to extend the ex-

his spouse's death in many cases the widow will find herself suddenly forced into a job market with which she is unfamiliar, and in which, because of her former economic dependency, she will have fewer skills to offer." (Footnotes omitted).

emption to needy men as well as needy women, but administrative efficiency is not an adequate justification for discriminations based purely on sex. *Frontiero* v. *Richardson,* 411 U.S. 677 (1973); *Reed* v. *Reed,* 404 U.S. 71 (1971).

It may be suggested that the State is entitled to prefer widows over widowers because their assumed need is rooted in past and present economic discrimination against women. But this is not a credible explanation of Florida's tax exemption; for if the State's purpose was to compensate for past discrimination against females, surely it would not have limited the exemption to women who are widows. Moreover, even if past discrimination is considered to be the criterion for current tax exemption, the State nevertheless ignores all those widowers who have felt the effects of economic discrimination, whether as a member of a racial group or as one of the many who cannot escape the cycle of poverty. It seems to me that the State in this case is merely conferring an economic benefit in the form of a tax exemption and has not adequately explained why women should be treated differently than men.

I dissent.

NOTES

1. What does *Kahn v. Shevin* portend with regard to state protective labor laws presently applying to women only when challenged under:
   a. The Equal Protection clause of the Fourteenth Amendment;
   b. Title VII;
   c. The Equal Rights Amendment, if and when it becomes part of the Constitution?

2. Is the result in *Kahn v. Shevin* reconcilable with *LaFleur,* p. 149 *infra?* With Justice Douglas's discussion of the merits in *DeFunis,* p. 139 *infra?*

3. Justices Brennan and Marshall, in their dissent, state: "While doubtless some widowers are in financial need, no one suggests that such need results from sex discrimination as in the case of widows." Doesn't this assertion reflect a too narrow view of the phenomenon of sex discrimination? How many widowers would not be in financial need had they not been obligated, as a matter of law and sex role expectations, to be the primary source of financial support for wives and children?

4. What equal-protection tests are being applied by Douglas? By Brennan? Why? Compare Douglas's test in *DeFunis,* p. 139 *infra.*

5. By providing an exemption for widows and not for elderly single women—or even young single women in need—isn't Florida promoting sex discrimination by rewarding those women who have won the "prize" of marrying a man, whom death has deprived them of? Does the fact that in the United States, as elsewhere, there are significantly fewer men than women of marriageable age have any bearing on this problem?

6. What will be the effect of *Kahn* on a whole range of legal rules in the domestic relations area which, on the surface at least, appear to favor females over males? Two cases reaching contrary results which were decided before the Supreme Court's decision in *Kahn* are: Husband v. Wife, Del. Sup. Ct., 42 U.S.L.W. 2550 (1974) (upholding statute authorizing divorce courts to award a wife, but not a

husband, a reasonable share of spouse's property. Neither "rational basis" nor "compelling state interest" tests for equal-protection purposes were violated by the statute, said the court); Murphy v. Murphy, Ga. Sup. Ct., Fulton County, 42 U.S.L.W. 2393 (1974) (Georgia statute allowing alimony to be awarded to wives only violates equal-protection and due-process guarantees).

Geduldig v. Aiello

United States Supreme Court, 1974
U.S.   , 94 S.Ct. 2485, 41 L.Ed.2d 256

MR. JUSTICE STEWART delivered the opinion of the Court.

For almost 30 years California has administered a disability insurance system that pays benefits to persons in private employment who are temporarily unable to work because of disability not covered by workmen's compensation. The appellees brought this action to challenge the constitutionality of a provision of the California program that, in defining "disability," excludes from coverage certain disabilities resulting from pregnancy. Because the appellees sought to enjoin the enforcement of this state statute, a three-judge court was convened pursuant to 28 U. S. C. § § 2281 and 2284. On the appellees' motion for summary judgment, the District Court, by a divided vote, held that this provision of the disability insurance program violates the Equal Protection Clause of the Fourteenth Amendment, and therefore enjoined its continued enforcement. 359 F. Supp. 792. The District Court denied a motion to stay its judgment pending appeal. The appellant thereupon filed a similar motion in this Court, which we granted. – U.S. –. We subsequently noted probable jurisdiction of the appeal. – U.S. –.

I

California's disability insurance system is funded entirely from contributions deducted from the wages of participating employees. Participation in the program is mandatory unless the employees are protected by a voluntary private plan approved by the State. Each employee is required to contribute one percent of his salary, up to an annual maximum of $85. These contributions are placed in the Unemployment Compensation Disability Fund, which is established and administered as a special trust fund within the state treasury. It is from this Disability Fund that benefits under the program are paid.

An individual is eligible for disability benefits if, during a one-year base period prior to his disability, he has contributed one percent of a minimum income of $300 to the Disability Fund. In the event he suffers a compensable disability, the individual can receive a "weekly benefit amount" of between $25 and $105, depending on the amount he earned during the highest quarter of the base period.[6]

6. § 2655. This provision has been amended, effective July 1, 1974, to provide for a maximum weekly benefit amount of $119.

Benefits are not paid until the eighth day of disability, unless the employee is hospitalized, in which case benefits commence on the first day of hospitalization. In addition to the "weekly benefit amount," a hospitalized employee is entitled to receive "additional benefits" of $12 per day of hospitalization. "Weekly benefit amounts" for any one disability are payable for 26 weeks so long as the total amount paid does not exceed one-half of the wages received during the base period. "Additional benefits" for any one disability are paid for a maximum of 20 days.

In return for his one-percent contribution to the Disability Fund, the individual employee is insured against the risk of disability stemming from a substantial number of "mental or physical illness[es] and mental or physical injur[ies]." West's Ann. Cal. Un. Ins. Code § 2626. It is not every disabling condition, however, that triggers the obligation to pay benefits under the program. As already noted, for example, any disability of less than eight days' duration is not compensable, except when the employee is hospitalized. Conversely, no benefits are payable for any single disability beyond 26 weeks. Further, disability is not compensable if it results from the individual's court commitment as a dipsomaniac, drug addict, or sexual psychopath. Finally, § 2626 of the Unemployment Insurance Code excludes from coverage certain disabilities that are attributable to pregnancy. It is this provision that is at issue in the present case.

Appellant is the Director of the California Department of Human Resources Development. He is responsible for the administration of the State's disability insurance program. Appellees are four women who have paid sufficient amounts into the Disability Fund to be eligible for benefits under the program. Each of the appellees became pregnant and suffered employment disability as a result of her pregnancy. With respect to three of the appellees, Carolyn Aiello, Augustina Armendariz, and Elizabeth Johnson, the disabilities were attributable to abnormal complications encountered during their pregnancies. The fourth, Jacqueline Jaramillo, experienced a normal pregnancy, which was the sole cause of her disability.

At all times relevant to this case, § 2626 of the Unemployment Insurance Code provided:

> " 'Disability' or 'disabled' includes both mental or physical illness and mental or physical injury. An individual shall be deemed disabled in any day in which, because of mental or physical condition, he is unable to perform his regular or customary work. *In no case shall the term 'disability' or 'disabled' include any injury or illness caused by or arising in connection with pregnancy up to the termination of such pregnancy and for a period of 28 days thereafter.*" (Emphasis added.)

Appellant construed and applied the final sentence of this statute to preclude the payment of benefits for any disability resulting from pregnancy. As a result, the appellees were ruled ineligible for disability benefits by reason of this provision, and they sued to enjoin its enforcement. The District Court, finding "that the exclusion of pregnancy-related disabilities is not based upon a classification having a rational and substantial relationship to a legitimate state purpose," held that the exclusion was unconstitutional under the Equal Protection Clause. 359 F. Supp., at 801.

Shortly before the District Court's decision in this case, the California Court of Appeal, in a suit brought by a woman who suffered an ectopic pregnancy, held that § 2626 does not bar the payment of benefits on account of disability that results from medical complications arising during pregnancy. *Rentzer* v. *California Unemployment Insurance Appeals Board,* 32 Cal. App. 3d 604 (2d App. Dist., 1973).[14] The state court construed the statute to preclude only the payment of benefits for disability accompanying normal pregnancy.[15] The appellant acquiesced in this construction and issued administrative guidelines that exclude only the payment of "maternity benefits"–*i. e.,* hospitalization and disability benefits for normal delivery and recuperation.

Although *Rentzer* was decided some 10 days before the District Court's decision in this case, there was apparently no opportunity to call the court's attention to it. The appellant, therefore, asked the court to reconsider its decision in light of the construction that the California Court of Appeal had given to § 2626 in the *Rentzer* case. By a divided vote, the court denied the motion for reconsideration. Although a more definitive ruling would surely have been preferable, we interpret the District Court's denial of the appellant's motion as a determination that its decision was not affected by the limiting construction given to § 2626 in *Rentzer*.

Because of the *Rentzer* decision and the revised administrative guidelines that resulted from it, the appellees Aiello, Armendariz, and Johnson, whose disabilities were attributable to causes other than normal pregnancy and delivery, became entitled to benefits under the disability insurance program, and their claims have since been paid. With respect to appellee Jaramillo, however, whose disability stemmed solely from normal pregnancy and childbirth, § 2626 continues to bar the payment of any benefits. It is evident that only Jaramillo continues to have a live controversy with the appellant as to the validity of § 2626. The claims of the other appellees have been mooted by the change that *Rentzer* worked in the construction and application of that provision. Thus, the issue before the Court on this appeal is whether the California disability insurance program invidiously discriminates against Jaramillo and others similarly situated by not paying insurance benefits for disability that accompanies normal pregnancy and childbirth.

---

14. In an earlier decision, the Court of Appeal had sustained § 2626 against an Equal Protection challenge by a female employee who had suffered disability as a result of normal pregnancy and delivery. *Clark* v. *California Emp. Stat. Comm.,* 166 Cal. App. 2d 326 (1966).

15. Section 2626 was later amended, and a new § 2626.2 was added, in order clearly to reflect this interpretation. The two sections now provide as follows:

"§ 2626 'Disability' or 'disabled' includes both mental or physical illness, mental or physical injury, and, to the extent specified in Section 2626.2, pregnancy. An individual shall be deemed disabled in any day in which, because of his physical or mental condition, he is unable to perform his regular or customary work.

"§ 2626.2 Benefits relating to pregnancy shall be paid under this part only in accordance with the following:

"(a) Disability benefits shall be paid upon a doctor's certification that the claimant is disabled because of an abnormal and involuntary complication of pregnancy, including but not limited to: puerperal infection, eclampsia, caesarian section delivery, ectopic pregnancy, and toxemia.

"(b) Disability benefits shall be paid upon a doctor's certification that a condition possibly arising out of pregnancy would disable the claimant without regard to the pregnancy, including but not limited to: anemia, diabetes, embolism, heart disease, hypertension, phlebitis, phlebothrombosis, pyelonephritis, thrombophlebitis, vaginitis, varicose veins, and venous thrombosis."

These amendments took effect on January 1, 1974.

II

It is clear that California intended to establish this benefit system as an insurance program that was to function essentially in accordance with insurance concepts.[16] Since the program was instituted in 1946, it has been totally self-supporting, never drawing on general state revenues to finance disability or hospital benefits. The Disability Fund is wholly supported by the one percent of wages annually contributed by participating employees. At oral argument, counsel for the appellant informed us that in recent years between 90% and 103% of the revenue to the Disability Fund has been paid out in disability and hospital benefits. This history strongly suggests that the one-percent contribution rate, in addition to being easily computable, bears a close and substantial relationship to the level of benefits payable and to the disability risks insured under the program.

Over the years California has demonstrated a strong commitment not to increase the contribution rate above the one-percent level. The State has sought to provide the broadest possible disability protection that would be affordable by all employees, including those with very low incomes. Because any larger percentage or any flat dollar-amount rate of contribution would impose an increasingly regressive levy bearing most heavily upon those with the lowest incomes, the State has resisted any attempt to change the required contribution from the one-percent level. The program is thus structured, in terms of the level of benefits and the risks insured, to maintain the solvency of the Disability Fund at a one-percent annual level of contribution.[17]

In ordering the State to pay benefits for disability accompanying normal pregnancy and delivery, the District Court acknowledged the State's contention "that coverage of these disabilities is so extraordinarily expensive that it would be impossible to maintain a program supported by employee contributions if these disabilities are included." 359 F. Supp., at 798. There is considerable disagreement between the parties with respect to how great the increased costs would actually be, but they would clearly be substantial.[18] For purposes of analysis the District Court accepted the State's estimate, which was in excess of $100 million annually, and stated that "it is clear that including these disabilities would not destroy the program. The increased costs could be accommodated quite easily by making reason-

---

16. In his message to the state legislature proposing the creation of this program, Governor Earl Warren stated:

"It is not possible for employees to obtain from private insurance companies protection against loss of wages or salary during sickness as adequately or cheaply as the protection could be obtained by diverting their 1% contribution for the support of a Disability Benefits Program."

California Senate Journal, January 23, 1946, p. 229. The California Supreme Court has concluded "that the legislative purpose in providing unemployment disability benefits ... was to provide an insurance program to pay benefits to individuals who are unemployed because of illness or injury...." *Garcia* v. *Industrial Accident Comm.*, 41 Cal. 2d 689, 692 (1954) (internal quotations omitted).

17. Section 2604 vests the Governor and the appellant with authority to modify the payment of benefits and to increase the waiting time for eligibility if such steps are necessary to forestall insolvency of the Disability Fund. But neither the Governor nor the appellant is authorized to increase the contribution rate under any circumstances.

18. Appellant's estimate of the increased cost of including normal pregnancy within the insured risks has varied between $120.2 million and $131 million annually, or between a 33% and 36% increase in the present amount of benefits paid under the program. On the other hand, appellee contends that the increased cost would be $48.9 million annually, or a 12% increase over present expenditures.

able changes in the contribution rate, the maximum benefits allowable, and the other variables affecting the solvency of the program." *Ibid.*

Each of these "variables"—the benefit level deemed appropriate to compensate employee disability, the risks selected to be insured under the program, and the contribution rate chosen to maintain the solvency of the program and at the same time to permit low-income employees to participate with minimal personal sacrifice—represents a policy determination by the State. The essential issue in this case is whether the Equal Protection Clause requires such policies to be sacrificed or compromised in order to finance the payment of benefits to those whose disability is attributable to normal pregnancy and delivery.

We cannot agree that the exclusion of this disability from coverage amounts to invidious discrimination under the Equal Protection Clause. California does not discriminate with respect to the persons or groups who are eligible for disability insurance protection under the program. The classification challenged in this case relates to the asserted under-inclusiveness of the set of risks that the State has selected to insure. Although California has created a program to insure most risks of employment disability, it has not chosen to insure all such risks, and this decision is reflected in the level of annual contribution exacted from participating employees. This Court has held that, consistently with the Equal Protection Clause, a State "may take one step at a time, addressing itself to the phase of the problem which seems most acute to the legislative mind. The legislature may select one phase of one field and apply a remedy there, neglecting the others. . . ." *Williams* v. *Lee Optical Co.,* 348 U. S. 483, 489; *Jefferson* v. *Hackney,* 406 U. S. 535 (1972). Particularly with respect to social welfare programs, so long as the line drawn by the State is rationally supportable, the courts will not interpose their judgment as to the appropriate stopping point. "[T]he Equal Protection Clause does not require that a State must choose between attacking every aspect of a problem or not attacking the problem at all." *Dandridge* v. *Williams,* 397 U.S. 471, 486-487 (1970).

The District Court suggested that moderate alterations in what it regarded as "variables" of the disability insurance program could be made to accommodate the substantial expense required to include normal pregnancy within the program's protection. The same can be said, however, with respect to the other expensive class of disabilities that are excluded from coverage—short-term disabilities. If the Equal Protection Clause were thought to compel disability payments for normal pregnancy, it is hard to perceive why it would not also compel payments for short-term disabilities suffered by participating employees.[19]

It is evident that a totally comprehensive program would be substantially more costly than the present program and would inevitably require state subsidy, a higher rate of employee contribution, a lower scale of benefits for those suffering insured disabilities, or some combination of these measures. There is nothing in the Constitution, however, that requires the State to subordinate or compromise its legitimate

---

19. The same could be said of disabilities
continuing beyond 26 weeks.

interests solely to create a more comprehensive social insurance program than it already has.

The State has a legitimate interest in maintaining the self-supporting nature of its insurance program. Similarly, it has an interest in distributing the available resources in such a way as to keep benefit payments at an adequate level for disabilities that are covered, rather than to cover all disabilities inadequately. Finally, California has a legitimate concern in maintaining the contribution rate at a level that will not unduly burden participating employees, particularly low-income employees who may be most in need of the disability insurance.

These policies provide an objective and wholly noninvidious basis for the State's decision not to create a more comprehensive insurance program than it has. There is no evidence in the record that the selection of the risks insured by the program worked to discriminate against any definable group or class in terms of the aggregate risk protection derived by that group or class from the program.[20] There is no risk from which men are protected and women are not. Likewise, there is no risk from which women are protected and men are not.[21]

The appellee simply contends that, although she has received insurance protection equivalent to that provided all other participating employees, she has suffered discrimination because she encountered a risk that was outside the program's protection. For the reasons we have stated, we hold that this contention is not a valid one under the Equal Protection Clause of the Fourteenth Amendment.

The stay heretofore issued by the Court is vacated, and the judgment of the District Court is

Reversed.

MR. JUSTICE BRENNAN, with whom MR. JUSTICE DOUGLAS and MR. JUSTICE MARSHALL join, dissenting.

Relying upon *Dandridge* v. *Williams,* 397 U. S. 471 (1970), and *Jefferson* v. *Hackney,* 406 U. S. 535 (1972), the Court today rejects respondents' equal protec-

---

20. The dissenting opinion to the contrary, this case is thus a far cry from cases like *Reed* v. *Reed,* 404 U. S. 71, and *Frontiero* v. *Richardson,* 411 U. S. 677, involving discrimination based upon gender as such. The California insurance program does not exclude anyone from benefit eligibility because of gender but merely removes one physical condition—pregnancy—from the list of compensable disabilities. While it is true that only women can become pregnant, it does not follow that every legislative classification concerning pregnancy is a sex-based classification like those considered in *Reed, supra,* and *Frontiero, supra.* Normal pregnancy is an objectively identifiable physical condition with unique characteristics. Absent a showing that distinctions involving pregnancy are mere pretexts designed to effect an invidious discrimination against the members of one sex or the other, lawmakers are constitutionally free to include or exclude pregnancy from the coverage of legislation such as this on any reasonable basis, just as with respect to any other physical condition.

The lack of identity between the excluded disability and gender as such under this insurance program becomes clear upon the most cursory analysis. The program divides potential recipients into two groups—pregnant women and nonpregnant persons. While the first group is exclusively female, the second includes members of both sexes. The fiscal and actuarial benefits of the program thus accrue to members of both sexes.

21. Indeed, the appellant submitted to the District Court data that indicated that both the annual claim rate and the annual claim cost are greater for women than for men. As the District Court acknowledged, "women contribute 28 per cent of the total disability insurance fund and receive back about 38 per cent of the fund in benefits." 359 F. Supp., at 800. Several *amici curiae* have represented to the Court that they have had a similar experience under private disability insurance programs.

tion claim and upholds the exclusion of pregnancy related disabilities from coverage under California's disability insurance program on the ground that the legislative classification rationally promotes the State's legitimate cost-saving interests in "maintaining the self-supporting nature of its insurance program[,] . . . distributing the available resources in such a way as to keep benefit payments at an adequate level for disabilities that are covered[,] . . . [and] maintaining the contribution rate at a level that will not unduly burden the participating employees. . . ." *Ante,* . . . Because I believe that *Reed* v. *Reed,* 404 U. S. 71 (1971), and *Frontiero* v. *Richardson,* 411 U. S. 677 (1973), mandate a stricter standard of scrutiny which the State's classification fails to satisfy, I respectfully dissent.

California's disability insurance program was enacted to supplement the State's unemployment insurance and workmen's compensation programs by providing benefits to wage earners to cushion the economic effects of income loss and medical expenses resulting from sickness or injury. The Legislature's intent in enacting the program was expressed clearly in § 2601 of the Unemployment Insurance Code:

> "The purpose of this part is to compensate in part for the wage loss sustained by individuals unemployed because of sickness or injury and to reduce to a minimum the suffering caused by unemployment resulting therefrom. This part shall be construed liberally in aid of its declared purpose to mitigate the evils and burdens which fall on the unemployed and disabled worker and his family."

To achieve the Act's broad humanitarian goals, the Legislature fashioned a pooled-risk disability fund covering all employees at the same rate of contribution,[1] regardless of individual risk.[2] The only requirement that must be satisfied before an employee becomes eligible to receive disability benefits is that the employee must have contributed one percent of a minimum income of $300 during a one year base-period. Unemp. Ins. Code § 2652. The "basic benefits," varying from $25 to $119 per week, depending upon the employee's base-period earnings, begin on the eighth day of disability or on the first day of hospitalization. Unemp. Ins. Code §§ 2655, 2627 (b), 2802. Benefits are payable for a maximum of 26 weeks, but may not exceed one-half of the employee's total base-period earnings. Unemp. Ins. Code § 2653. Finally, compensation is paid for virtually all disabling conditions without regard to cost, voluntariness, uniqueness, predictability, or "normalcy" of the disability.[3] Thus, for example, workers are compensated for costly disabilities

1. An employee must contribute one percent of his annual wages, not exceeding a total contribution of $85 per year ($95 for calendar year 1974 and thereafter). Unemp. Ins. Code §§ 2901, 984, 985. The ceiling on wages subject to the one percent contribution rate, of course, introduces a regressive element in the contribution scheme. Perhaps in recognition of this fact, the disability benefits schedule is designed to grant proportionately greater benefits to more poorly paid workers. Unemp. Ins. Code § 2655.

2. California deliberately decided not to classify employees on the basis of actuarial data. Thus, the contribution rate for a particular group of employees is not tied to that group's predicted rate of disability claims. 359 F. Supp. 792, 800.

3. While the Act technically excludes from coverage individuals under court commitment for dipsomania, drug addiction, or sexual psychopathy, Unemp. Ins. Code § 2678, the Court was informed by the Deputy Attorney General of California at oral argument that court commitment for such disabilities is "a fairly archaic practice" and that "it would be unrealistic to say that they constitute valid exclusions." Tr. of Oral Arg., at 13.

such as heart attacks, voluntary disabilities such as cosmetic surgery or sterilization, sex and race unique disabilities such as prostatectomies or sickle-cell anemia, pre-existing conditions inevitably resulting in disability such as degenerative arthritis or cataracts, and "normal" disabilities such as removal of irritating wisdom teeth or other orthodonia.

Despite the Act's broad goals and scope of coverage, compensation is denied for disabilities suffered in connection with a "normal" pregnancy—disabilities suffered only by women. Unemp. Ins. Code §§ 2626, 2626.2. Disabilities caused by preg-nancy, however, like other physically disabling conditions covered by the Act, require medical care, often include hospitalization, anesthesia and surgical proced-ures, and may involve genuine risk to life.[4] Moreover, the economic effects caused by pregnancy related disabilities are functionally indistinguishable from the effects caused by any other disability: wages are lost due to a physical inability to work, and medical expenses are incurred for the delivery of the child and for post-partum care.[5] In my view, by singling out for less favorable treatment a gender-linked disability peculiar to women, the State has created a double standard for disability compensation: a limitation is imposed upon the disabilities for which women workers may recover, while men receive full compensation for all disabilities suf-fered, including those that affect only or primarily their sex, such as prostatec-tomies, circumcision, hemophilia and gout. In effect, one set of rules is applied to females and another to males. Such dissimilar treatment of men and women, on the basis of physical characteristics inextricably linked to one sex, inevitably consti-tutes sex discrimination.

The same conclusion has been reached by the Equal Employment Opportunity Commission, the federal agency charged with enforcement of Title VII of the Civil Rights Act of 1964, as amended by the Equal Employment Opportunity Act of 1972, 42 U. S. C. (Supp. II) § 2000e *et seq.,* which prohibits employment discrim-ination on the basis of sex. In guidelines issued pursuant to Title VII and designed

---

4. On March 2, 1974, the American Col-lege of Obstetricians and Gynecologists adopted the following Policy Statement on Pregnancy-related Disabilities:

"Pregnancy is a physiological process. All pregnant patients, however, have a variable degree of disability on an individual basis, as indicated below, during which time they are unable to perform their usual activities. (1) In an uncomplicated pregnancy, disability occurs near the termination of pregnancy, during labor, delivery and the peurperium. The pro-cess of labor and peurperium is disabling in itself. The usual duration of such disability is approximately six to eight weeks. (2) Compli-cations of a pregnancy may occur which give rise to other disability. Examples of such complications include toxemia, infection, hemorrhage, ectopic pregnancy and abortion. (3) A woman with preexisting disease which in itself is not disabling, may become disabled with the addition of pregnancy. Certain patients with heart disease, diabetes, hyper-tensive cardiovascular disease, renal disease, and other systemic conditions may become disabled during their pregnancy because of the adverse effect pregnancy has upon these conditions.

"The onset, termination and cause of the disability, related to pregnancy, can only be determined by a physician."
See Brief for Appellees, at 59-60.

5. Nearly two-thirds of all women who work do so of necessity: either they are un-married or their husbands earn less than $7,000 per year. See United States Depart-ment of Labor, Women's Bureau, Why Women Work (Rev. ed. 1972); United States Department of Labor, Employment Standards Administration, The Myth and Reality (1973). Moreover, this Court recognized in *Kahn* v. *Shevin,* – U. S. –, – (1974), that "data compiled by the Women's Bureau of the United States Department of Labor shows that in 1972 women working full time had a median income which was only 57.9% of the male median—a figure actually six points lower than had been achieved in 1955."

to prohibit the disparate treatment of pregnancy disabilities in the employment context,[6] the EEOC has declared that:

> "Disabilities caused or contributed to by pregnancy, miscarriage, abortion, childbirth, and recovery therefrom are, for all job-related purposes, temporary disabilities and should be treated as such under any health or temporary disability insurance or sick leave plan available in connection with employment. Written and unwritten employment policies and practices involving such as the commencement and duration of sick leave, the availability of extensions, the accrual of seniority and other benefits and privileges, reinstatement, and payment under any health or temporary disability insurance or sick leave plan, formal or informal, shall be applied to disability due to pregnancy or childbirth on the same terms and conditions as they are applied to other temporary disabilities." 29 CFR § 1604.10 (b) (1973).[7]

In the past, when a legislative classification has turned on gender, the Court has justifiably applied a standard of judicial scrutiny more strict than that generally accorded economic or social welfare programs. Compare *Reed* v. *Reed, supra,* and *Frontiero* v. *Richardson, supra,* with *Dandridge* v. *Williams, supra,* and *Jefferson* v. *Hackney, supra.* Yet, by its decision today, the Court appears willing to abandon that higher standard of review without satisfactorily explaining what differentiates the gender-base classification employed in this case from those found unconstitutional in *Reed* and *Frontiero.* The Court's decision threatens to return men and women to a time when "traditional" equal protection analysis sustained legislative classifications that treated differently members of a particular sex solely because of their sex. See, *e.g., Muller* v. *Oregon,* 208 U. S. 412 (1908); *Goesaert* v. *Cleary,* 335 U. S. 464 (1948); *Hoyt* v. *Florida,* 368 U. S. 57 (1961).

I cannot join the Court's apparent retreat. I continue to adhere to my view that "classifications based upon sex, like classifications based upon race, alienage, or national origin, are inherently suspect, and must therefore be subjected to strict judicial scrutiny." *Frontiero* v. *Richardson, supra,* 411 U. S., at 688. When, as in this case, the State employs a legislative classification that distinguishes between beneficiaries solely by reference to gender-linked disability risks, "[t]he Court is not . . . free to sustain the statute on the ground that it rationally promotes legitimate governmental interests; rather, such suspect classifications can be sustained only when the State bears the burden of demonstrating that the challenged legislation serves overriding or compelling interests that cannot be achieved either by a more carefully tailored legislative classification or by the use of feasible, less drastic means." *Kahn* v. *Shevin,* — U. S. —, -- (1974) (BRENNAN, J., dissenting).

6. "The Commission carefully scrutinized both the employer practices and their crucial impact on women for a substantial period of time and then issued its Guidelines after it became increasingly apparent that systematic and pervasive discrimination against women was frequently found in employers' denial of employment opportunity and benefits to women on the basis of the childbearing role, performed solely by women." Brief of the United States Equal Employment Opportunity Commission as *amicus curiae,* at 10.

7. See also the proposed "Sex Discrimination Guidelines" issued by the Department of Labor pursuant to Executive Order 11246, virtually adopting the EEOC's pregnancy related disabilities guideline, 38 Fed. Reg. 35336, 35338 (Dec. 27, 1973) (proposed § 60-20 (h) (2), 41 CFR).

The State has clearly failed to meet that burden in the present case. The essence of the State's justification for excluding disabilities caused by a normal pregnancy from its disability compensation scheme is that covering such disabilities would be too costly. To be sure, as presently funded, inclusion of normal pregnancies "would be substantially more costly than the present program."[8] *Ante,* p. 10. The present level of benefits for insured disabilities could not be maintained without increasing the employee contribution rate, raising or lifting the yearly contribution ceiling, or securing State subsidies. But whatever role such monetary considerations may play in traditional equal protection analysis, the State's interest in preserving the fiscal integrity of its disability insurance program simply cannot render the State's use of a suspect classification constitutional. For while "a State has a valid interest in preserving the fiscal integrity of its programs[,] . . . a State may not accomplish such a purpose by invidious distinctions between classes of its citizens. . . . The saving of welfare costs cannot justify an otherwise invidious classification." *Shapiro* v. *Thompson,* 394 U. S. 618, 633 (1969). Thus, when a statutory classification is subject to strict judicial scrutiny, the State "must do more than show that denying [benefits to the excluded class] saves money." *Memorial Hospital* v. *Maricopa County,* – U. S. –, – (1974). See also *Graham* v. *Richardson,* 403 U. S. 365, 374-375 (1971).[9]

Moreover, California's legitimate interest in fiscal integrity could easily have been achieved through a variety of less drastic, sexually neutral means. As the District Court observed:

"Even using [the State's] estimate of the cost of expanding the program to include pregnancy-related disabilities, however, it is clear that including these disabilities would not destroy the program. The increased costs could be accommodated quite easily by making reasonable changes in the contribution rate, the maximum benefits allowable, and the other variables affecting the solvency of the program. For example, the entire cost increase estimated by defendant could be met by requiring workers to contribute an additional amount of approximately .364 percent of their salary and increasing the maximum annual contribution to about $119." 359 F. Supp. 792, 798.

I would therefore affirm the judgment of the District Court.

NOTES

1. In the second paragraph of footnote 20, in which the majority concludes that the "fiscal and actuarial benefits of the program thus accrue to members of both

8. However, "[i]t is important to remember, especially in the cost context, that if an employee is being paid his regular pay while disabled, he cannot collect disability pay. Therefore, it follows that any alleged financial burden on the State will be greatly diminished when employers adhere to Title VII and treat pregnancy-related disabilities the same as other disabilities by allowing women to use accumulated sick leave and possibly annual leave as well." Brief of the United States Equal Employment Commission as *amicus, curiae,* at 21 n. 12.

9. Similarly, under the EEOC's Guidelines on Discrimination Because of Sex, "It shall not be a defense under Title VII to a charge of sex discrimination in benefits that the cost of such benefits is greater with respect to one sex than the other." 29 CFR § 1604.9 (e).

sexes," is it not engaging in a type of judicial legerdemain? When the majority says, "The program divides potential recipients into two groups—pregnant women and nonpregnant persons. While the first group is exclusively female, the second includes members of both sexes," is it correct? Isn't even a nonpregnant woman being discriminated against by the program in being forewarned by it that any future pregnancy of hers will not be covered?

2. What bearing will the *Aiello* decision have on Title VII cases in which women (or men) have been denied equal employment opportunity because of physical characteristics unique to their own sex? *Cf. Doe v. Osteopathic Hospital of Wichita, Inc.,* at p. 319 of the main volume. See also the problem set forth in note 2, p. 353 of the main volume.

3. Is the majority, as the dissent claims, returning to traditional equal-protection analysis? Would the result in *Aiello* necessarily be different were the ERA in force? *Cf.* Kanowitz, Women and the Law: The Unfinished Revolution, p. 195-96 (1969).

4. When the majority states (footnote 20) that "The California insurance program does not exclude anyone from benefit eligibility because of gender but merely removes one physical condition—pregnancy—from the list of compensable disabilities," is it, in effect, resurrecting the "sex-plus" doctrine presumably buried in *Phillips v. Martin Marietta,* p. 315 of the main volume?

5. Now that a majority of the Court has upheld the exclusion from the California disability insurance program of disabilities resulting from normal pregnancy, what arguments would you urge upon the California legislature for (or against) amendment of the statute to include such disabilities?

Page 528. Following problem, add:

DeFunis v. Odegaard
Supreme Court of Washington, 1973
82 Wash.2d 11, 507 P.2 1169

Defendants, who include members of the Board of Regents of the University of Washington, the President of the University, and the Dean and certain members of the Admissions Committee of the University of Washington School of Law, appeal from a judgment ordering them to admit plaintiff Marco DeFunis, Jr., as a first-year student to the University of Washington School of Law, as of September 22, 1971.

Broadly phrased, the major question presented herein is whether the law school may, in consonance with the equal protection provisions of the state and federal constitutions, consider the racial or ethnic background of applicants as one factor in the selection of students.

Marco DeFunis, Jr. (hereinafter plaintiff), his wife, and his parents commenced an action in the superior court, alleging that plaintiff, an applicant for admission to the University of Washington School of Law (hereinafter law school) for the class commencing September 1971, had been wrongfully denied admission in that no preference was given to residents of the state of Washington in the admissions process and that persons were admitted to the law school with lesser qualifications than those of plaintiff. The complaint asked that the court order the defendants to admit and enroll plaintiff in the law school in the fall of 1971 and, upon the failure of defendants to do so, that plaintiffs recover damages in the sum of not less than $50,000.

... After a nonjury trial, the court ruled that in denying plaintiff admission to the law school, the University of Washington had discriminated against him in violation of the equal protection of the laws guaranteed by the fourteenth amendment to the United States Constitution.

Law school admissions pose a complex problem, and require a sensitive balancing of diverse factors. To gain insight into the complicated process of selecting first-year law students, and to better appreciate the essence of plaintiff's complaint against the law school, we turn first to the circumstances and operative facts—as delineated by the record—from which this litigation arises.

Under RCW 28B.20.130(3), the Board of Regents of the University of Washington has the power and duty to establish entrance requirements for students seeking admission to the University. The dean and faculty of the law school, pursuant to the authority delegated to them by the Board of Regents and the President of the University, have established a Committee on Admissions and Readmissions to determine who shall be admitted to the law school. For the academic year September 15, 1970, to June 15, 1971, the committee was composed of five faculty members and two student members; on June 7, 1971, the faculty of the law school expanded the membership of the committee to six faculty members and three student members. The chairman estimated that the committee spent over 1,300 hours in the selection process for the 1971-72 first-year class.

The number of qualified applicants to the law school has increased dramatically in recent years. In 1967, the law school received 618 applications; in 1968, 704; in 1969, 860; and in 1970, 1026 applications were received. The law school received 1601 applications for admission to the first-year class beginning September, 1971. Under the University's enrollment limitation there were only 445 positions allotted to the law school, and of these the number available for the first-year class was between 145 and 150. The chairman of the admissions committee stated that most of these applicants would be regarded as qualified by admissions standards at this and other comparable law schools in recent years. Hence, the task of selection is difficult, time-consuming and requires the exercise of careful and informed discretion, based on the evidence appearing in the application files. While many applicants are relatively easy to select for admission because of very outstanding qualifications, and others are relatively easy to reject, the middle group of candidates is much more difficult to assess. Plaintiff was in this latter category.

Applicants for admission to the law school must have earned an undergraduate degree and taken the Law School Admission Test (LSAT) administered by the Education Testing Service of Princeton, New Jersey. They must also submit with their written application a copy of transcripts from all schools and colleges which they have attended prior to application for admission, together with statements from their undergraduate dean of students and letters of recommendation from faculty members in their major field of study. They may submit additional letters of recommendation and statements. The application for admission gives the applicant the option to indicate his "dominant" ethnic origin. The admissions process does not include personal interviews and does not reveal whether applicants are poor or affluent.

The committee's basic criteria for selecting students are expressed in the "Guide for Applicants," a copy of which plaintiff received with his 1971 application:

> We below describe the process we applied to determine the class that entered the University of Washington School of Law in September 1970. We anticipate that the same process will be applied in determining membership in the class of 1971.
>
> *   *   *   *   *   *
>
> In assessing applications, we began by trying to identify applicants who had the potential for outstanding performance in law school. We attempted to select applicants for admission from that group on the basis of their ability to make significant contributions to law school classes and to the community at large.

For the purpose of a preliminary ranking of the applicants for the class of 1974, the junior-senior undergraduate grade point average and the Law School Admissions Test scores[1] for each applicant were combined through a formula to yield a predicted first-year of law school grade average for the applicant. This preliminary index number is called the Predicted First-Year Average (PFYA). The relative weight of grades and test scores in this formula was determined on the basis of past experience at the law school. The same formula is used for all applicants in a given year. If an applicant has taken the LSAT more than once in the past 3 years, the average score is employed rather than the latest score; this is done to offset a learning effect which statistical studies by the Educational Testing Service indicates occurs as the result of the multiple taking of the test.

Plaintiff's PFYA as determined by the law school, was 76.23. This figure was calculated by using a formula combining plaintiff's junior-senior grade point average of 3.71, average LSAT score of 582 (512 plus 566 plus 668, divided by 3)[2] and average writing test score component of 61 (62 plus 58 plus 64, divided by 3).

Ranking of applicants by PFYA was used to help organize the committee's processing of the applications. On the basis of the previous year's applicant group, the committee decided that most promising applicants for the class of 1974 would be defined as applicants with predicted first-year law school averages over 77. Applicants with PFYAs above 77 were reviewed and decided by the full committee as they came in, in order to reach an early decision as to the acceptance of such students. Each of these files was assigned to a committee member for thorough review and for presentation to the committee.

Applicants with PFYAs below 74.5 were reviewed by the chairman of the committee, and were either rejected by him, or placed in a group for later review by the

1. The Law School Admissions Test yields two scores for each candidate, a general law aptitude score and a writing ability score.

2. Plaintiff took the Law School Admissions test on three different occasions: August 1969, November 1969 and December 1970.

full committee. The decision of rejection or committee review of an application was based on the chairman's judgment derived from information in the applicant's file indicating whether the applicant had a significantly better potential for law study than the relatively low predicted first-year average tended to indicate. Cases of doubt were to be resolved in favor of deferring judgment until committee review could be undertaken.

Two exceptions were made in regard to applicants with PFYAs below 74.5. First, the law school had established a policy that persons who had been previously admitted but who were unable to enter, or forced to withdraw from, the law school because of induction into the military service, had a right to reenroll if they re-applied immediately upon honorable completion of their tour of duty. Second, all files of "minority" applicants (which the committee defined for this purpose as including Black Americans, Chicano Americans, American Indians and Philippine Americans[3] were considered by the full committee as warranting their attention, regardless of the PFYA of the individual applicant.

Applicants with predicted first-year averages between 74.5 and 76.99 were accumulated and held until the applications deadline had passed and essentially all the applications were complete and ready for review, so that the critical decisions as to the remainder of the incoming class could be made with a relatively complete view of qualified applicants not therebefore admitted. Plaintiff's application, pre-senting a 76.23 predicted first-year average, was placed in this third category. Included for consideration at that time, in addition to the minority group and those with PFYAs between 74.5 and 77, were some applicants with PFYAs above 77 upon whom the committee had reserved judgment, feeling that such applicants were not as promising as their PFYAs seemed to indicate.

These "close cases,"–*i.e.,* where the applicant was neither clearly outstanding nor clearly deficient–required the most effort of the committee. In selecting the applicants from this narrow range, the committee used the process described in its Guide for Applicants, a copy of which was sent to all applicants:

> We gauged the potential for outstanding performance in law school not only from the existence of high test scores and grade point averages, but also from careful analysis of recommendations, the quality of work in difficult analytical seminars, courses, and writing programs, the academic standards of the school attended by the applicant, the applicant's graduate work (if any), and the nature of the applicant's employment (if any), since graduation.
>
> An applicant's ability to make significant contributions to law school classes and the community at large was assessed from such factors as his extracurricular and community activities, employment, and general back-ground.
>
> We gave no preference to, but did not discriminate against, either Washing-ton residents or women in making our determinations. An applicant's racial

---

3. The chairman of the admissions com-mittee testified that Asian-Americans, *e.g.,* were not treated as "minority" applicants for admissions purposes, since a significant num-ber could be admitted on the same basis as general applicants.

As used herein, the term "minority" refers to and includes only Black Americans, Chi-cano Americans, American Indians and Philip-pine Americans.

or ethnic background was considered as one factor in our general attempt to convert formal credentials into realistic predictions.

Each file to be reviewed by the full committee was first assigned and read by a committee member who reported on its contents to the committee. There followed a discussion on the applicants under consideration, leading to a committee vote on the disposition of the application. Assignment of files to the committee member for initial reading was usually on a random basis. The files of Black applicants, however, were assigned to and separately read by both Professor Geoffrey Crooks and Mr. Vincent Hayes, the two committee members thought best equipped to report to the full committee on the contents of the file. Professor Crooks worked with minority applications during the summer of 1970 as director of the school's Council on Legal Education Opportunities (CLEO) program[4] and Mr. Hayes, a second-year Black law student, who previously served as director of the Governor's Multi-Service Center in Seattle, a job involving considerable personnel evaluation. Applications of Chicanos, American Indians and Filipinos were reviewed by Associate Dean Robert S. Hunt for presentation to the committee.

In considering minority applicants, the committee was guided by a University-wide policy which sought to eliminate the continued effects of past segregation and discrimination against Blacks, Chicanos, American Indians and other disadvantaged racial and ethnic minority groups. At trial, the President of the University of Washington testified as to the origin of this policy:

> More and more it became evident to us that just an open door, as it were, at the point of entry to the University, somehow or other seemed insufficient to deal with what was emerging as the greatest internal problem of the United States of America, a problem which obviously could not be resolved without some kind of contribution being made not only by the schools, but obviously, also, by the colleges in the University and the University of Washington, in particular, given the racial distribution of this state.
>
> * * *
>
> So that was the beginning of a growing awareness that just an open-door sheer equality in view of the cultural circumstances that produced something other than equality, was not enough; that some more positive contribution had to be made to the resolution of this problem in American life, and something had to be done by the University of Washington.

Thus, the University sought to achieve a reasonable representation within the student body of persons from these groups which have been historically suppressed by encouraging their enrollment within the various programs offered at the University. Policies for admission of minorities throughout the University recognized that the conventional "mechanical" credentializating system does not always produce good indicators of the full potential of such culturally separated or deprived in-

---

4. A federally (OEO) funded program, sponsored by the American Bar Association, the American Association of Law Schools, the National Bar Association and the Law School Admission Council, which provides summer training programs and financial assistance to disadvantaged college students seeking admission to law school.

dividuals, and that to rely solely on such formal credentials could well result in unfairly denying to qualified minority persons the chance to pursue the educational opportunities available at the University.

The law school sought to carry forward this University policy in its admission program, not only to obtain a reasonable representation from minorities within its classes, but to increase participation within the legal profession by persons from racial and ethnic groups which have been historically denied access to the profession and which, consequently, are grossly underrepresented within the legal system. In doing so, the Admissions Committee followed certain procedures which are the crux of plaintiff's claimed denial of equal protection of the laws.

First, in reviewing the files of minority applicants, the committee attached less weight to the PFYA in making a total judgmental evaluation as to the relative ability of the particular applicant to succeed in law school. Also, the chairman testified that although the same standard was applied to all applicants (*i.e.,* the relative probability of the individual succeeding in law school), minority applicants were directly compared to one another, but were not compared to applicants outside of the minority group. The committee sought to identify, within the minority category, those persons who had the highest probability of succeeding in law school. Thus, the law school included within its admitted group minority applicants whose PFYAs were lower than those of some other applicants, but whose entire record showed the committee that they were capable of successfully completing the law school program.[5]

As a result of this process, the committee admitted a group of minority applicants, placed a group of such applicants on a waiting list, and rejected other minority applications. The dean of the law school testified that the law school has no fixed admissions quota for minority students, but that the committee sought a reasonable representation of such groups in the law school. He added that the law school has accepted no unqualified minority applicants, but only those whose records indicated that they were capable of successfully completing the law school program.

The admissions committee sent letters of acceptance to over 200 applicants. Normal attrition among those invited was expected to reduce this group to produce a class of about 150. Against the possibility of unusually high attrition among the group of accepted applicants, the committee placed approximately 155 additional applicants on a waiting list. The waiting list was ranked in approximate quartiles, with 46 applicants in the highest quartile, 38 applicants in the second quartile, 36 applicants in the third quartile, and 33 applicants in the fourth or lowest quartile. The remaining applicants—those receiving neither offers of acceptance nor waiting list assignments—received letters of denial. Plaintiff received an invitation to be placed on the waiting list and he was ranked in the fourth or lowest quartile. On July 21, 1971, the rate of attrition from the admitted applicants appearing to be within normal ranges, the committee decided to send letters of denial to those applicants in the third and fourth quartiles on the waiting list. Plaintiff was thus

5. For example, many of the minority group applicants were first screened through special compensatory summer programs, operated primarily by CLEO.

notified on August 2, 1971, that he was neither admitted nor any longer on the waiting list. As of August 1, 1971, 275 students were admitted to the freshman law school class and 55 students remained on the waiting list, making a total of 330 students.

Out of the 275 students given notice of admission, 127 were nonresidents of the state of Washington. Out of the 55 on the waiting list, 23 were nonresidents of the state of Washington. Thus, of the 330 applicants admitted or waiting, 180 were residents of the state of Washington. Ultimately, 32 nonresidents (21.6 per cent of the entering class) actually enrolled in the first-year class.

Because of the judgmental factors in the admissions process, as outlined, the ultimate determination of applicants to whom admission was offered did not follow exactly the relative ranking of PFYAs. Of those invited, 74 had lower PFYAs than plaintiff; 36 of these were minority applicants, 22 were returning from military service, and 16 were applicants judged by the committee as deserving invitations on the basis of other information contained in their files. Twenty-nine applicants with higher PFYAs than plaintiff's were denied admission. Of the 36 minority group students invited 18 actually enrolled in the first-year class.

The trial court found that some minority applicants with college grades and LSAT scores so low that had they been of the white race their applications would have been summarily denied, were given invitations for admission; that some such students were admitted instead of plaintiff; that since no more than 150 applicants were to be admitted to the law school, the admission of less qualified students resulted in a denial of places to those better qualified; and that plaintiff had better "qualifications" than many of the students admitted by the committee. The trial court also found that plaintiff was and is fully qualified and capable of satisfactorily attending the law school.

The trial court concluded that there is no constitutional restriction upon admitting nonresidential students; and no laws or regulations provide preference to residential students over nonresidential students for admission to the University of Washington School of Law; that, in denying plaintiff admission to the law school, the University of Washington discriminated against him and did not accord to him equal protection of the laws as guaranteed by the fourteenth amendment to the United States Constitution; and therefore, that plaintiff should be admitted to the law school for the class of 1974, beginning September 22, 1971.[6]

[The court held that plaintiff had standing to assert the constitutional questions, though there was "no way of knowing that plaintiff would have been admitted to the law school, even had no minority student been admitted."]

II.

The essence of plaintiff's Fourteenth Amendment argument is that the law school violated his right to equal protection of the laws by denying him admission,

6. At time of oral argument in this court it was stated that plaintiff had actually been admitted to the law school in September, 1971, and was still in attendance. Due to the conditions under which plaintiff was admitted and the great public interest in the continuing issues raised by this appeal, we do not consider the case to be moot.

yet accepting certain minority applicants with lower PFYAs than plaintiff who, but for their minority status, would not have been admitted.[8]

To answer this contention we consider three implicit, subordinate questions: (A) whether race can ever be considered as one factor in the admissions policy of a state law school or whether racial classifications are *per se* unconstitutional because the equal protection of the laws requires that law school admissions be "color blind"; (B) if consideration of race is not *per se* unconstitutional, what is the appropriate standard of review to be applied in determining the constitutionality of such a classification; and (C) when the appropriate standard is applied does the specific minority admissions policy employed by the law school pass constitutional muster?[9]

In Brown v. Board of Education [347 U.S. 483, 74 S.Ct. 686, 98 L.Ed. 873 (1954)], the Supreme Court addressed a question of primary importance at page 493, 74 S.Ct. at page 691:

> Does segregation of children in public schools solely on the basis of race, even though the physical facilities and other "tangible" factors may be equal, deprive the children of the minority group of equal educational opportunities? We believe that it does.

The Court in *Brown* held the equal protection clause of the Fourteenth Amendment prohibits state law from requiring the operation of racially segregated, dual school systems of public education and requires that the system be converted into a unitary, nonracially segregated system. In so holding, the Court noted that segregation inevitably stigmatizes Black children:

> To separate them from others of similar age and qualifications solely because of their race generates a feeling of inferiority as to their status in the community that may affect their hearts and minds in a way unlikely ever to be undone.

Brown v. Board of Education, *supra,* at page 494, 74 S.Ct. at page 691. Moreover, "The impact is greater when it has the sanction of the law; for the policy of separating the races is usually interpreted as denoting the inferiority of the negro group." *Id.* at page 494, 74 S.Ct. at page 691.

Brown did not hold that all racial classifications are *per se* unconstitutional; rather, it held that invidious racial classifications—*i.e.,* those that stigmatize a racial

8. Our review is specifically limited to a consideration of the alleged constitutional infirmities in the law school's admissions policy and procedures. Beyond question, it would be inappropriate for this court to determine the actual composition of the first year class through an independent evaluation of each applicant's file, substituting our criteria and judgment for those of the Admissions Committee. In regard to the scope of judicial review in this area, the United States Supreme Court has stated that:

> In seeking to define even in broad and general terms how far this remedial power extends it is important to remember that judicial powers may be exercised only on

the basis of a constitutional violation. Remedial judicial authority does not put judges automatically in the shoes of school authorities whose powers are plenary. Judicial authority enters only when local authority defaults.

Swann v. Charlotte-Mecklenburg Board of Education, 402 U.S. 1, 16, 91 S.Ct. 1267, 1276, 28 L.Ed.2d 554 (1971).

9. Considering the statutory delegation of power to establish entrance requirements for students to the University, no serious question is raised as to whether the action of the law school here complained of constitutes "state action" within the meaning of the Fourteenth Amendment.

group with the stamp of inferiority—are unconstitutional. Even viewed in a light most favorable to plaintiff, the "preferential" minority admissions policy administered by the law school is clearly not a form of invidious discrimination. The goal of this policy is not to separate the races, but to bring them together. And, as has been observed,

> Preferential admissions do not represent a covert attempt to stigmatize the majority race as inferior; nor is it reasonable to expect that a possible effect of the extension of educational preferences to certain disadvantaged racial minorities will be to stigmatize whites.

O'Neil, Preferential Admissions: Equalizing the Access of Minority Groups to Higher Education, 80 Yale L.J. 699, 713 (1971).

While Brown v. Board of Education, *supra,* certainly provides a starting point for our analysis of the instant case, we do not agree with the trial court that *Brown* is dispositive here. Subsequent decisions of the United States Supreme Court have made it clear that in some circumstances a racial criterion *may* be used—and indeed in some circumstances *must* be used—by public educational institutions in bringing about racial balance. School systems which were formerly segregated de jure[10] now have an affirmative duty to remedy racial imbalance.

In Green v. County School Board, 391 U.S. 430, 88 S.Ct. 1689, 20 L.Ed.2d 716 (1968), the Supreme Court considered a school board's adoption of a "freedom-of-choice" plan which allowed a student to choose his own public school. No student was assigned or admitted to school on the basis of race. In holding that, on the facts presented, the plan did not satisfy the board's duty to create a unitary, nonracial system, the Court stated at pages 437-440, 88 S.Ct. at page 1694:

> In the context of the state-imposed segregated pattern of long standing, the fact that in 1965 the Board opened the doors of the former "white" school to Negro children and of the "Negro" school to white children merely begins, not ends, our inquiry whether the Board has taken steps adequate to abolish its dual, segregated system.

> *   *   *   *   *   *

> The burden on a school board today is to come forward with a plan that promises realistically to work, and promises realistically to work *now.*

As Judge Sobeloff has put it,

---

10. "De jure" segregation generally refers to "segregation directly intended or mandated by law or otherwise issuing from an official racial classification." Hobson v. Hansen, 269 F.Supp. 401, 492 (D.D.C. 1967), aff'd sub nom. Smuck v. Hobson, 132 U.S.App.D.C. 372, 408 F.2d 175 (1969), or, in other words, to segregation which has, or had, the sanction of law. In the context of public education the United States Supreme Court has expanded the meaning of the term "de jure segregation" [T]o comprehend any situation in which the activities of school authorities have had a racially discriminatory impact con-

tributing to the establishment or continuation [of racial imbalance] . . .
State ex rel. Citizens Against Mandatory Bussing v. Brooks, 80 Wash.2d 121, 130, 492 P.2d 536, 542 (1972).
Where the segregation is inadvertent and without the assistance or collusion of school authorities, and is not caused by any "state action," but rather by social, economic and other determinants, it will be referred to as "de facto" herein. *See* Fiss, Racial Imbalance in the Public Schools: the Constitutional Concepts, 78 Harv. L. Rev. 564, 565-66, 584, 598 (1965).

" 'Freedom of choice' is not a sacred talisman; it is only a means to a constitutionally required end—the abolition of the system of segregation and its effects. If the means prove effective, it is acceptable, but if it fails to undo segregation, other means must be used to achieve this end. The school officials have the continuing duty to take whatever action may be necessary to create a 'unitary, nonracial system.' " Bowman v. County School Board, 382 F.2d 326, 333 (C.A.4th Cir. 1967) (concurring opinion).

Pursuing this principle further, the Supreme Court in Swann v. Charlotte-Mecklenburg Board of Education, 402 U.S. 1, 16, 91 S.Ct. 1267, 1276, 28 L.Ed.2d 554 (1971), unanimously held that school authorities, in seeking to achieve a unitary, nonracial system of public education, need not be "color-blind," but may consider race as a valid criterion when considering admissions and producing a student body:

School authorities are traditionally charged with broad power to formulate and implement educational policy and might well conclude, for example, that in order to prepare students to live in a pluralistic society each school should have a prescribed ratio of Negro to white students reflecting the proportion for the district as a whole. To do this as an educational policy is within the broad discretionary powers of school authorities; absent a finding of a constitutional violation, however, that would not be within the authority of a federal court.

The Supreme Court then approved the District Court's opinion requiring the school authorities to consider race in determining the composition of individual schools:

As we said in *Green,* a school authority's remedial plan or a district court's remedial decree is to be judged by its effectiveness. Awareness of the racial composition of the whole school system is likely to be a useful starting point in shaping a remedy to correct past constitutional violations.

Swann v. Charlotte-Mecklenburg Board of Education, *supra,* at page 25, 91 S.Ct. at page 1280.

Thus, the Constitution is color conscious to prevent the perpetuation of discrimination and to undo the effects of past segregation. In holding invalid North Carolina's anti-bussing law, which flatly forbade assignment of any student on account of race or for the purpose of creating a racial balance or ratio in the schools and which prohibited bussing for such purposes, the Court stated:

[T]he statute exploits an apparently neutral form to control school assignment plans by directing that they be "color blind"; that requirement, against the background of segregation, would render illusory the promise of Brown v. Board of Education, 347 U.S. 483, 74 S.Ct. 686, 98 L.Ed. 873 (1954). Just as the race of students must be considered in determining whether a constitutional violation has occurred, so also must race be considered in formulating a remedy.

North Carolina State Board of Education v. Swann, 402 U.S. 43, 45, 91 S.Ct. 1284, 1286, 28 L.Ed.2d 586 (1971). *Accord,* United States v. Jefferson County Board of Education, 372 F.2d 836 (5th Cir. 1966), aff'd en banc, 380 F.2d 385 (1967), cert. denied sub nom. Board of Education of Bessemer v. United States, 389 U.S. 840, 88 S.Ct. 77, 19 L.Ed.2d 104 (1967).

Clearly, consideration of race by school authorities does not violate the Fourteenth Amendment where the purpose is to bring together, rather than separate, the races. The "minority" admissions policy of the law school, aimed at insuring a reasonable representation of minority persons in the student body, is not invidious. Consideration of race is permissible to carry out the mandate of *Brown,* and, as noted, has been required in some circumstances.

However, plaintiff contends that cases such as Green v. County School Board, *supra,* and Swann v. Charlotte-Mecklenburg Board of Education, *supra,* are inapposite here since none of the students there involved were deprived of an education by the plan to achieve a unitary school system. It is questionable whether defendants deprived plaintiff of a legal education by denying him admission.[11] But even accepting this contention, arguendo, the denial of a "benefit" on the basis of race is not necessarily a *per se* violation of the Fourteenth Amendment, if the racial classification is used in a compensatory way to promote integration.

For example, in Porcelli v. Titus, 431 F.2d 1254 (3d Cir. 1970), cert. denied, 402 U.S. 944, 91 S.Ct. 1612, 29 L.Ed.2d 112 (1971), a group of white teachers alleged that the school board had bypassed them in abolishing the regular promotion schedule and procedure for selecting principals and vice-principals, and had given priority to Black candidates in order to increase the integration of the system's faculty. In upholding the board's judgment to suspend the ordinary promotion system upon racial considerations, the court stated:

> State action based partly on considerations of color, when color is not used per se, and in furtherance of a proper governmental objective, is not necessarily a violation of the Fourteenth Amendment.

Porcelli v. Titus, *supra,* at page 1257.

Similarly, the Eighth Circuit concluded that in order to eradicate the effects of past discrimination,

> [I]t would be in order for the district court to mandate that one out of every three persons hired by the [Minneapolis] Fire Department would be a minority individual who qualifies until at least 20 minority persons have been so hired.

Carter v. Gallagher, 452 F.2d 315, 331 (8th Cir. 1971); cert. denied 406 U.S. 950, 92 S.Ct. 2045, 32 L.Ed.2d 338 (1972). Thus, the court ordered the department to hire minority applicants, although in doing so a more qualified nonminority applicant might be bypassed. *Cf.* Contractors Ass'n of Eastern Pennsylvania v. Secretary

11. Plaintiff alleged in his complaint that he had previously applied to, and been accepted by, the law school at each of the following universities: University of Oregon, University of Idaho, Gonzaga University and Willamette University.

of Labor, 442 F.2d 159 (3d Cir. 1971), cert. denied, 404 U.S. 854, 92 S.Ct. 98, 30 L.Ed.2d 95 (1971).

We conclude that the consideration of race as a factor in the admissions policy of a state law school is not a *per se* violation of the equal protection clause of the Fourteenth Amendment. We proceed, therefore, to the question of what standard of review is appropriate to determine the constitutionality of such a classification.

B.

Generally, when reviewing a state-created classification alleged to be in violation of the equal protection clause of the Fourteenth Amendment, the question is whether the classification is reasonably related to a legitimate public purpose. And, in applying this "rational basis" test "[A] discrimination will not be set aside if any state of facts reasonably may be conceived to justify it." McGowan v. Maryland, 366 U.S. 420, 426, 81 S.Ct. 1101, 1105, 6 L.Ed.2d 393 (1961).

However, where the classification is based upon race, a heavier burden of justification is imposed upon the state. In overturning Virginia's antimiscegenation law, the Supreme Court explained this stricter standard of review:

> The clear and central purpose of the Fourteenth Amendment was to eliminate all official state sources of invidious racial discrimination in the States. [Citations omitted.]
>
> ... At the very least, the Equal Protection Clause demands that racial classifications, especially suspect in criminal statutes, be subjected to the "most rigid scrutiny," [citation omitted] and, if they are ever to be upheld, they must be shown to be necessary to the accomplishment of some permissible state objective, independent of the racial discrimination which it is the object of the Fourteenth Amendment to eliminate ...
>
> There is patently no legitimate overriding purpose independent of invidious racial discrimination which justifies this classification.

Loving v. Virginia, 388 U.S. 1, 10-11, 87 S.Ct. 1817, 1823, 18 L.Ed.2d 1010 (1967). *Accord,* McLaughlin v. Florida, 379 U.S. 184, 85 S.Ct. 283, 13 L.Ed.2d 222 (1964); Hunter v. Erickson, 393 U.S. 385, 89 S.Ct. 557, 21 L.Ed.2d 616 (1969).

It has been suggested that the less strict "rational basis" test should be applied to the consideration of race here, since the racial distinction is being used to redress the effects of past discrimination; thus, because the persons normally stigmatized by racial classifications are being benefited, the action complained of should be considered "benign" and reviewed under the more permissive standard. However, the minority admissions policy is certainly not benign with respect to nonminority students who are displaced by it. *See* O'Neil, Preferential Admissions: Equalizing the Access of Minority Groups to Higher Education, 80 Yale L.J. 699, 710 (1971).

The burden is upon the law school to show that its consideration of race in admitting students is necessary to the accomplishment of a compelling state interest.

C.

It can hardly be gainsaid that the minorities have been, and are, grossly under-represented in the law schools—and consequently in the legal profession—of this state and this nation.[12] We believe the state has an overriding interest in promoting integration in public education. In light of the serious underrepresentation of minority groups in the law schools, and considering that minority groups partic-ipate on an equal basis in the tax support of the law school, we find the state interest in eliminating racial imbalance within public legal education to be com-pelling.

Plaintiff contends, however, that any discrimination in this case has been de facto, rather than de jure. Thus, reasons plaintiff, since the law school itself has not actively discriminated against minority applicants, it may not attempt to remedy racial imbalance in the law school student body, and, consequently, throughout the legal profession. We disagree.

In State ex rel. Citizens Against Mandatory Bussing v. Brooks, 80 Wash.2d 121, 128, 492 P.2d 536, 541 (1972), we held that whether the nature of segregation is de jure or de facto is of no consequence where a voluntary plan of eliminating racial imbalance is adopted by school officials:

> Reason impels the conclusion that, if the Constitution supports court di-rected mandatory bussing to desegregate schools in a system which is dual "de jure," then such bussing is within the appropriate exercise of the discre-tion of school authorities in a system which is dual "de facto."

This conclusion is supported by the reasoning of the district court in Barksdale v. Springfield School Committee, 237 F.Supp. 543, 546 (D.Mass.1965), vacated on other grounds, 348 F.2d 261 (1st Cir. 1965):

> It is neither just nor sensible to proscribe segregation having its basis in affirmative state action while at the same time failing to provide a remedy for segregation which grows out of discrimination in housing, or other economic or social factors.

Significantly, this case does not present for review a court order imposing a program of desegregation. Rather, the minority admissions policy is a voluntary

---

12. Report of Black Lawyers and Judges in the United States, 1960-70, 91st Cong., 2d Sess., 116 Cong.Rec. 30786 (1970); U.S. Dept. of Commerce, Bureau of Census, Gen-eral Population Characteristics of the State of Washington, Tables 17 and 18 (1970); Office of Program Planning and Fiscal Management of the State of Washington, Pocket Data Book (1971); Rosen, Equalizing Access to Legal Education: Special Programs for Law Stu-dents Who Are Not Admissible by Traditional Criteria, 1970 U.Tol.L.Rev. 321 (1970); Ed-wards, A New Role for the Black Law Grad-uates—A Reality or an Illusion? 69 Mich.L. Rev. 1407 (1971); Gelhorn, The Law Schools and the Negro, 1968 Duke L.J. 1069 (1968); Reynoso, Laraza, the Law and the Law Schools, 1970 U.Tol.L.Rev. 809 (1970); Toles, Black Population and Black Judges, 17 Student Lawyer J. 20 (Feb. 1972); O'Neil, Preferential Admissions: Equalizing Access to Legal Education, 1970 U.Tol.L.Rev. 281 (1970); Atwood, Survey of Black Law Stu-dent Enrollment, 16 Student Lawyer J. 18 (June 1971); Comment, Selected Bibliogra-phy: Minority Group Participation in the Legal Profession, 1970 U.Tol.L.Rev. 935 (1970).

In relying on statistical evidence to estab-lish the underrepresentation of minority groups in the legal profession, defendants are supported by ample precedent. See, e.g., Hob-son v. Hansen, *supra,* footnote 10.

plan initiated by school authorities. Therefore, the question before us is not whether the Fourteenth Amendment *requires* the law school to take affirmative action to eliminate the continuing effects of de facto segregation; the question is whether the Constitution *permits* the law school to remedy racial imbalance through its minority admissions policy. In refusing to enjoin school officials from implementing a plan to eradicate de facto school segregation by the use of explicit racial classifications, the Second Circuit observed: "That there may be no constitutional duty to act to undo de facto segregation, however, does not mean that such action is unconstitutional." Offermann v. Nitkowski, 378 F.2d 22, 24 (2d Cir. 1967).

The de jure-de facto distinction is not controlling in determining the constitutionality of the minority admissions policy voluntarily adopted by the law school.[13] Further, we see no reason why the state interest in eradicating the continuing effects of past racial discrimination is less merely because the law school itself may have previously been neutral in the matter.

The state also has an overriding interest in providing *all* law students with a legal education that will adequately prepare them to deal with the societal problems which will confront them upon graduation. As the Supreme Court has observed, this cannot be done through books alone:

> [A]lthough the law is a highly learned profession, we are well aware that it is an intensely practical one. The law school, the proving ground for legal learning and practice, cannot be effective in isolation from the individuals and institutions with which the law interacts. Few students and no one who has practiced law would choose to study in an academic vacuum, removed from the interplay of ideas and the exchange of views with which the law is concerned.

Sweatt v. Painter, 339 U.S. 629, 634, 70 S.Ct. 848, 850, 94 L.Ed. 1114 (1950).

The legal profession plays a critical role in the policy making sector of our society, whether decisions be public or private, state or local. That lawyers, in making and influencing these decisions, should be cognizant of the views, needs and demands of all segments of society is a principle beyond dispute. The educational interest of the state in producing a racially balanced student body at the law school is compelling.

Finally, the shortage of minority attorneys—and, consequently, minority prosecutors, judges and public officials—constitutes an undeniably compelling state interest.[14] If minorities are to live within the rule of law, they must enjoy equal representation within our legal system.

Once a constitutionally valid state interest has been established, it remains for the state to show the requisite connection between the racial classification employed and that interest. The consideration of race in the law school admissions

---

13. We do not, therefore, reach the question of whether there is an inherent cultural bias in the Law School Admission Test, or in the methods of teaching and testing employed by the law school, which perpetuates racial imbalance to such an extent as to constitute de jure segregation.

14. *See* O'Neil, Preferential Admissions: Equalizing Access to Legal Education, *supra*, footnote 12.

policy meets the test of necessity here because racial imbalance in the law school and the legal profession is the evil to be corrected, and it can only be corrected by providing legal education to those minority groups which have been previously deprived.

It has been suggested that the minority admissions policy is not necessary, since the same objective could be accomplished by improving the elementary and secondary education of minority students to a point where they could secure equal representation in law schools through direct competition with nonminority applicants on the basis of the same academic criteria. This would be highly desirable, but 18 years have passed since the decision in Brown v. Board of Education, *supra,* and minority groups are still grossly underrepresented in law schools. If the law school is forbidden from taking affirmative action, this underrepresentation may be perpetuated indefinitely. No less restrictive means would serve the governmental interest here; we believe the minority admissions policy of the law school to be the only feasible "plan that promises realistically to work, and promises realistically to work *now.*" Green v. County School Board, *supra,* 391 U.S. at page 439, 88 S.Ct. at page 1694.

We conclude that defendants have shown the necessity of the racial classification herein to the accomplishment of an overriding state interest, and have thus sustained the heavy burden imposed upon them under the equal protection provision of the Fourteenth Amendment.

There remains a further question as to the scope of the classification. A validly drawn classification is one "which includes all [and only those] persons who are similarly situated with respect to the purpose of the law." Tussman & ten-Broek, The Equal Protection of the Laws, 37 Calif.L.Rev. 341, 346 (1949). The classification used by defendants does not include all racial minorities, but only four (Blacks, Chicanos, Indians and Philippine Americans). However, the purpose of the racial classification here is to give special consideration to those racial minority groups which are underrepresented in the law schools and legal profession, and which cannot secure proportionate representation if strictly subjected to the standardized mathematical criteria for admission to the law school.

In selecting minority groups for special consideration, the law school sought to identify those groups most in need of help. The chairman of the admissions committee testified that Asian-Americans, *e.g.,* were not treated as minority applicants for admissions purposes since a significant number could be admitted on the same basis as general applicants. In light of the purpose of the minority admissions policy, the racial classification need not include all racial minority groups.[15] The state may identify and correct the most serious examples of racial imbalance, even though in so doing it does not provide an immediate solution to the entire problem of equal representation within the legal system.

We hold that the minority admissions policy of the law school, and the denial by the law school of admission to plaintiff, violate neither the equal protection clause

15. *See* O'Neil, Preferential Admissions: Equalizing the Access of Minority Groups to   Higher Education, 80 Yale L.J. 699, 750 (1971).

of the fourteenth amendment to the United States Constitution nor Article 1, § 12 of the Washington State Constitution.[16]

III.

Apart from his equal protection argument, plaintiff contends that the procedures employed by the law school in selecting first-year students constitute arbitrary and capricious administrative action, and that the law school's denial of admission to plaintiff pursuant to these procedures must be set aside.

We recently reaffirmed our long standing test of arbitrary and capricious action:

> Arbitrary and capricious action of administrative bodies means willful and unreasoning action, without consideration and in disregard of facts or circumstances. Where there is room for two opinions, action is not arbitrary or capricious when exercised honestly and upon due consideration, even though it may be believed that an erroneous conclusion has been reached.

DuPont-Fort Lewis School Dist. 7 v. Bruno, 79 Wash.2d 736, 739, 489 P.2d 171, 174 (1971). Plaintiff must carry the burden of proof on this issue. State ex rel. Longview Fire Fighters Union, Local 828 v. Longview, 65 Wash.2d 568, 572, 399 P.2d 1 (1965).

In determining whether the denial of plaintiff's application to the law school constitutes arbitrary and capricious action, we turn first to the ultimate admissions goals of the law school, pursuant to which the policy and procedures of the admissions committee have been formulated. In light of the tremendous increase in the number of qualified applicants, the law school sought to identify applicants with the potential for outstanding performance in the law school, and then "to select applicants for admission from that group on the basis of their ability to make significant contributions to law school classes and to the community at large." The guide for applicants also stated that the criteria to be applied by the law school in the selection process would not be limited to numerical indicators such as test scores and grade point averages, but would also include several other factors requiring the exercise of judgmental evaluation. Among these other factors were recommendations, the quality of work in difficult analytical seminars and writing programs, the academic standards of the applicant's undergraduate school, and the nature of the applicant's graduate work or employment (if any) since graduation. The guide added that race would be considered as one factor in the law school's attempt to convert formal credentials into realistic predictions.

Plaintiff first contends that no standards were applied by the committee in its evaluation of these criteria for admission. However, the trial court specifically refused to make a finding of fact proposed by plaintiff that:

> [T]he Admissions Committee selected and denied students for admission to

---

16. As we have held, the equal protection clause of U.S.Const., amend. 14, and the privileges and immunities clause of Const. art. 1, § 12, have the same import, and we apply them as one. Markham Adv. Co. v. State, 73 Wash.2d 405, 427, 439 P.2d 248 (1968), appeal dismissed, 393 U.S. 316, 89 S.Ct. 553, 21 L.Ed.2d 512 (1969).

the University of Washington School of Law with no set standards or procedures.

We particularly note that while race was a major factor, it was not the only factor considered by the committee in reviewing minority applications. No minority quota was established; rather, a reasonable representation of such groups in the law school was sought. Also, the dean of the law school testified (and the trial court did not find otherwise) that only "qualified" minority applicants were admitted— *i.e.,* minority persons whose entire record showed the committee that they were capable of successfully completing the law school program. Many minority applicants were denied admission. The trial court did find that some minority students admitted would have been summarily denied had they been white, since their predicted first-year averages were relatively low. Also, the court found that some minority students were admitted with "lower qualifications" than plaintiff. Thus, the record overwhelmingly indicates that the admissions committee did employ predetermined standards and procedures in selecting students.

Plaintiff further contends that the committee failed to consider all applicants on the same basis, but instead judged minority applicants by different standards. In reviewing the files of applicants, the committee did ask the same fundamental question in every case: what is the relative probability of the individual succeeding in law school and making significant contributions to law school classes and the community at lárge? However, minority applicants were directly compared to one another under this test, but were not compared to nonminority applicants.

The question thus raised is whether, in selecting those applicants most likely to make significant contributions to law school classes and to the community at large, it is arbitrary and capricious for the admissions committee to consider race as a factor in admitting qualified minority applicants whose strict academic credentials yield a lower PFYA than that of some nonminority applicants who are not admitted. The answer depends on whether race is relevant to the goals of the law school's admission program as stated in the guide for applicants.

The thrust of plaintiff's objection here is that the action of the committee was arbitrary because, in admitting students, it deviated from the relative numerical ranking provided by the PFYAs. Thus, argues plaintiff, by taking subjective (*i.e.,* nonmathematical) factors into consideration, and weighting them differently for different applicants, the committee arbitrarily denied him admission. We do not agree that the exercise of judgment in evaluating an applicant's file constitutes arbitrary and capricious action. Nor do we find an abuse of that judgment here.

The President of the University testified that the decision to consider race in interpreting a minority applicant's numerical grade averages and test scores was reached because of the opinion within the University that such standardized indicators inherently exclude a disproportionate number of minority applicants.

*   *   *

"Basic intelligence must have the means of articulation to manifest itself fairly in a testing process." Griggs v. Duke Power Co., 401 U.S. 424, 430, 91 S.Ct. 849, 853,

28 L.Ed.2d 158 (1971). We express no opinion as to whether the LSAT bears a cultural bias which renders the test less reliable as a predictor of law school performance for minority students than for others. But this is certainly a factor which the law school may consider in its discretion. *See* Hobson v. Hansen, *supra,* 269 F.Supp. at page 484; O'Neil, Preferential Admissions: Equalizing Access to Legal Education, 1970 U.Tol.L.Rev. 281, 303 (1970). It would be unnecessary, of course, for the law school to consider race in interpreting the standardized numerical indicators for nonminority students, because the alleged bias operates *in favor* of those applicants.

The fallacy of plaintiff's argument is the assumption that, but for the special consideration given minority applicants, selection decisions by the committee would have been based solely upon objective, measurable mathematical projections of the academic performance of applicants. Actually, although the PFYA was a very important factor, it was not the sole determinative factor for any group of students. Rather, the committee utilized the PFYA as a starting point in making its judgment as to the fundamental criterion for admission: the applicant's potential for contributing to law school classes and to the community. That the committee considered more than the standardized numerical indicators in reviewing the files of all students is indicated by the fact that 16 *non*minority, general applicants were admitted with lower PFYAs than plaintiff.

Moreover, we question the assumption that a minority applicant is ipso facto "less qualified" than a nonminority applicant who has a higher predicted first-year average. When judging "qualifications," the primary criterion of the law school in admitting students must be remembered. In light of the gross underrepresentation of minorities in the legal system, can it be said with such certainty as to leave no room for differing opinions that a white applicant with a higher PFYA will make a greater contribution to the law school and the community? We think not. While the probability of applicant achieving high grades in his first year of law school is an important criterion for admission, it is not the sole permissible criterion.

Where the criteria for admissions are not arbitrary and capricious, we will not vitiate the judgment of the admissions committee unless a constitutional violation is shown. Considering the debatable nature of the criteria, we do not find the consideration of race in the admission of those minority applicants who indicate competence to successfully complete the law school program to be arbitrary and capricious. Law school admissions need not become a game of numbers; the process should remain sensitive and flexible, with room for informed judgment in interpreting mechanical indicators. The committee may consider the racial or ethnic background of an applicant when interpreting his standardized grades and test scores.

As a final point, plaintiff argues that the consideration of race here was arbitrary because no inquiry was made into the background of each minority applicant to make certain that the individual was in fact educationally, economically and culturally deprived. However, the mere fact that a minority applicant comes from a relatively more affluent home does not mean that he has not been subjected to psychological harm through discrimination. *See* Hobson v. Hansen, *supra,* 269 F.Supp. at page 482. Likewise, every minority lawyer is critically needed, whether he be rich or poor. A showing of actual deprivation is unnecessary for the accomplishment of the compelling state interests here.[17]

Plaintiff has failed to show that the policy and procedures of the law school in denying him admission were so unreasoned and in disregard of the facts and circumstances as to constitute arbitrary and capricious action.

IV.

Plaintiff also contends that Article 9, § 1 of the Washington State Constitution[18] and certain of the statutes governing the University of Washington[19] require preference to be given Washington residents over nonresidents in admission to the school of law, and that in failing to give this preference to plaintiff, the law school wrongfully denied him admission. The trial court ruled against plaintiff's contention on this issue. We agree with the trial court.

* * *

The judgment of the trial court is reversed.

The foregoing opinion was prepared by Justice Marshall A. Neill while a member of this court. It is adopted by the undersigned as the opinion of the court.

FINLEY, HAMILTON, STAFFORD, WRIGHT and UTTER, JJ., and TUTTLE, J. pro tem., concur.

[Concurrence of Justice Wright and dissent of Chief Justice Hale are omitted.]

NOTES

1. On April 23, 1974, the United States Supreme Court, in a 5-4 per curiam decision, vacated the judgment of the Supreme Court of Washington on the ground of mootness. Specifically, the majority held that "Because the petitioner will complete his law school studies at the end of the term for which he has now registered regardless of any decision this Court might reach on the merits of this litigation, we conclude that the Court cannot, consistently with the limitations of Art. III of the Constitution, consider the substantive constitutional issues tendered by the parties." DeFunis v. Odegaard,   U.S.   , 94 S.Ct. 1704, 40 L.Ed.2d 164 (1974). Of the four dissenting members of the Court—Justices Brennan, Douglas, White, and Marshall—who believed that the issues in the case were not moot, only Justice Douglas expressed any view on the merits. First, he suggested grave doubts as to the validity of the Predicted First-Year Average as an "admissions tool" because of deficiencies he discerned in both the Law School Admissions Test and the Undergraduate Grade Point Averages as predictors of precise gradations in future performance as law student or lawyer. But since neither party had challenged the validity of the PFYA, Justice Douglas proceeded to examine the basic constitutional issues as he saw them (94 S.Ct. at 1713):

17. *See generally* O'Neil, Preferential Admissions: Equalizing the Access of Minority Groups to Higher Education, *supra*, at 751.
18. Art. 9 "§ 1 *preamble* It is the paramount duty of the state to make ample provision for the education of all children residing within its borders . . ."
19. RCW 28B.20.020, 28B.15.011 et seq., and 28B.10.800.

The Equal Protection Clause did not enact a requirement that Law Schools employ as the sole criterion for admissions a formula based upon the LSAT and undergraduate grades, nor does it proscribe law schools from evaluating an applicant's prior achievements in light of the barriers that he had to overcome. A Black applicant who pulled himself out of the ghetto into a junior college may thereby demonstrate a level of motivation, perseverance and ability that would lead a fairminded admissions committee to conclude that he shows more promise for law study than the son of a rich alumnus who achieved better grades at Harvard. That applicant would not be offered admission because he is Black, but because as an individual he has shown he has the potential, while the Harvard man may have taken less advantage of the vastly superior opportunities offered him. Because of the weight of the prior handicaps that Black applicant may not realize his full potential in the first year of law school, or even in the full three years, but in the long pull of a legal career his achievements may far outstrip those of his classmates whose earlier records appeared superior by conventional criteria. There is currently no test available to the admissions committee that can predict such possibilities with assurance, but the committee may nevertheless seek to gauge it as best as it can, and weigh this factor in its decisions. Such a policy would not be limited to Blacks, or Chicanos or Filipinos or American Indians, although undoubtedly groups such as these may in practice be the principal beneficiaries of it. But a poor Appalachian white, or a second generation Chinese in San Francisco, or some other American whose lineage is so diverse as to defy ethnic labels, may demonstrate similar potential and thus be accorded favorable consideration by the committee.

The difference between such a policy and the one presented by this case is that the committee would be making decisions on the basis of individual attributes, rather than according a preference solely on the basis of race. To be sure, the racial preference here was not absolute—the committee did not admit all applicants from the four favored groups. But it did accord all such applicants a preference by applying, to an extent not precisely ascertainable from the record, different standards by which to judge their applications, with the result that the committee admitted minority applicants who, in the school's own judgment, were less promising than other applicants who were rejected. Furthermore, it is apparent that because the admissions committee compared minority applicants only with one another, it was necessary to reserve some proportion of the class for them, even if at the outset a precise number of places were not set aside,[12] That proportion, apparently 15 to

---

12. At the outset the committee may have chosen only a range, with the precise number to be determined later in the process as the total number of minority applicants, and some tentative assessment of their quality, could be determined. . . .

The fact that the Committee did not set a precise number in advance is obviously irrelevant to the legal analysis. Nor does it matter that there is some minimal level of achievement below which the Committee would not reach in order to achieve its stated goal as to the proportion of the class reserved for minority groups, so long as the Committee was willing, in order to achieve that goal, to admit minority applicants who, in the committee's own judgment, were less qualified than other rejected applicants and who would not otherwise have been admitted.

20%, was chosen because the school determined it to be "reasonable," although no explanation is provided as to how that number rather than some other was found appropriate. Without becoming embroiled in a semantic debate over whether this practice constitutes a "quota," it is clear that given the limitation on the total number of applicants who could be accepted, this policy did reduce the total number of places for which DeFunis could compete—solely on account of his race. Thus, as the Washington Supreme Court concluded, whatever label one wishes to apply to it, "the minority admissions program is certainly not benign with respect to nonminority students who are displaced by it." 82 Wn.2d 11,–,507 P.2d 1169,–. A finding that the state school employed a racial classification in selecting its students subjects it to the strictest scrutiny under the Equal Protection Clause.

The consideration of race as a measure of an applicant's qualification normally introduces a capricious and irrelevant factor working an invidious discrimination, *Anderson* v. *Martin,* 375 U.S. 399, 402; *Loving* v. *Virginia,* 388 U.S. 1, 10; *Harper* v. *Virginia Board of Elections,* 383 U.S. 663, 668. Once race is a starting point educators and courts are immediately embroiled in competing claims of different racial and ethnic groups that would make difficult manageable standards consistent with the Equal Protection Clause. "The clear and central purpose of the Fourteenth Amendment was to eliminate all official state sources of invidious racial discrimination in the States." *Loving, supra,* at 10. The law school's admissions policy cannot be reconciled with that purpose, unless cultural standards of a diverse rather than a homogeneous society are taken into account. The reason is that professional persons, particularly lawyers, are not selected for life in a computerized society. The Indian who walks to the beat of Chief Seattle of the Muckleshoot Tribe in Washington has a different culture than Examiners at Law Schools.

The key to the problem is the consideration of each application *in a racially neutral way.* Since LSAT reflects questions touching on cultural backgrounds, the admissions committee acted properly in my view in setting minority applications apart for separate processing. These minorities have cultural backgrounds that are vastly different from the dominant Caucasian. Many Eskimos, American Indians, Filipinos, Chicanos, Asian Indians, Burmese, and Africans come from such disparate backgrounds that a test sensitively tuned for most applicants would be wide of the mark for many minorities.

The melting pot is not designed to homogenize people, making them uniform in consistency. The melting pot as I understand it is a figure of speech that depicts the wide diversities tolerated by the First Amendment under one flag. See Morrison and Emmager [sic], The Growth of the American Republic (1950) vol. II, c. VIII. Minorities in our midst who are to serve actively in our public affairs should be chosen on talent and character alone not on cultural orientation or leanings.

I do know, coming as I do from Indian country—in Washington, that many of the young Indians know little about Adam Smith or Karl Marx but are deeply imbued with the spirit and philosophy of Chief Robert B. Jim of the Yakimas, Chief Seattle of the Muckleshoots and Chief Joseph of the Nez Perce which offer competitive attitudes towards life, fellow man, and nature.

I do not know the extent to which Blacks in this country are imbued with ideas of African Socialism. Leopold Senghor and Sekon [*sic*] Torae [*sic*], most articulate of African leaders, have held that modern African political philosophy is not oriented either to marxism or to capitalism. How far the reintroduction into educational curricula of ancient African art and history has reached the minds of young Afro-Americans I do not know. But at least as respects Indians, Blacks, and Chicanos—as well as those from Asian cultures—I think a separate classification of these applicants is warranted, lest race be a subtle force in eliminating minority members of cultural differences.

Insofar as LSAT tests reflect the dimensions and orientation of the Organization Man they do a disservice to minorities. I personally know that admissions tests were once used to eliminate Jews. How many other minorities they aim at I do not know. My reaction is that the presence of an LSAT test is sufficient warrant for a school to put racial minorities into a separate class in order better to probe their capacities and potentials.

This does not mean that a separate LSAT test be designed for minority racial groups, although that might be a possibility. The merits of the present controversy cannot in my view be resolved on this record. A trial would involve the disclosure of hidden prejudices, if any, against certain minorities and the manner in which substitute measurements of one's talents and character were employed in the conventional tests, I could agree with the majority of the Washington Supreme Court only, if on the record, it could be said that the law school's selection was racially neutral. The case, in my view, should be remanded for a new trial to consider, *inter alia*, whether the established LSAT tests should be eliminated so far as racial minorities are concerned.

This does not mean that a separate LSAT test must be designed for minority racial groups, although that might be a possibility. The reason for the separate treatment of minorities as a class is to make more certain that racial factors do not militate *against an applicant or on his behalf*.[18]

There is no constitutional right for any race to be preferred. The years of slavery did more than retard the progress of Blacks. Even a greater wrong was done the whites by creating arrogance instead of humility and by encouraging the growth of the fiction of a superior race. There is no superior person by

18. We are not faced here with a situation where barriers are overtly or covertly put in the path of members of one racial group which are not required by others. There was also no showing that the purpose of the school's policy was to eliminate arbitrary and irrelevant barriers to entry by certain racial groups into the legal profession groups. *Griggs* v. *Duke Power Co.,* 401 U.S. 424. In *Swann* v. *Charlotte-Mecklenburg Board of Education,* 402 U.S. 1, 16, we stated that as a matter of educational policy school authorities could, within their broad discretion, prescribe that each school within their district have a prescribed ratio of Negro to white students reflecting the proportion for the district as a whole, in order to disestablish a dual school system. But there is a crucial difference between the policy suggested in *Swann* and that under consideration here: the *Swann* policy would impinge on no person's constitutional rights, because no one would be excluded from a public school and no one has a right to attend a segregated public school.

constitutional standards. A DeFunis who is white is entitled to no advantage by reason of that fact; nor is he subject to any disability, no matter his race or color. Whatever his race, he had a constitutional right to have his application considered on its individual merits in a racially neutral manner.

The slate is not entirely clean. First, we have held that *pro rata* representation of the races is not required either on juries, see *Cassell* v. *Texas,* 339 U.S. 282, 286-287, or in public schools, *Swann, supra,* at 24. Moreover, in *Hughes* v. *Superior Court,* 339 U.S. 460, we reviewed the contempt convictions of pickets who sought by their demonstration to force an employer to prefer Negroes to whites in his hiring of clerks, in order to ensure that 50% of the employees were Negro. In finding that California could constitutionally enjoin the picketing there involved we quoted from the opinion of the California Supreme Court, which noted that the pickets would "make the right to work for Lucky dependent not on fitness for the work nor on an equal right of all, regardless of race, to compete in an open market, but, rather, on membership in a particular race. If petitioners were upheld in their demand then other races, white, yellow, brown, and red, would have equal rights to demand discriminatory hiring on a racial basis." *Id.,* at 463-464. We then noted that

> "[t]o deny to California the right to ban picketing in the circumstances of this case would mean that there could be no prohibition of the pressures of picketing to secure proportional employment on ancestral grounds of Hungarians in Cleveland, of Poles in Buffalo, of Germans in Milwaukee, of Portuguese in New Bedford, of Mexicans in San Antonio, of the numerous minority groups in New York, and so on through the whole gamut of racial and religious concentrations in various cities." *Ibid.*

The reservation of a proportion of the law school class for members of selected minority groups is fraught with similar dangers, for one must immediately determine which groups are to receive such favored treatment and which are to be excluded, the proportions of the class that are to be allocated to each, and even the criteria by which to determine whether an individual is a member of a favored group. There is no assurance that a common agreement can be reached, and first the schools, and then the courts, will be buffeted with the competing claims. The University of Washington included Filipinos, but excluded Chinese and Japanese; another school may limit its program to Blacks, or to Blacks and Chicanos. Once the Court sanctioned racial preferences such as these, it could not then wash its hands of the matter, leaving it entirely in the discretion of the school, for then we would have effectively overruled *Sweatt* v. *Painter,* 339 U.S. 629, and allowed imposition of a "zero" allocation.[19] But what standard is the Court to apply

---

19. *Sweatt* held that a State could not justify denying a black admission to its regular law school by creating a new law school for blacks. We held that the new law school did not meet the requirements of "equality" set forth in *Plessy* v. *Ferguson,* 163 U.S. 537.

when a rejected applicant of Japanese ancestry brings suit to require the University of Washington to extend the same privileges to his group? The committee might conclude that the population of Washington is now 2% Japanese, and that Japanese also constitute 2% of the Bar, but that had they not been handicapped by a history of discrimination, Japanese would now constitute 5% of the Bar, or 20%. Or alternatively the Court could attempt to assess how grievously each group has suffered from discrimination, and allocate proportions accordingly; if that were the standard the current University of Washington policy would almost surely fall, for there is no western State which can claim that it has always treated Japanese and Chinese in a fair and evenhanded manner. See, *e.g., Yick Wo* v. *Hopkins,* 118 U.S. 356; *Terrace* v. *Thompson,* 263 U.S. 197; *Oyama* v. *California,* 332 U.S. 633. This Court has not sustained a racial classification since the wartime cases of *Korematsu* v. *United States,* 323 U.S. 214 (1944), and *Hirabayashi* v. *United States,* 320 U.S. 81 (1943), involving curfews and and relocations imposed upon Japanese-Americans.[20]

Nor obviously will the problem be solved if next year the law school included only Japanese and Chinese, for then Norwegians and Swedes, the Poles and the Italians, the Puerto Ricans and the Hungarians, and all other groups which form this diverse Nation would have just complaints.

The key to the problem is consideration of such applications *in a racially neutral way.* Abolition of the LSAT test would be a start. The invention of substitute tests might be made to get a measure of an applicant's cultural background, perception, ability to analyze, and his or her relation to groups. They are highly subjective, but unlike the LSAT they are not concealed but in the open. A law school is not bound by any legal principle to admit students by mechanical criteria which are insensitive to the potential of such an applicant which may be realized in a more hospitable environment. It will be necessary under such an approach to put more effort into assessing each individual than is required when LSAT scores and undergraduate grades

---

The student, we said, was entitled to "legal education equivalent to that offered by the state to students of other races. Such education is not available to him in a separate law school as offered by the state." 339 U.S., at 635.

20. Those cases involved an exercise of the war power, a great leveller of other rights. Our Navy was sunk at Pearl Harbor and no one knew where the Japanese fleet was. We were advised on oral argument that if the Japanese landed troops on our west coast nothing could stop them west of the Rockies. The military judgment was that, to aid in the prospective defense of the West Coast, the enclaves of Americans of Japanese ancestry should be moved inland, lest the invaders by donning civilian clothes would wreck even more serious havoc on our western ports. The decisions were extreme and went to the verge of war time power; and they have been severely criticized. It is, however, easy in retrospect to denounce what was done, as there actually was no attempted Japanese invasion of our country. While our Joint Chief of Staff was worrying about Japanese soldiers landing on the west coast, they actually were landing in Burma and at Kota Bharu in Malaya. But those making plans for defense of the Nation had no such knowledge and were planning for the worst. Moreover, the day we decided *Korematsu* we also decided *Ex parte Endo,* 323 U.S. 283, holding that while evacuation of the Americans of Japanese ancestry was allowable under extreme war conditions, their detention after evacuation was not. We said:

"A citizen who is concededly loyal presents no problem of espionage or sabotage. Loyalty is a matter of the heart and mind, not of race, creed, or color. He who is loyal is by definition not a spy or a saboteur. When the power to detain is derived from the power to protect the war effort against espionage and sabotage, detention which has no relationship to that objective is unauthorized." *Id.,* at 302.

dominate the selection process. Interviews with the applicant and others who know him is a time-honored test. Some schools currently run summer programs in which potential students who likely would be bypassed under conventional admissions criteria are given the opportunity to try their hand at law courses, and certainly their performance in such programs could be weighed heavily. There is, moreover, no bar to considering an individual's prior achievements in light of the racial discrimination that barred his way, as a factor in attempting to assess his true potential for a successful legal career. Nor is there any bar to considering on an individual basis, rather than according to racial classifications, the likelihood that a particular candidate will more likely employ his legal skills to service communities that are not now adequately represented than will competing candidates. Not every student benefited by such an expanded admissions program would fall into one of the four racial groups involved here, but it is no drawback that other deserving applicants will also get an opportunity they would otherwise have been denied. Certainly such a program would substantially fulfill the law school's interest in giving a more diverse group access to the legal profession. Such a program might be less convenient administratively than simply sorting students by race, but we have never held administrative convenience to justify racial discrimination.

The argument is that a "compelling" state interest can easily justify the racial discrimination that is practiced here. To many "compelling" would give members of one race even more than *pro rata* representation. The public payrolls might then be deluged say with Chicanos because they are as a group the poorest of the poor and need work more than others, leaving desperately poor individual Blacks and whites without employment. By the same token large quotas of blacks or browns could be added to the Bar, waiving examinations required of other groups, so that it would be better racially balanced.[22] The State, however, may not proceed by racial classification to force strict population equivalencies for every group in every occupation, overriding individual preferences. The Equal Protection Clause commands the elimination of racial barriers, not their creation in order to satisfy our theory as to how society ought to be organized. The purpose of the University of Washington

22. In *Johnson* v. *Committee on Examinations,* 407 U.S. 915, we denied certiorari in a case presenting a similar issue. There the petitioner claimed that the bar examiners reconsidered the papers submitted by failing minority applicants whose scores were close to the cutoff point, with the result that some minority applicants were admitted to the Bar although they initially had examination scores lower than those of white applicants who were failed.

As the Arizona Supreme Court denied Johnson admission summarily, in an original proceeding, there were no judicial findings either sustaining or rejecting his factual claims of racial bias, putting the case in an awkward posture for review here. Johnson subsequently brought a civil rights action in Federal District Court, seeking both damages and injunctive relief. The District Court dismissed the action and the Court of Appeals affirmed, holding that the lower federal courts did not have jurisdiction to review the decisions of the Arizona Supreme Court on admissions to the state bar. −F.2d−. Johnson then sought review here and we denied his motion for leave to file a petition for mandamus, prohibition and/or certiorari on February 18, 1974. *Johnson* v. *Wilmer,* 414 U.S.−. Thus in the entire history of the case no court had ever actually sustained Johnson's factual contentions concerning racial bias in the bar examiner's procedures. *DeFunis* thus appears to be the first case here squarely presenting the problem.

cannot be to produce Black lawyers for Blacks, Polish lawyers for Poles, Jewish lawyers for Jews, Irish lawyers for the Irish. It should be to produce good lawyers for Americans and not to place First Amendment barriers against anyone.[23] That is the point at the heart of all our school desegregation cases, from *Brown* v. *Board of Education,* 347 U.S. 483, through *Swann* v. *Charlotte-Mecklenburg Board of Educ.,* 402 U.S. 1. A segregated admissions process creates suggestions of stigma and caste no less than a segregated classroom, and in the end it may produce that result despite its contrary intentions. One other assumption must be clearly disapproved, that Blacks or Browns cannot make it on their individual merit. That is a stamp of inferiority that a State is not permitted to place on any lawyer.

If discrimination based on race is constitutionally permissible when those who hold the reins can come up with "compelling" reasons to justify it, then constitutional guarantees acquire an accordionlike quality. Speech is closely brigaded with action when it triggers a fight, *Chaplinsky* v. *New Hampshire,* 315 U.S. 568, as shouting "fire" in a crowded theatre triggers a riot. It may well be that racial strains, racial susceptibility to certain diseases, racial sensitiveness to environmental conditions that other races do not experience may in an extreme situation justify differences in racial treatment that no fairminded person would call "invidious" discrimination. Mental ability is not in the category. All races can compete fairly at all professional levels. So far as race is concerned, any state sponsored preference to one race over another in that competition is in my view "invidious" and violative of the Equal Protection Clause.

The problem tendered by this case is important and crucial to the operation of our constitutional system; and educators must be given leeway. It may well be that a whole congeries of applicants in the marginal group defy known methods of selection. Conceivably, an admissions committee might conclude that a selection by lot of say the last 20 seats is the only fair solution. Courts are not educators; their expertise is limited; and our task ends with the inquiry whether, judged by the main purpose of the Equal Protection Clause—the protection against racial discrimination[24]—there has been an "invidious" discrimination.

We would have a different case if the suit were one to displace the applicant who was chosen in lieu of DeFunis. What the record would show con-

23. Underlying all cultural background tests are potential ideological issues that have plagued bar associations and the courts. *In re Summers,* 325 U.S. 561, involved the denial of the practice of law to a man who could not conscientiously bear arms. The vote against him was five to four. *Konigsberg* v. *State Bar,* 353 U.S. 252, followed, after remand, by *Konigsberg* v. *State Bar,* 366 U.S. 36, resulted in barring one from admission to a state bar because of his refusal to answer questions concerning Communist Party membership. He, too, was excluded five to four. *Schware* v. *Board of Bar Examiners,* 353 U.S. 232, was, however, admitted to practice even though he had about 10 years earlier been a member of the Communist Party. But in *In re Anastaplo,* 366 U.S. 82, a five-to-four decision barred a man from admission to a state bar not because he invoked the Fifth Amendment when asked about membership in the Communist Party but because he asserted that the First Amendment protected him from that inquiry, *Baird* v. *State Bar of Arizona,* 401 U.S. 1, held by a divided vote that a person could not be kept out of the state bar for refusing to answer whether he had ever been a member of the Communist Party; and *In re Stolar,* 401 U.S. 23.

24. See *Slaughter House Cases,* 16 Wall. 36, 81.

cerning his potentials would have to be considered and weighed. The educational decision, provided proper guidelines were used, would reflect an expertise that courts should honor. The problem is not tendered here because the physical facilities were apparently adequate to take DeFunis in addition to the others. My view is only that I cannot say by the tests used and applied he was invidiously discriminated against because of his race.

I cannot conclude that the admissions procedure of the Law School of the University of Washington that excluded DeFunis is violative of the Equal Protection Clause of the Fourteenth Amendment. The judgment of the Washington Supreme Court should be vacated and the case remanded for a new trial.

2. Since Justice Douglas agrees with the Washington Supreme Court that "the minority admissions program is certainly not benign with respect to nonminority students who are displaced by it," how could he have reached the result he did, and written the opinion for the majority, in *Kahn v. Shevin, supra* p. 104? Stated differently, was the preferential tax exemption at issue in *Kahn* "benign" with respect to widowers who were denied such an exemption?

3. Is Justice Douglas's insistence in *DeFunis* upon taking account of individual attributes of "minority" law school applicants, while categorically rejecting the right of a state institution to grant blanket preferential treatment to them based upon race, reconcilable with the result in *Kahn* approving blanket preferences to widows regardless of their actual financial situations and of the actual financial situations of widowers in Florida?

4. What kind of equal-protection test would Justice Douglas apply in *DeFunis?* Compare his test in *Kahn,* p. 106 *supra.* If they differ, how can this be explained?

5. Are similar preferential admissions needed or desirable for women students?

6. If the United States Supreme Court, when it confronts the merits, ultimately holds that a preferential admissions policy for women students *(cf. Kahn v. Shevin, supra)* does not violate the Equal Protection Clause, would the same result necessarily obtain under the Equal Rights Amendment? *Cf.* Testimony of Professor Thomas Emerson, p. 544 of main volume.

7. Following *DeFunis,* the United States Supreme Court unanimously upheld a federal statute, 25 U.S.C. § 472, which required an employment preference for qualified Indians over non-Indians for certain jobs within the federal Bureau of Indian Affairs. Morton v. Mancari,   U.S.   , 94 S.Ct. 2474, 41 L.Ed.2d 290, 42 U.S.L.W. 4933 (1974). In *Mancari,* the Court first held that the earlier statutory preference for Indians was not repealed by the Equal Employment Opportunity Act of 1972. It then examined the constitutional issue as follows:

> We still must decide whether, as the appellees contend, the preference constitutes invidious racial discrimination in violation of the Due Process Clause of the Fifth Amendment. *Bolling* v. *Sharpe,* 347 U. S. 497 (1954). The District Court, while pretermitting this issue, said, "[W]e could well hold that the statute must fail on constitutional grounds." 359 F. Supp., at 591.
>
> Resolution of the instant issue turns on the unique legal status of Indian tribes under federal law and upon the plenary power of Congress, based on a

history of treaties and the assumption of a "guardian-ward" status, to legislate on behalf of federally-recognized Indian tribes. The plenary power of Congress to deal with the special problems of Indians is drawn both explicitly and implicitly from the Constitution itself. Article I, § 8, cl. 3, provides Congress with the power to "regulate Commerce . . . with the Indian Tribes," and thus, to this extent, singles Indians out as a proper subject for separate legislation. Article II, § 2, cl. 2, gives the President the power, by and with the advice and consent of the Senate, to make treaties. This has often been the source of the Government's power to deal with the Indian tribes. The Court has described the origin and nature of the special relationship:

> "In the exercise of the war and treaty powers, the United States overcame the Indians and took possession of their lands, sometimes by force, leaving them an uneducated, helpless and dependent people, needing protection against the selfishness of others and their own improvidence. Of necessity, the United States assumed the duty of furnishing that protection, and with it the authority to do all that was required to perform that obligation and to prepare the Indians to take their place as independent, qualified members of the modern body politic." *Board of County Comm'rs* v. *Seber*, 318 U. S. 705, 715 (1943).

See also *United States* v. *Kayama*, 118 U. S. 375, 383-384 (1886).

Literally every piece of legislation dealing with Indian tribes and reservations, and certainly all legislation dealing with the BIA, single out for special treatment a constituency of tribal Indians living on or near reservations. If these laws, derived from historical relationships and explicitly designed to help only Indians, were deemed invidious racial discrimination, an entire Title of the United States Code (25 U. S. C.) would be effectively erased and the solemn commitment of the Government toward the Indians would be jeopardized. See *Simmons* v. *Eagle Seelatsee*, 244 F. Supp. 808, 814 n. 13 (ED Wash. 1965), aff'd, 384 U. S. 209 (1966).

It is in this historical and legal context that the constitutional validity of the Indian preference is to be determined. As discussed above, Congress in 1934 determined that proper fulfillment of its trust required turning over to the Indians a greater control of their own destinies. The overly paternalistic approach of prior years had proved both exploitative and destructive of Indian interests. Congress was united in the belief that institutional changes were required. An important part of the Indian Reorganization Act was the preference provision here at issue.

Contrary to the characterization made by appellees, this preference does not constitute "racial discrimination." Indeed, it is not even a "racial" preference.[24] Rather, it is an employment criterion reasonably designed to further

---

24. The preference is not directed towards a "racial" group consisting of "Indians"; instead, it applies only to members of "federally recognized" tribes. This operates to exclude many individuals who are racially to be classified as "Indians." In this sense, the pref-

the cause of Indian self-government and to make the BIA more responsive to the needs of its constituent groups. It is directed to participation by the governed in the governing agency. The preference is similar in kind to the constitutional requirement that a United States Senator, when elected, be "an Inhabitant of that State for which he shall be chosen," Art. I, § 3, cl. 3, or that a member of a city council reside within the city governed by the council. Congress has sought only to enable the BIA to draw more heavily from among the constituent group in staffing its projects, all of which, either directly or indirectly, affect the lives of tribal Indians. The preference, as applied, is granted to Indians not as a discrete racial group, but, rather, as members of quasi-sovereign tribal entities whose lives and activities are governed by the BIA in a unique fashion. See n. 24, *supra.* In the sense that there is no other group of people favored in this manner, the legal status of the BIA is truly *sui generis.*[25] Furthermore, the preference applies only to employment in the Indian service. The preference does not cover any other government agency or activity, and we need not consider the obviously more difficult question that would be presented by a blanket exemption for Indians from all civil service examinations. Here, the preference is reasonably and directly related to a legitimate, nonracially based goal. This is the principal characteristic that generally is absent from proscribed forms of racial discrimination.

On numerous occasions this Court specifically has upheld legislation that singles out Indians for particular and special treatment. See, *e. g., Board of County Comm'rs* v. *Seber,* 318 U. S. 705 (1943) (federally granted tax immunity); *McClanahan* v. *Arizona State Tax Comm'n,* 411 U. S. 164 (1973) (same); *Simmons* v. *Eagle Seelatsee,* 384 U. S. 209 (1966), affirming, 244 F. Supp. 808 (ED Wash. 1965) (statutory definition of tribal membership, with resulting interest in trust estate); *Williams* v. *Lee,* 358 U. S. 217 (1959) (tribal courts and their jurisdiction over reservation affairs). Cf. *Morton* v. *Ruiz,* – U. S. – (1974) (federal welfare benefits for Indians "on or near" reservations). This unique legal status is of long standing, see *Cherokee Nation* v. *Georgia,* 5 Pet. 1 (1831); *Worcester* v. *Georgia,* 6 Pet. 515 (1832), and its sources are diverse. See, generally, U. S. Dept. of Interior, Federal Indian Law (1958); Comment, The Indian Battle for Self-Determination, 58 Cal. L. Rev.

---

erence is political rather than racial in nature. The eligibility criteria appear in 44 BIAM 335, 3.1:

"1 Policy—An Indian has preference in appointment in the Bureau. To be eligible for preference in appointment, promotion, and training, an individual must be one-fourth or more degree Indian blood and be a member of a Federally-recognized tribe. It is the policy for promotional consideration that where two or more candidates who meet the established qualification requirements are available for filling a vacancy, if one of them is an Indian, he shall be given preference in filling the vacancy. In accordance with the policy statement approved by the Secretary, the Com-

missioner may grant exceptions to this policy by approving the selection and appointment of non-Indians, when he considers it in the best interest of the Bureau.

"This program does not restrict the right of management to fill positions by methods other than through promotion. Positions may be filled by transfers, reassignment, reinstatement, or initial appointment." App. 92.

25. Senator Wheeler described the BIA as "an entirely different service from anything else in the United States." Hearings before the Senate Committee on Indian Affairs on S. 2755 and S. 3645 (Part 2), 73d Cong., 2d Sess., 256 (1934).

445 (1970). As long as the special treatment can be tied rationally to the fulfillment of Congress' unique obligation toward the Indians, such legislative judgments will not be disturbed. Here, where the preference is reasonable and rationally designed to further Indian self-government, we cannot say that Congress' classification violates due process.

Does the above indicate how the Court will rule, when it finally confronts the merits, on a preferential hiring policy for racial or ethnic minorities, or for women, designed to redress the effects of past discrimination by: (a) the individual employer involved; (b) society at large?

EE. DUE PROCESS ONCE AGAIN

Cleveland Board of Education v. LaFleur
United States Supreme Court, 1974
U.S.   , 94 S.Ct. 791, 39 L.Ed.2d 52

MR. JUSTICE STEWART delivered the opinion of the Court.

The respondents in No. 72-777 and the petitioner in No. 72-1129 are female public school teachers. During the 1970-1971 school year, each informed her local school board that she was pregnant; each was compelled by a mandatory maternity leave rule to quit her job without pay several months before the expected birth of her child. These cases call upon us to decide the constitutionality of the school boards' rules.

I

Jo Carol LaFleur and Ann Elizabeth Nelson, the respondents in No. 72-777, are junior high school teachers employed by the Board of Education of Cleveland, Ohio. Pursuant to a rule first adopted in 1952, the school board requires every pregnant school teacher to take a maternity leave without pay, beginning five months before the expected birth of her child. Application for such leave must be made no later than two weeks prior to the date of departure. A teacher on maternity leave is not allowed to return to work until the beginning of the next regular school semester which follows the date when her child attains the age of three months. A doctor's certificate attesting to the health of the teacher is a prerequisite to return; an additional physical examination may be required. The teacher on maternity leave is not promised re-employment after the birth of the child; she is merely given priority to reassignment to a position for which she is qualified. Failure to comply with the mandatory maternity leave provisions is grounds for dismissal.

Neither Mrs. LaFleur nor Mrs. Nelson wished to take an unpaid maternity leave; each wanted to continue teaching until the end of the school year. Because of the mandatory maternity leave rule, however, each was required to leave her job in

March of 1971. The two women then filed separate suits in the United States District Court for the Northern District of Ohio under 42 U.S.C. § 1983, challenging the constitutionality of the maternity leave rule. The District Court tried the cases together, and rejected the plaintiffs' arguments. 326 F. Supp. 1208. A divided panel of the United States Court of Appeals for the Sixth Circuit reversed, finding the Cleveland rules in violation of the Equal Protection Clause of the Fourteenth Amendment. 465 F.2d 1184.

The petitioner in No. 72-1129, Susan Cohen, was employed by the School Board of Chesterfield County, Virginia. That school board's maternity leave regulation requires that a pregnant teacher leave work at least four months prior to the expected birth of her child. Notice in writing must be given to the school board at least six months prior to the expected birth date. A teacher on maternity leave is declared re-eligible for employment when she submits written notice from a physician that she is physically fit for re-employment, and when she can give assurances that care of the child will cause minimal interferences with her job responsibilities. The teacher is guaranteed re-employment no later than the first day of the school year following the date upon which she is declared re-eligible.

Mrs. Cohen informed the Chesterfield County School Board in November 1970, that she was pregnant and expected the birth of her child about April 28, 1971. She initially requested that she be permitted to continue teaching until April 1, 1971. The school board rejected the request, as it did Mrs. Cohen's subsequent suggestion that she be allowed to teach until January 21, 1971, the end of the first school semester. Instead, she was required to leave her teaching job on December 18, 1970. She subsequently filed this suit under 42 U.S.C. § 1983 in the United States District Court for the Eastern District of Virginia. The District Court held that the school board regulation violates the Equal Protection Clause, and granted appropriate relief. 326 F. Supp. 1159. A divided panel of the Fourth Circuit affirmed, but, on rehearing *en banc,* the Court of Appeals upheld the constitutionality of the challenged regulation in a 4-3 decision. 474 F.2d 395.

We granted certiorari in both cases, 411 U.S. 947, in order to resolve the conflict between the Courts of Appeals regarding the constitutionality of such mandatory maternity leave rules for public school teachers.[8]

---

8. The practical impact of our decision in the present cases may have been somewhat lessened by several recent developments. At the time that the teachers in these cases were placed on maternity leave, Title VII of the Civil Rights Act of 1964, 42 U.S.C. § 2000e *et seq.,* did not apply to state agencies and educational institutions. 42 U.S.C. §§ 2000e-1 and 2000e(b) (1970). On March 27, 1972, however, the Equal Employment Act of 1972 amended Title VII to withdraw those exemptions. Pub. L. 92-261; 86 Stat. 103. Shortly thereafter, the Equal Employment Opportunity Commission promulgated guidelines providing that a mandatory leave or termination policy for pregnant women presumptively violates Title VII. 29 CFR § 1604.10, 37 Fed. Reg. 6837. While the statutory amendments and the administrative regulations are of course inapplicable to the cases now before us, they will affect like suits in the future.

In addition, a number of other federal agencies have promulgated regulations similar to those of the Equal Employment Opportunity Commission, forbidding discrimination against pregnant workers with regard to sick leave policies. See *e.g.,* 5 CFR § 630.401(b) (Civil Service Commission); 41 CFR § 60-20.3(g) (Office of Federal Contract Compliance). See generally Koontz, Childbirth and Child Rearing Leave: Job-Related Benefits, 17 N.Y.L.F. 480, 487-490; Comment, Love's Labors Lost: New Conceptions of Maternity Leaves, 7 Harv. Civ. Rights-Civ. Lib. L. Rev. 260, 280-281. We of course express no opinion as to the validity of any of these regulations.

II

This Court has long recognized that freedom of personal choice in matters of marriage and family life is one of the liberties protected by the Due Process Clause of the Fourteenth Amendment. *Roe* v. *Wade,* 410 U.S. 113; *Loving* v. *Virginia,* 388 U.S. 1, 12; *Griswold* v. *Connecticut,* 381 U.S. 479; *Pierce* v. *Society of Sisters,* 268 U.S. 510; *Meyer* v. *Nebraska,* 262 U.S. 390. See also *Prince* v. *Massachusetts,* 321 U.S. 158; *Skinner* v. *Oklahoma,* 316 U.S. 535. As we noted in *Eisenstadt* v. *Baird,* 405 U.S. 438, 453, there is a right "to be free from unwarranted governmental intrusion into matters so fundamentally affecting a person as the decision whether to bear or beget a child."

By acting to penalize the pregnant teacher for deciding to bear a child, overly restrictive maternity leave regulations can constitute a heavy burden on the exercise of these protected freedoms. Because public school maternity leave rules directly affect "one of the basic civil rights of man," *Skinner* v. *Oklahoma, supra,* at 541, the Due Process Clause of the Fourteenth Amendment requires that such rules must not needlessly, arbitrarily, or capriciously impinge upon this vital area of a teacher's constitutional liberty. The question before us in these cases is whether the interests advanced in support of the rules of the Cleveland and Chesterfield County School Boards can justify the particular procedures they have adopted.

The school boards in these cases have offered two essentially overlapping explanations for their mandatory maternity leave rules. First, they contend that the firm cut-off dates are necessary to maintain continuity of classroom instruction, since advance knowledge of when a pregnant teacher must leave facilitates the finding and hiring of a qualified substitute. Secondly, the school boards seek to justify their maternity rules by arguing that at least some teachers become physically incapable of adequately performing certain of their duties during the latter part of pregnancy. By keeping the pregnant teacher out of the classroom during these final months, the maternity leave rules are said to protect the health of the teacher and her unborn child, while at the same time assuring that students have a physically capable instructor in the classroom at all times.[9]

It cannot be denied that continuity of instruction is a significant and legitimate educational goal. Regulations requiring pregnant teachers to provide early notice of their condition to school authorities undoubtedly facilitate administrative planning

---

9. The records in these cases suggest that the maternity leave regulations may have originally been inspired by other, less weighty, considerations. For example, Dr. Mark C. Schinnerer, who served as Superintendent of Schools in Cleveland at the time the leave rule was adopted testified in the District Court that the rule had been adopted in part to save pregnant teachers from embarrassment at the hands of giggling schoolchildren; the cut-off date at the end of the fourth month was chosen because this was when the teacher "began to show." Similarly, at least several members of the Chesterfield County School Board thought a mandatory leave rule was justified in order to insulate schoolchildren from the sight of conspicuously pregnant women. One member of the school board thought that it was "not good for the school system" for students to view pregnant teachers, "because some of the kids say, my teacher swallowed a watermelon, things like that."

The school boards have not concluded in this Court that these considerations can serve as a legitimate basis for a rule requiring pregnant women to leave work; we thus note the comments only to illustrate the possible role of outmoded taboos in the adoption of the rules. Cf. *Green* v. *Waterford Board of Education,* 473 F.2d 629, 635 (CA2) ("Whatever may have been the reaction in Queen Victoria's time, pregnancy is no longer a dirty word.").

toward the important objective of continuity. But, as the Court of Appeals for the Second Circuit noted in *Green* v. *Waterford Board of Education,* 472 F.2d 629, 635:

> "Where a pregnant teacher provides the Board with a date certain for commencement of leave, however, that value [continuity] is preserved; an arbitrary leave date set at the end of the fifth month is no more calculated to facilitate a planned and orderly transition between the teacher and a substitute than is a date fixed closer to confinement. Indeed, the latter . . . would afford the Board more, not less, time to procure a satisfactory long-term substitute." (Footnote omitted.)

Thus, while the advance notice provisions in the Cleveland and Chesterfield County rules are wholly rational and may well be necessary to serve the objective of continuity of instruction, the absolute requirements of termination at the end of the fourth or fifth month of pregnancy are not. Were continuity the only goal, cutoff dates much later during pregnancy would serve as well or better than the challenged rules, providing that ample advance notice requirements were retained. Indeed, continuity would seem just as well attained if the teacher herself were allowed to choose the date upon which to commence her leave, at least so long as the decision were required to be made and notice given of it well in advance of the date selected.[10]

In fact, since the fifth or sixth months of pregnancy will obviously begin at different times in the school year for different teachers, the present Cleveland and Chesterfield County rules may serve to hinder attainment of the very continuity objectives that they are purportedly designed to promote. For example, the beginning of the fifth month of pregnancy for both Mrs. LaFleur and Mrs. Nelson occurred during March of 1971. Both were thus required to leave work with only a few months left in the school year, even though both were fully willing to serve through the end of the term.[11] Similarly, if continuity were the only goal, it seems ironic that the Chesterfield County rule forced Mrs. Cohen to leave work in mid-December 1970 rather than at the end of the semester in January, as she requested.

We thus conclude that the arbitrary cut-off dates embodied in the mandatory leave rules before us have no rational relationship to the valid state interest of preserving continuity of instruction. As long as the teacher is required to give substantial advance notice of her condition, the choice of firm dates later in pregnancy would serve the boards' objectives just as well, while imposing a far lesser burden on the women's exercise of constitutionally protected freedom.

The question remains as to whether the fifth and sixth month cut-off dates can be justified on the other ground advanced by the school boards—the necessity of

---

10. It is of course possible that either premature childbirth or complications in the later stages of pregnancy might upset even the most careful plans of the teacher, the substitute, and the school board. But there is nothing in these records to indicate that such emergencies could not be handled, as are all others, through the normal use of the emergency substitute teacher process. See *Green* v. *Waterford Board of Education,* 473 F.2d, at 635-636.

11. Indeed, it is somewhat difficult to view the Cleveland mandatory leave rule as seriously furthering the goal of continuity, since the rules require only two weeks' advance notice before the leave is to commence.

keeping physically unfit teachers out of the classroom. There can be no doubt that such an objective is perfectly legitimate, both on educational and safety grounds. And, despite the plethora of conflicting medical testimony in these cases, we can assume *arguendo* that at least some teachers become physically disabled from effectively performing their duties during the latter stages of pregnancy.

The mandatory termination provisions of the Cleveland and Chesterfield County rules surely operate to insulate the classroom from the presence of potentially incapacitated pregnant teachers. But the question is whether the rules sweep too broadly. See *Shelton* v. *Tucker,* 364 U.S. 479. That question must be answered in the affirmative, for the provisions amount to a conclusive presumption that every pregnant teacher who reaches the fifth or sixth month of pregnancy is physically incapable of continuing. There is no individualized determination by the teacher's doctor—or the school board's—as to any particular teacher's ability to continue at her job. The rules contain an irrebuttable presumption of physical incompetency, and that presumption applies even when the medical evidence as to an individual woman's physical status might be wholly to the contrary.

As the Court noted last Term in *Vlandis* v. *Kline,* 412 U.S. 441, 446, "permanent irrebuttable presumptions have long been disfavored under the Due Process Clauses of the Fifth and Fourteenth Amendments." In *Vlandis,* the Court declared unconstitutional, under the Due Process Clause, a Connecticut statute mandating an irrebuttable presumption of nonresidency for the purposes of qualifying for reduced tuition rates at a state university. We said in that case, 412 U.S., at 452:

> "[I]t is forbidden by the Due Process Clause to deny an individual the resident rates on the basis of a permanent and irrebuttable presumption of non-residence, when that presumption is not necessarily or universally true in fact, and when the state has reasonable alternative means of making the crucial determination."

Similarly, in *Stanley* v. *Illinois,* 405 U.S. 645, the Court held that an Illinois statute containing an irrebuttable presumption that unmarried fathers are incompetent to raise their children violated the Due Process Clause. Because of the statutory presumption, the State took custody of all illegitimate children upon the death of the mother, without allowing the father to attempt to prove his parental fitness. As the Court put the matter:

> "It may be, as the State insists, that most unmarried fathers are unsuitable and neglectful parents. It may also be that Stanley is such a parent and that his children should be placed in other hands. But all unmarried fathers are not in this category; some are wholly suited to have custody of their children." *Id.,* at 654 (footnotes omitted).

Hence, we held that the State could not conclusively presume that any particular unmarried father was unfit to raise his child; the Due Process Clause required a more individualized determination. See also *United States Dept. of Agriculture* v. *Murry,* 413 U.S. 508; *id.,* at 514-517 (concurring opinion); *Bell* v. *Burson,* 402 U.S. 535; *Carrington* v. *Rash,* 380 U.S. 89.

These principles control our decision in the cases before us. While the medical experts in these cases differed on many points, they unanimously agreed on one— the ability of any particular pregnant woman to continue at work past any fixed time in her pregnancy is very much an individual matter. Even assuming *arguendo* that there are some women who would be physically unable to work past the particular cut-off dates embodied in the challenged rules, it is evident that there are large numbers of teachers who are fully capable of continuing work for longer than the Cleveland and Chesterfield County regulations will allow. Thus, the conclusive presumption embodied in these rules, like that in *Vlandis,* is neither "necessarily nor universally true," and is violative of the Due Process Clause.

The school boards have argued that the mandatory termination dates serve the interest of administrative convenience, since there are many instances of teacher pregnancy, and the rules obviate the necessity of case-by-case determinations. Certainly, the boards have an interest in devising prompt and efficient procedures to achieve their legitimate objectives in this area. But, as the Court stated in *Stanley* v. *Illinois, supra,* at 656:

> "[T]he Constitution recognizes higher values than speed and efficiency. Indeed, one might fairly say of the Bill of Rights in general, and the Due Process Clause in particular, that they were designed to protect the fragile values of a vulnerable citizenry from the overbearing concern for efficiency and efficacy that may characterize praiseworthy government officials no less, and perhaps more, than mediocre ones." (Footnote omitted.)

While it might be easier for the school boards to conclusively presume that all pregnant women are unfit to teach past the fourth or fifth month or even the first month, of pregnancy, administrative convenience alone is insufficient to make valid what otherwise is a violation of due process of law.[13] The Fourteenth Amendment requires the school boards to employ alternative administrative means, which do not so broadly infringe upon basic constitutional liberty, in support of their legitimate goals.[14]

We conclude, therefore, that neither the necessity for continuity of instruction nor the state interest in keeping physically unfit teachers out of the classroom can justify the sweeping mandatory leave regulations that the Cleveland and Chester-

13. This is not to say that the only means for providing appropriate protection for the rights of pregnant teachers is an individualized determination in each case and in every circumstance. We are not dealing in these cases with maternity leave regulations requiring a termination of employment at some firm date during the last few weeks of pregnancy. We therefore have no occasion to decide whether such regulations might be justified by considerations not presented in these records—for example, widespread medical consensus about the "disabling" effect of pregnancy on a teacher's job performance during these latter days, or evidence showing that such firm cutoffs were the only reasonable method of avoiding the possibility of labor beginning while some teacher was in the classroom, or proof that adequate substitutes could not be procured without at least some minimal lead time and certainty as to the dates upon which their employment was to begin.

14. The school boards have available to them reasonable alternative methods of keeping physically unfit teachers out of the classroom. For example, they could require the pregnant teacher to submit to medical examination by a school board physician, or simply require each teacher to submit a current certification from her obstetrician as to her ability to continue work. Indeed, when evaluating the physical ability of a teacher to *return* to work, each school board in this case relies upon precisely such procedures. See nn. 1 and 5 *supra;* see also text *infra,* at ____.

field County School Boards have adopted. While the regulations no doubt represent a good-faith attempt to achieve a laudable goal, they cannot pass muster under the Due Process Clause of the Fourteenth Amendment, because they employ irrebuttable presumptions that unduly penalize a female teacher for deciding to bear a child.

III

In addition to the mandatory termination provisions, both the Cleveland and Chesterfield County rules contain limitations upon a teacher's eligibility to return to work after giving birth. Again, the school boards offer two justifications for the return rules—continuity of instruction and the desire to be certain that the teacher is physically competent when she returns to work. As is the case with the leave provisions, the question is not whether the school board's goals are legitimate, but rather whether the particular means chosen to achieve those objectives unduly infringe upon the teachers' constitutional liberty.

Under the Cleveland rule, the teacher is not eligible to return to work until the beginning of the next regular school semester following the time when her child attains the age of three months. A doctor's certificate attesting to the teacher's health is required before return; an additional physical examination may be required at the option of the school board.

The respondents in No. 72-777 do not seriously challenge either the medical requirements of the Cleveland rule or the policy of limiting eligibility to return to the next semester following birth. The provisions concerning a medical certificate or supplemental physical examination are narrowly drawn methods of protecting the school board's interest in teacher fitness; these requirements allow an individualized decision as to teacher's condition, and thus avoid the pitfalls of the presumptions inherent in the leave rules. Similarly, the provision limiting eligibility to return to the semester following delivery is a precisely drawn means of serving the school board's interest in avoiding unnecessary changes in classroom personnel during any one school term.

The Cleveland rule, however, does not simply contain these reasonable medical and next-semester eligibility provisions. In addition, the school board requires the mother to wait until her child reaches the age of three months before the return rules begin to operate. The school boards have offered no reasonable justification for this supplemental limitation, and we can perceive none. To the extent that the three months provision reflects the school board's thinking that no mother is fit to return until that point in time, it suffers from the same constitutional deficiences that plague the irrebuttable presumption in the termination rules.[15] The presump-

---

15. It is clear that the factual hypothesis of such a presumption—that no mother is physically fit to return to work until her child reaches the age of three months—is neither necessarily nor universally true. See R. Benson, Handbook of Obstetrics and Gynecology 209 (4th ed. 1971) (patient may return to "full activity or employment" if course of progress up to fourth or fifth week is normal). Cf. Comment, Love's Labor Lost: New Conceptions of Maternity Leaves, 7 Harv. Civ. Rights-Civ. Lib. L. Rev. 260, 262 n. 11, 287 n. 145.

Of course, it may be that the Cleveland rule is based upon another theory—that new mothers are too busy with their children within the first three months to allow a return to work. Viewed in that light, the rule remains a conclusive presumption, whose underlying factual assumptions can hardly be said to be universally valid.

tion, moreover, is patently unnecessary, since the requirement of a physician's certificate or a medical examination fully protects the school's interests in this regard. And finally, the three month provision simply has nothing to do with continuity of instruction, since the precise point at which the child will reach the relevant age will obviously occur at a different point throughout the school year for each teacher.

Thus, we conclude that the Cleveland return rule, insofar as it embodies the three months age provision, is wholly arbitrary and irrational, and hence violates the Due Process Clause of the Fourteenth Amendment. The age limitation serves no legitimate state interest, and unnecessarily penalizes the female teacher for asserting her right to bear children.

We perceive no such constitutional infirmities in the Chesterfield County rule. In that school system, the teacher becomes eligible for reemployment upon submission of a medical certificate from her physician; return to work is guaranteed no later than the beginning of the next school year following the eligibility determination.[16] The medical certificate is both a reasonable and narrow method of protecting the school board's interest in teacher fitness, while the possible deferring of return until the next school year serves the goal of preserving continuity of instruction. In short, the Chesterfield County rule manages to serve the legitimate state interests here without employing unnecessary presumptions that broadly burden the exercise of protected constitutional liberty.

IV

For the reasons stated, we hold that the mandatory termination provisions of the Cleveland and Chesterfield County maternity regulations violate the Due Process Clause of the Fourteenth Amendment, because of their use of unwarranted conclusive presumptions that seriously burden the exercise of protected constitutional liberty. For similar reasons, we hold the three months' provision of the Cleveland return rule unconstitutional.

Accordingly, the judgment in No. 72-777 is affirmed; the judgment in No. 72-1129 is reversed, and the case is remanded to the Court of Appeals for the Fourth Circuit for further proceedings consistent with this opinion.

It is so ordered.

MR. JUSTICE DOUGLAS concurs in the result.

MR. JUSTICE POWELL, concurring in the result.

I concur in the Court's result, but I am unable to join its opinion. In my view

---

16. The Virginia rule also requires that the teacher give assurances that care of the child will not unduly interfere with her job duties. While such a requirement has within it the potential for abuse, there is no evidence on this record that the assurances required here are anything more than those routinely sought by employers from prospective employees—that the worker is willing to devote full attention to job duties. Nor is there any evidence in this record that the school authorities do not routinely accept the woman's assurances of her ability to return.

these cases should not be decided on the ground that the mandatory maternity leave regulations impair any right to bear children or create an "irrebuttable presumption." It seems to me that equal protection analysis is the appropriate frame of reference.

These regulations undoubtedly add to the burdens of childbearing. But certainly not every government policy that burdens childbearing violates the Constitution. Limitations on the welfare benefits a family may receive that do not take into account the size of the family illustrate this point. See *Dandridge* v. *Williams,* 397 U.S. 47 1 (1970). Undoubtedly Congress could, as another example, constitutionally seek to discourage excessive population growth by limiting tax deductions for dependents. That would represent an intentional governmental effort to "penalize" childbearing. See *ante,* at 7. The regulations here do not have that purpose. Their deterrent impact is wholly incidental. If some intentional efforts to penalize childbearing are constitutional, and if *Dandridge, supra,* means what I think it does, then certainly these regulations are not invalid as an infringement of any right to procreate.

I am also troubled by the Court's return to the "irrebuttable presumption" line of analysis of *Stanley* v. *Illinois,* 405 U.S. 645 (1972) (POWELL, J., not participating), and *Vlandis* v. *Kline,* 412 U.S. 441 (1973). Although I joined the opinion of the Court in *Vlandis* and continue fully to support the result reached there, the present cases have caused me to re-examine the "irrebuttable presumption" rationable. This has led me to the conclusion that the Court should approach that doctrine with extreme care. There is much to what MR. JUSTICE REHNQUIST says in his dissenting opinion, *post,* at _____, about the implications of the doctrine for the traditional legislative power to operate by classification. As a matter of logic, it is difficult to see the terminus of the road upon which the Court has embarked under the banner of "irrebuttable presumptions." If the Court nevertheless uses "irrebuttable presumption" reasoning selectively, the concept at root often will be something else masquerading as a due process doctrine. That something else, of course, is the Equal Protection Clause.

These cases present precisely the kind of problem susceptible to treatment by classification. Most school teachers are women, a certain percentage of them are pregnant at any given time, and pregnancy is a normal biological function possessing, in the great majority of cases, a fairly well defined term. The constitutional difficulty is not that the boards attempted to deal with this problem by classification. Rather, it is that the boards chose irrational classifications.

A range of possible school board goals emerge from the cases. Several may be put to one side. The records before us abound with proof that a principal purpose behind the adoption of the regulations was to keep visibly pregnant teachers out of the sight of school children. The boards do not advance this today as a legitimate objective, yet its initial primacy casts a shadow over these cases. Moreover, most of the after-the-fact rationalizations proposed by these boards are unsupported in the records. The boards emphasize teacher absenteeism, classroom discipline, the safety of school children, and the safety of the expectant mother and her unborn child. No doubt these are legitimate concerns. But the boards have failed to demonstrate that these interests are in fact threatened by the continued employment of pregnant teachers.

To be sure, the boards have a legitimate and important interest in fostering continuity of teaching. And, even a normal pregnancy may at some point jeopardize that interest. But the classifications chosen by these boards, so far as we have been shown, are either contraproductive or irrationally overinclusive even with regard to this significant, nonillusory goal. Accordingly, in my opinion these regulations are invalid under rational basis standards of equal protection review.[2]

In speaking of continuity of teaching, the boards are referring in part to their valid interest in reducing the number of times a new teacher is assigned to a given class. It is particularly appropriate to avoid teacher turnover in the middle of a semester, since continuity in teaching approach as well as teacher-pupil relationships are otherwise impaired. That aspect of the Cleveland regulation limiting a teacher's eligibility to return to the classroom to the semester following delivery, which the Court approves, *ante,* at 16, rationally serves this legitimate state interest. But the four and five month prebirth leave periods of the two regulations and the three month post-birth provision of the Cleveland regulation do not. As the Court points out, *ante,* at 10, such cutoff points are more likely to prevent continuity of teaching than to preserve it. Because the cutoff dates occur throughout the school year, they inevitably result in the removal of many capable teachers from the classroom in the middle or near the end of a semester, thus provoking the disruption the boards hope to avoid.

The boards' reference to continuity of teaching also encompasses their need to assure constant classroom coverage by teachers who are up to the task. This interest is obviously legitimate. No one disputes that a school board must concern itself with the physical and emotional capabilities of its teachers. But the objectionable portions of these regulations appear to be bottomed on factually unsupported assumptions about the ability of pregnant teachers to perform their jobs. The overwhelming weight of the medical testimony adduced in these cases is that most teachers undergoing normal pregnancies are quite capable of carrying out their responsibilities until some ill-defined point a short period prior to term. Certainly the boards have made little effort to contradict this conclusion. Thus, it appears that by forcing all pregnant teachers undergoing a normal pregnancy from the classroom so far in advance of term, the regulations compel large numbers of able-bodied teachers to quit work.[3] Once more, such policies inhibit, rather than further, the goal of continuity of teaching. For no apparent reason, they remove teachers from their students and require the use of substitutes.

The boards' reliance on the goal of continuity of teaching also takes into account

2. I do not reach the question whether sex-based classifications invoke strict judicial scrutiny, *e.g, Frontiero* v. *Richardson,* 411 U.S. 677 (1973), or whether these regulations involve sex classifications at all. Whether the challenged aspects of the regulations constitute sex classifications or disability classifications, they must at least rationally serve some legitimate articulated or obvious state interest. While there are indeed some legitimate state interests at stake here, it has not been shown that they are rationally furthered by the challenged portions of these regulations.

3. Teachers who undergo abnormal pregnancies may well be disabled, either temporarily or for a substantial period. But as I read the Court, boards may deal with abnormal pregnancies like any other disability. *Ante,* at 9, n. 10.

their obvious planning needs. Boards must know when pregnant teachers will temporarily cease their teaching responsibilities, so that substitutes may be scheduled to fill the vacancies. And, planning requires both notice of pregnancy and a fixed termination date. It appears, however, that any termination date serves the purpose.[4] The choice of a cutoff date that produces several months of forced unemployment is thus wholly unnecessary to the planning of the boards. Certainly nothing in the records of these cases is the contrary.

For the above reasons, I believe the linkage between the boards' legitimate ends and their chosen means is too attenuated to support those portions of the regulations overturned by the Court. Thus, I concur in the Court's result. But I think it is important to emphasize the degree of latitude the Court, as I read it, has left the boards for dealing with the real and recurrent problems presented by teacher pregnancies. Boards may demand in every case "substantial advance notice of [pregnancy]...." *Ante,* at 10. Subject to certain restrictions, they may require all pregnant teachers to cease teaching "at some firm date during the last few weeks of pregnancy...." *Id.,* at 14, n. 13.[5] The Court further holds that boards may in all cases restrict re-entry into teaching to the outset of the school term following delivery. *Id.,* at 16.

In my opinion, such class-wide rules for pregnant teachers are constitutional under traditional equal protection standards.[6] School boards, confronted with sensitive and widely variable problems of public education, must be accorded latitude in the operation of school systems and in the adoption of rules and regulations of general application. *E.g., San Antonio Independent School District* v. *Rodriguez,* 411 U.S. 1, 42-43 (1973). A large measure of discretion is essential to the effective discharge of the duties vested in these local, often elective, governmental units. My concern with the Court's opinion is that, if carried to logical extremes, the emphasis on individualized treatment is at war with this need for discretion. Indeed, stringent insistence on individualized treatment may be quite impractical in a large school district with thousands of teachers.

But despite my reservations as to the rationale of the majority, I nevertheless conclude that in these cases the gap between the legitimate interests of the boards and the particular means chosen to attain them is too wide. A restructuring generally along the lines indicated in the Court's opinion seems unavoidable. Accordingly, I concur in its result.

4. One may question, however, whether planning needs are well served by the mere two-week gap between notice and departure set forth in the Cleveland regulation. The brief notice the Cleveland board has allowed itself casts some doubt on that board's reliance on planning needs.

5. The Court's language does not specify a particular prebirth cutoff point, and we need not decide that issue, as these boards have attempted to support only four- and five-month dates. In light of the Court's language, however, I would think that a four-week prebirth period would be acceptable. I do not agree with the Court's view of the stringent standards a board must meet to justify a reasonable prebirth cutoff date. See *ante,* at 14, n. 13. Nothing in the Constitution man-

dates the heavy burden of justification the Court has imposed on the boards in this regard. If school boards must base their policies on a "widespread medical consensus..." the "only reasonable method..." for accomplishing a goal, or a demonstration that needed services will otherwise be impossible to obtain, *ibid.,* they may be seriously handicapped in the performance of their duties.

6. As the Court notes, these cases arose prior to the recent amendment extending Tit. VII of the Civil Rights Act of 1964, 42 U.S.C. § 2000e *et seq.* to state agencies and educational institutions. Pub. L. 92-261; 83 Stat. 103. See *ante,* at 5-6, n. 8. Like the Court, I do not address the impact of Tit. VII on mandatory maternity leave regulations.

MR. JUSTICE REHNQUIST, with whom THE CHIEF JUSTICE joins, dissenting.

The Court rests its invalidation of the school regulations involved in these cases on the Due Process Clause of the Fourteenth Amendment, rather than on any claim of sexual discrimination under the Equal Protection Clause of that Amendment. My Brother STEWART thereby enlists the Court in another quixotic engagement in his apparently unending war on irrebuttable presumptions. In this case we are told that although a regulation "requiring a termination of employment at some firm date during the last few weeks of pregnancy" (n. 13, opinion of the Court), might pass muster, the regulations here challenged requiring termination at the end of the fourth or fifth month of pregnancy violate due process of law.

As THE CHIEF JUSTICE pointed out in his dissent last year in *Vlandis* v. *Kline*, 412 U.S. 441, "literally thousands of state statutes create classifications permanent in duration, which are less than perfect, as all legislative classifications are, and might be improved on by individualized determinations. . . ." *Id.,* at 462. Hundreds of years ago in England, before Parliament came to be thought of as a body having general lawmaking power, controversies were determined on an individualized basis without benefit of any general law. Most students of government consider the shift from this sort of determination, made on an *ad hoc* basis by the king's representative, to a relatively uniform body of rules enacted by a body exercising legislative authority, to have been a significant step forward in the achievement of a civilized political society. It seems to me a little late in the day for this Court to weigh in against such an established consensus.

Countless state and federal statutes draw lines such as those drawn by the regulations here which, under the Court's analysis, might well prove to be arbitrary in individual cases. The District of Columbia Code, for example, draws lines with respect to age for several purposes. The Code requires that a person to be eligible to vote be 18 years of age, that a male be 18 and a female be 16 before a valid marriage may be contracted, that alcoholic beverages not be sold to a person under age 21 years, or beer or light wines to any person under the age of 18 years. A resident of the District of Columbia must be 16 years of age to obtain a permit to operate motor vehicle, and the District of Columbia delegate to the United States Congress must be 25 years old. Nothing in the Court's opinion clearly demonstrates why its logic would not equally well sustain a challenge to these laws from a 17-year-old who insists that he is just as well informed for voting purposes as an 18-year-old, from a 20-year-old who insists that he is just as able to carry his liquor as a 21-year-old, or from the numerous other persons who fall on the outside of lines drawn by these and similar statutes.

More closely in point is the jeopardy in which the Court's opinion places longstanding statutes providing for mandatory retirement of government employees. 5 U.S.C. § 8335 provides with respect to Civil Service employees:

"(a) Except as otherwise provided by this section, an employee who becomes seventy years of age and completes fifteen years of service shall be automatically separated from the service. . . ."

It was pointed out by my Brother STEWART only last year in his concurring opinion in *Roe* v. *Wade,* 410 U.S. 113, 169, "The 'liberty' protected by the Due Process Clause of the Fourteenth Amendment covers more than those freedoms explicitly named in the Bill of Rights. See . . . *Truax* v. *Reich,* 239 U.S. 33, 41." In *Truax* v. *Reich,* the Court said:

> "It requires no argument to show that the right to work for a living and the common occupations of the community is of the very essence of the personal freedom and opportunity that it was the purpose of the Amendment to secure." 239 U.S. 33, 41.

Since this right to pursue an occupation is presumably on the same lofty footing as the right of choice in matters of family life, the Court will have to strain valiantly in order to avoid having today's opinion lead to the invalidation of mandatory retirement statutes for governmental employees. In that event federal, state, and local governmental bodies will be remitted to the task, thankless both for them and for the employees involved, of individual determinations of physical impairment and senility.

It has been said before, *Williamson* v. *Lee Optical Co.,* 348 U.S. 483, but it bears repeating here: All legislation involves the drawing of lines, and the drawing of lines necessarily results in particular individuals who are disadvantaged by the line drawn being virtually indistinguishable for many purposes from those individuals who benefit from the legislative classification. The Court's disenchantment with "irrebuttable presumptions," and its preference for "individualized determination," is in the last analysis nothing less than an attack upon the very notion of lawmaking itself.

The lines drawn by the school boards in the city of Cleveland and Chesterfield County in these cases require pregnant teachers to take forced leave at a stage of their pregnancy when medical evidence seems to suggest that a majority of them might well be able to continue teaching without any significant possibility of physical impairment. But so far as I am aware, the medical evidence also suggests that in some cases there may be physical impairment at the stage of pregnancy fastened on by the regulations in question, and that the probability of physical impairment increases as the pregnancy advances. If legislative bodies are to be permitted to draw a general line anywhere short of the delivery room, I can find no judicial standard of measurement which says the ones drawn here were invalid. I therefore dissent.

NOTES

1. Does the result in *LaFleur*—and in *Stanley* v. *Illinois,* p. 288 of main volume— have any bearing on the problem set forth on pp. 527-28 of the main volume?

2. Does Justice Powell, in preferring an equal-protection rationale for the decision, base this on the sex-discriminatory implications of the rules in dispute? Are there sex-discriminatory implications in those rules? What are they?

Page 529. Before "Hearings . . . etc.," insert:

As of May 16, 1974, thirty-three states had ratified the ERA. These included two—Nebraska and Tennessee—that first ratified but then voted to withdraw their earlier ratifications. Whether such withdrawals are effective may become a crucial question if, in 1979, the necessary thirty-eight ratifying state legislatures include any that have done this. What effect should be given to such withdrawals?

In Coleman v. Miller, 307 U.S. 433, 450 (1939), the United States Supreme Court declared:

> [T]he question of the efficacy of ratifications by state legislatures, in the light of previous rejection or attempted withdrawal, should be regarded as a political question pertaining to the political departments, with the ultimate authority in the Congress in the exercise of its control over the promulgation of the adoption of the amendment.

Since the facts in *Coleman* involved only a previous rejection, the Court's reference to a previous withdrawal is clearly dictum. Moreover, in the light of Baker v. Carr, 369 U.S. 186 (1962) and Powell v. McCormick, 395 U.S. 486 (1969), which drastically limited the circumstances under which the "political question" ground for judicial noninterference will succeed, there is a serious question whether, should the supposed situation occur in 1979, the Court would hold that the matter is for Congressional resolution only.

Among other reasons that might impel the Court to conclude that judicial resolution of the question is appropriate are:

    a. Amending the federal constitution is difficult enough—only 26 out of more than 1500 attempts have succeeded—without placing additional hurdles in the ratification process.

    b. If the state legislatures have second thoughts about the earlier ratification amendment, the avenue of repeal is open to them. Compare Amendments XVIII and XXI.

    c. Finally, the cases and congressional practices had developed the rule that "a state could reverse any action rejecting ratification, but once it had acted favorably, its power had expired." Heckman, Ratification of a Constitutional Amendment: Can a State Change Its Mind?, 6 Conn. L. Rev. 28, 33 (1973).

If the Court should rule, when squarely confronted with the problem of the effect to be given to a state's withdrawal of an earlier ratification, that this is a "political question" to be decided by Congress alone, Congress's resolution of the problem is far from predictable. For one thing, Congress, not being a court, is not bound by its precedents. Thus it would not necessarily follow its practice with regard to the XIVth and XVth amendments, both of which were deemed ratified by Congress, though, to make up the required number of ratifying states, some that had purported to withdraw earlier ratifications had to be counted. See article by Heckman, cited above. Moreover, overwhelming U.S. Senate approval and apparent House sympathy toward proposed legislation on the convention method of amending the federal constitution suggest current congressional sentiment is opposed to earlier practices. Specifically, S. 1272, introduced in the First Session of the 93rd Congress, which is a copy of S. 215 approved by an 84-to-0 vote of the Senate in the 92d Congress, provides, in Section 13(a):

(a) Any State may rescind its ratification of a proposed amendment by the same process by which it ratified the proposed amendment, except that no state may rescind when there are existing valid ratifications of such amendments by three-fourths of the States.

If such legislation is enacted, does it necessarily govern instances where amendments have been proposed by Congress, rather than by a constitutional convention? In the light of *Powell v. McCormick, supra,* does Congress have the power to prescribe such a rule? See Note, Proposed Legislation on the Convention Method of Amending the United States Constitution, 85 Harv. L. Rev. 1612, 1637-38 (1972).

Because of such unanswered questions, much may depend on whether the United States Supreme Court ultimately adheres to its dictum in *Coleman v. Miller* that the effectiveness of a state's withdrawal of an earlier ratification is a "political question."

Chapter 9

Sex Roles and Pornography

Page 611. Following note 4, add:

5. In Miller v. California, 413 U.S. 15, 93 S.Ct. 2607, 37 L.Ed.2d 419 (1973), a 5-4 majority of the United States Supreme Court enunciated the latest standards for testing state statutes designed to regulate "obscene" materials. Said Mr. Chief Justice Burger for the majority (93 S.Ct. 2614-20):

"[W]e now confine the permissible scope of such regulation to works which depict or describe sexual conduct. That conduct must be specifically defined by the applicable state law, as written or authoritatively construed. A state offense must also be limited to works which, taken as a whole, appeal to the prurient interest in sex, which portray sexual conduct in a patently offensive way, and which, taken as a whole, do not have serious literary, artistic, political, or scientific value.

The basic guidelines for the trier of fact must be: (a) whether "the average person, applying contemporary community standards" would find that the work, taken as a whole, appeals to the prurient interest, . . . (b) whether the work depicts or describes, in a patently offensive way, sexual conduct specifically defined by the applicable state law, and (c) whether the work, taken as a whole, lacks serious literary, artistic, political, or scientific value. We do not adopt as a constitutional standard the *"utterly* without redeeming social value" test of Memoirs v. Massachusetts, . . . that concept has never commanded the adherence of more than three Justices at one time. . . .[7] If a state law that regulates obscene material is thus limited, as written or construed, the First Amendment values applicable to the States through the Fourteenth Amendment are adequately protected by the ultimate power of appellate courts to conduct an independent review of constitutional claims when necessary. . . .

We emphasize that it is not our function to propose regulatory schemes for the States. That must await their concrete legislative efforts. It is possible, however, to give a few plain examples of what a state statute could define for regulation under the second part (b) of the standard announced in this opinion, *supra:*

(a) Patently offensive representations or descriptions of ultimate sexual acts, normal or perverted, actual or simulated.

(b) Patently offensive representation or descriptions of masturbation, excretory functions, and lewd exhibition of the genitals.

Sex and nudity may not be exploited without limit by films or pictures exhibited or sold in places of public accommodation any more than live sex and nudity can be exhibited or sold without limit in such public places.[8] At a minimum, prurient, patently offensive depiction or description of sexual conduct must have serious literary, artistic, political, or scientific value to merit First Amendment protection. . . .

For example, medical books for the education of physicians and related personnel necessarily use graphic illustrations and descriptions of human anatomy. In resolving the inevitably sensitive questions of fact and law, we must continue to rely on the jury system, accompanied by the safeguards that judges, rules of evidence, presumption of innocence and other protective features provide, as we do with rape, murder and a host of other offenses against society and its individual members. . . .

Under the holdings announced today, no one will be subject to prosecution

7. "A quotation from Voltaire in the flyleaf of a book will not constitutionally redeem an otherwise obscene publication . . ." Kois v. Wisconsin, *supra,* 408 U.S., at 231, 92 S.Ct., at 2246 (1972). See Memoirs v. Massachusetts, *supra,* 383 U.S., at 461, 86 S.Ct., at 999 (1966) (White, J., dissenting). We also reject, as a constitutional standard, the ambiguous concept of "social importance." See *id.,* at 462, 86 S.Ct., at 999 (White, J., dissenting).

8. Although we are not presented here with the problem of regulating lewd public conduct itself, the States have greater power to regulate nonverbal, physical conduct than to suppress depictions or descriptions of the

same behavior. In United States v. O'Brien, 391 U.S. 367, 377, 88 S.Ct. 1673, 1679, 20 L.Ed.2d 672 (1968), a case not dealing with obscenity, the Court held a State regulation of conduct which itself embodied both speech and nonspeech elements to be "sufficiently justified if . . . it furthers an important or substantial government interest; if the government interest is unrelated to the suppression of free expression; and if the incidental restrictions on alleged First Amendment freedoms is no greater than is essential to the furtherance of that interest." See California v. LaRue, 409 U.S. 109, 117-118, 93 S.Ct. 390, 396-397, 34 L.Ed.2d 342 (1972).

for the sale or exposure of obscene materials unless these materials depict or describe patently offensive "hard core" sexual conduct specifically defined by the regulating state law, as written or construed. We are satisfied that these specific prerequisites will provide fair notice to a dealer in such materials that his public and commercial activities may bring prosecution. . . .

It is certainly true that the absence, since *Roth,* of a single majority view of this Court as to proper standards for testing obscenity has placed a strain on both state and federal courts. But today, for the first time since *Roth* was decided in 1957, a majority of this Court has agreed on concrete guidelines to isolate "hard core" pornography from expression protected by the First Amendment. . . .

Under a national Constitution, fundamental First Amendment limitations on the powers of the States do not vary from community to community, but this does not mean that there are, or should or can be, fixed, uniform national standards of precisely what appeals to the "prurient interest" or is "patently offensive." These are essentially questions of fact, and our nation is simply too big and too diverse for this Court to reasonably expect that such standards could be articulated for all 50 States in a single formulation, even assuming the prerequisite consensus exists. When triers of fact are asked to decide whether "the average person, applying contemporary community standards" would consider certain materials "prurient," it would be unrealistic to require that the answer be based on some abstract formulation. The adversary system, with lay jurors as the usual ultimate fact-finders in criminal prosecutions, has historically permitted triers-of-fact to draw on the standards of their community, guided always by limiting instructions on the law. To require a State to structure obscenity proceedings around evidence of a *national* "community standard" would be an exercise in futility.

As noted before, this case was tried on the theory that the California obscenity statute sought to incorporate the tripartite test of *Memoirs.* This, a "national" standard of First Amendment protection enumerated by a plurality of this Court, was correctly regarded at the time of trial as limiting state prosecution under the controlling case law. The jury, however, was explicitly instructed that, in determining whether the "dominant theme of the material as a whole . . . appeals to the prurient interest" and in determining whether the material "goes substantially beyond customary limits of candor and affronts contemporary community standards of decency" it was to apply "contemporary community standards of the State of California." . . .

We conclude that neither the State's alleged failure to offer evidence of "national standards," nor the trial court's charge that the jury consider state community standards, were constitutional errors. Nothing in the First Amendment requires that a jury must consider hypothetical and unascertainable "national standards" when attempting to determine whether certain materials are obscene as a matter of fact. Chief Justice Warren pointedly commented in his dissent in Jacobellis v. Ohio, *supra,* 378 U.S., at 200, 84 S.Ct., at 1685:

"It is my belief that when the Court said in *Roth* that obscenity is to be defined by reference to 'community standards,' it meant community standards—not a national standard, as is sometimes argued. I believe that there is no provable 'national standard'. . . . At all events, this Court has not been able to enunciate one, and it would be unreasonable to expect local courts to divine one."

It is neither realistic nor constitutionally sound to read the First Amendment as requiring that the people of Maine or Mississippi accept public depiction of conduct found tolerable in Las Vegas, or New York City. . . .[13]

People in different States vary in their tastes and attitudes, and this diversity is not to be strangled by the absolutism of imposed uniformity. As the Court made clear in Mishkin v. New York, 383 U.S. 502, 508-509, 86 S.Ct. 958, 963, 16 L.Ed.2d 56 (1966), the primary concern with requiring a jury to apply the standard of "the average person, applying contemporary community standards" is to be certain that, so far as material is not aimed at a deviant group, it will be judged by its impact on an average person, rather than a particularly susceptible or sensitive person—or indeed a totally insensitive one. See Roth v. United States, *supra,* 354 U.S., at 489, 77 S.Ct., at 1311 (1957). Compare the now discredited test in Regina v. Hicklin [1868] L.R. 3 Q.B. 360. We hold the requirement that the jury evaluate the materials with reference to "contemporary standards of the State of California" serves this protective purpose and is constitutionally adequate.

---

13. In Jacobellis v. Ohio, 378 U.S. 184, 84 S.Ct. 1676, 12 L.Ed.2d 793 (1964), two Justices argued that application of "local" community standards would run the risk of preventing dissemination of materials in some places because sellers would be unwilling to risk criminal conviction by testing variations in standards from place to place. *Id.,* 378 U.S., at 193-195, 84 S.Ct., at 1681-1682 (opinion of Brennan, J., joined by Goldberg, J.). The use of "national" standards, however, necessarily implies that materials found tolerable in some places, but not under the "national" criteria, will nevertheless be unavailable where they are acceptable. Thus, in terms of danger to free expression, the potential for suppression seems at least as great in the application of a single nationwide standard as in allowing distribution in accordance with local tastes, a point which Justice Harlan often emphasized. See Roth v. United States, *supra,* 354 U.S., at 506, 77 S.Ct., at 1320 (1957).

Petitioner also argues that adherence to a "national standard" is necessary "in order to avoid unconscionable burdens on the free flow of interstate commerce." As noted before, p. 2611, n. 1, *supra,* the application of domestic state police powers in this case did not intrude on any congressional powers under Art. I, § 8, cl. 3, for there is no indication that appellant's materials were ever distributed interstate. Petitioner's argument would appear without substance in any event. Obscene material may be validly regulated by a State in the exercise of its traditional local power to protect the general welfare of its population despite some possible incidental effect on the flow of such materials across state lines.

Chapter 10

Sex Roles and the Media

Page 626. Following note 4, add:

5. In Columbia Broadcasting System, Inc. v. Democratic National Committee, 412 U.S. 94, 93 S.Ct. 2080, 36 L.Ed.2d 772 (1973), a majority of the members of the United States Supreme Court held that the Fairness Doctrine did not require a broadcast licensee to sell time to "responsible entities" to present their views on public issues. In the Court's view, the Fairness Doctrine merely requires a broadcaster to give adequate coverage of important issues and fairly reflect differing viewpoints; it does not confer any right upon *individuals or groups* to command the use of broadcast facilities.

Chapter 11

Sex Roles, Sex Preferences, and Appearance

Page 651. At end of note 3, add:

In United States v. Caesar, 368 F. Supp. 328 (1973), the Mann Act was challenged for discriminating unreasonably against males in violation of the Fifth Amendment. Rejecting this challenge, the court stated (368 F. Supp. at 333): "Although only females qualify as victims of the crimes, both males and females may qualify as perpetrators."

Page 651. Following note 7, add:

8. Code of Ordinances, City of Houston, Texas, Sec. 28-42.4 (1972) provides: "It shall be unlawful for any person to appear on any public street, sidewalk, alley, or other public thoroughfare dressed with the designed intent to disguise his or her true sex as that of the opposite sex." A male transvestite, i.e., one who habitually dressed in female attire, was convicted under this ordinance. Review was denied by the United States Supreme Court in Mayes v. Texas, Docket No. 73-627, 42 U.S.L.W. 3551 (1974). What arguments would be available to the convicted defendant in challenging the constitutionality of the ordinance on its face? As applied to him?

Index

170

PREGNANCY
Disability insurance for
  Complications arising from, 51-52
  Normal pregnancy, 110-19

PRIVACY, RIGHT OF
And abortion, 2-24

PRISON TERMS
Sex-based inequalities in, 88

SOCIAL SECURITY
Discrimination against widowers, 101-3
Sex-based differences in retirement age eliminated, 1

STATE ACTION, 87

SUPPORT
Father's primary liability for child support, 90-92

TITLE VII
  See Employment

TOPLESSNESS
And sex-based discrimination, 88-89

TRANSVESTITES, 167

UNWRITTEN LAW DEFENSE
Repealed in New Mexico, 30

SS   COPY 3

QUEENS BOROUGH PUBLIC LIBRARY

CENTRAL LIBRARY
89-11 Merrick Boulevard
Jamaica, New York 11432

All items may be borrowed for 28 days and are due on latest date stamped on card in pocket.

A charge is made for each day, including Sundays and holidays, that this item is overdue.

SORRY NO RENEWALS